Genesis – the Book with Seventy Faces
A guide for the family

Esther Takac

Illustrations by Anna Pignataro

Book design by Dalit Bar

Genesis: the Book with Seventy Faces
Published by Pitspopany Press
Text Copyright © 2008 by Esther Takac
Illustrations Copyright © 2008 by Anna Pignataro
Project Coordinator: Esther Takac
Cover Design: Dalit Bar
Typesetting & Book design: Dalit Bar
Editor: Yaacov Peterseil
Editorial & production manager: Daniella Barak

All rights reserved. No part of this book may be used or reproduced or transmitted in any form or by any means, electronic or mechanical, including photocopying, recording, or by any information storage and retrieval system, without written permission from the publisher.

Pitspopany Press titles may be purchased for fund-raising programs by schools and organizations by contacting:

40 E. 78th Street Suite 16D
New York, NY 10021

Distributed in England by Menasche Scharf
Tel: 44 0845 698 0044
E-mail: pitspop@netvision.net.il
Web Site: www.pitspopany.com

Printed in Israel

In memory of my grandparents

With love for my children, to share with their children

למען ידעו דור אחרון

That the generation to come might know   Psalms 78:6

Contents

Foreword by Avivah Zornberg 7

For adults – How to read this book 9

For kids – How to see seventy faces 13

Bereshit 15

Noah 35

Lech Lecha 57

Vayeira 75

Chayei Sarah 97

Toldot 115

Vayetse 137

Vayishlach 153

Vayeshev 169

Miketz 185

Vayigash 203

Vayechi 215

Endnotes 230

Biblical commentators and commentaries 238

Bibliography 239

Acknowledgments 241

FOREWORD

Genesis -the Book with Seventy Faces offers parents and children a rich and imaginative resource for studying the Book of Genesis together. Drawing from many sources, ancient and modern, Esther Takac has lovingly and with great devotion created a guide to multiple understandings of the narratives – theological, psychological, ethical, ecological – in such a way as to stimulate discussion and curiosity in children of all ages.

She writes clearly and poetically, raising the spiritual and moral issues as they have been discussed throughout the ages in midrashic elaborations and traditional and modern commentaries. She addresses her young readers directly, challenging them to bring their intelligence and their sense of morality to bear on the stories, as well as their ability to respond to nuances in the text. She represents the exegetical traditions fairly and responsibly, while inviting the reader to participate in the sacred work of understanding the biblical text. When she addresses older children, she adds more detail, stimulating her reader to study the range of commentary for him/herself. Her experience as both mother and psychologist enriches her work.

The Jewish tradition of learning and re-learning, uncovering new questions and new layers of meaning, is honoured here, as children are exposed to this unfolding of sacred texts. Respect for the ancient and openness to the modern characterize this work. The illustrations, too, beautifully evoke a sense of both the familiar and the sacred.

This promises to be a valuable – and unique – contribution to the Jewish children's bookshelf, and one for which the time is right. The interest in studying authentic traditional materials is increasing in the Jewish world; parents will find this book a fine and aesthetic resource for sharing their own interest with their children. I hope these Seventy Faces succeed in reaching many Jewish families and in enriching their Jewish experience of the biblical narratives.

Avivah Zornberg

Carpin berry

daffodil

HOW TO READ THIS BOOK

Genesis – the Book with Seventy Faces is a guide for the family. It invites children and parents to join in a journey exploring the richness of the Genesis stories and the treasury of interpretation and commentary written about them.

Why do we need a guide?

Today, in the midst of our busy lives, we crave stories that provide a sense of meaning, belonging and wonder. The Genesis stories contain these, and a telling of things sacred, so often absent from our contemporary lives. But while we have these stories in our own Jewish tradition, the full richness of the stories is often difficult to access. At times the plain text of the story seems perplexing and inappropriate to our twenty-first century way of thinking. Closer study of the text, and familiarity with the many volumes of interpretation and commentary, both traditional and contemporary, is often necessary to enable one to more fully enjoy the richness of the stories.

As Barry Holtz describes in *Back to the Sources – Reading the Classic Jewish Texts*, traditional Jews rarely speak about "reading" the Torah, rather one talks about "studying" or "learning" Torah. While we sit alone to read a book, studying or learning Torah implies something very different. It involves pondering, discussing and debating the text with others. It also involves referring to the insights and interpretations of the many commentators throughout the centuries who themselves studied the text.

So in order to really understand the Torah text one needs to study it: the way each word and the order of words in a sentence has meaning, the repetitions and parallels across the stories, the examination of biblical heroes – their weaknesses as well as their strengths. One becomes involved in a centuries-long discussion of ethics and morality, for the Genesis stories deal with the big issues of morality, philosophy, heroes and fallen heroes, and our place in the world. As a precious stone sparkles more exquisitely when it is rubbed and polished, so too the meaning and beauty of the stories shine more brightly as they are rubbed and polished by the centuries of Jewish learning.

But many readers do not have the time for such study, and the volumes of commentary are intimidating. Much commentary is not easily accessible as it is written in Hebrew, Aramaic or Rashi script; other commentary in English is more accessible but complex. I learnt that although the Genesis stories and the commentaries about them are full of richness, poetry, moral dilemmas and spiritual insights, to many this part of our tradition remains largely a foreign country, unvisited, inaccessible. And so the concept of a guide evolved. As a guidebook can give you a glimpse and help you find your way around in a foreign country, so this book hopes to give you a glimpse and help you find your way around the Genesis stories and commentaries. But just as the guidebook does not replace visiting the country so reading this book is not the same as actually travelling through the Torah text and studying the commentaries yourself. Other rich experiences await those who go on to immerse themselves in the foreign language, sights and smells of the original texts.

Seventy faces to a story

The concept of a story with multiple layers of meaning sounds like a modern idea but it is based on a very old source. A Talmudic saying tells that the Torah has seventy different faces. Depending on your perspective, you see and understand a different "face", a different interpretation or dimension of the story. The concept of the seventy faces suggests that the biblical text has multiple meanings – no one meaning is the only "true" meaning. This echoes our contemporary understanding that stories, and human experience, are complex and multifaceted.

Different layers for different ages in the family

This book contains the twelve parashiot of Genesis, each parasha being the weekly section of the Torah that is read in synagogue. The stories are told in separate layers, to cater for the span of ages in the family.

Reading and sharing stories with others is one of life's joys. Children, teenagers and adults love to talk about the stories they are reading. With it's multiple layers on each page, *Genesis – the Book with Seventy Faces* allows children and parents to enjoy reading together.

The first layer – in large colored type – is a retelling of the story. While it is not an actual translation (the parasha is far too long to present in its entirety, instead significant verses have been selected, others have been summarized or omitted), it is essentially very similar to the biblical story, and the corresponding chapter and verse references are given. The retelling is my own, based on numerous translations of the Bible. I have tried to use language that is poetic and sparse, as is the actual Hebrew in the Torah, and make it child-friendly as well. If only this layer is read, it provides a simple and sequential retelling of the biblical narrative suitable for younger children. This retelling provides a basis for the layer of commentary following.

The second layer presents some of the "seventy faces" of the story as based on the commentaries. Over the centuries many hundreds of different commentaries and interpretations on the Torah have been written. In fact Barry Holtz suggests that the whole of Jewish literature can be seen as a kind of vast inverted pyramid, with the Bible at the base. This structure expands outwards enormously to include the Mishnah and Talmud, the Midrashic literature, the medieval rabbinic commentators and the mystical tradition. Added to this we have today a growing body of commentaries by contemporary scholars. For clarity I have organized these different commentaries and interpretations into genres. However the reader needs to be aware that this is a simplified division; each genre builds upon and draws on earlier commentaries, and the distinctions between genres are not always clear. In this book each genre is introduced by a tagline, e.g. Midrash says, Sages of Old tell etc. The different genres are as follows:

Midrash – The word "Midrash" is derived from the Hebrew *lidrosh*, meaning "to search out." The sparse style of the Torah is such that there is little detail – the thoughts, feelings and motivations of characters are rarely given. Midrash fills in these gaps. Also when scholars studying the Torah came upon a word or expression that seemed strange or superfluous in the text, they sought to understand – *lidrosh* – what new idea or nuance the Torah wished to convey by using it. For thousands of years classic rabbinic Midrash developed in the *beit midrash* or study-houses and resulted in a highly respected body of interpretive literature.

Midrash is focused on either Halakhic (legal) or Aggadic (narrative) material, the latter being the focus of the retellings here. Aggadic Midrash can be divided into three historical categories: the early period (400–640 C.E.) such as *Bereishit Rabbah*, the middle period (640–1000 C.E.) such as *Midrash Tanchuma*, and the late period (1000–1200 C.E.) such as *Midrash Tehillim*. From the beginning of the twelfth century scholars in various countries assembled anthologies of Midrash such as *Midrash HaGadol* and *Yalkut Shim'oni*.

Sages of Old – This genre includes all the traditional rabbinic commentators from 200 C.E. to 1800 C.E., however it mostly draws upon the work of the medieval commentators. It was only in the Middle Ages that running direct commentaries on the biblical text (such as Rashi's) developed. The traditional Jewish edition of the Torah, *Mikra'ot Gedolot*, was designed in the medieval period. It has the Hebrew text of the Bible surrounded by a number of commentaries. As Professor in Bible Edward Greenstein writes: "The great medieval commentaries continue to serve as the major companions to the Bible for those who study the text in the original Hebrew. The most distinctive personalities among the medieval commentators virtually sit in the room and share their opinions with the serious student." These reknowned personalities include Rashi, Rashbam, and Ibn Ezra.

Scholars of our Time – This genre includes all contemporary commentators, men and women. As was true for the majority of Western literature prior to the nineteenth century, the Sages of Old, the traditional rabbinic commentators, were almost all men. Today both men and women study the texts and write commentaries. We are blessed in our times to witness an enormous blossoming in women's learning; in fact, there are more learned Jewish women now than during any other period in history. Today women are actively engaging with the biblical text, responding to the stories – to the men and women in them – from a woman's perspective.

The commentaries cited in Scholars of our Time reflect a rich and diverse range of viewpoints including literary, psychological, legal, feminist and philosophical perspectives. I have drawn on the work of a broad range of scholars including Nehama Leibowitz, R. Samson Raphael Hirsch, Naomi Rosenblatt, R. Joseph Telushkin, Elie Wiesel, Nahum Sarna, James Kugel, Gunther Plaut and many others. I have particularly drawn on the work of Avivah Zornberg, whose book *The Beginning of Desire: Reflections on Genesis* has enormously enriched my understanding and appreciation of Genesis.

Legend – Jewish legend is related to Aggadic (narrative) Midrash, but it is less focused on interpreting the Torah text. These legends, sprinkled throughout the rabbinic literature, are often about magical events, biblical characters, the lives of the Rabbis. Sometimes they are almost like fairy tales, and as such easily cross the line into folk literature. Many of these stories serve to illustrate the biblical text, others are quite independent of it and are included because they have a moral or historical message, or simply because the stories are too good to be left out. Some of the legends have similarities to those of other cultures, and have been transmuted into specifically Jewish stories.

Kabbalah – Jewish mysticism is a complex system of thought that aims to reveal an understanding of God's essence. The mystic's path to God is through the Torah, as the Torah is seen to be the "clothing" of God. The most famous text of Kabbalah, the *Zohar*, published in the medieval period, is a commentary on the Torah expressed in symbolic language.

So the second layer distils a broad range of commentaries into a form that is user-friendly for the family. As such it provides a guide into the vast world of Jewish learning. It offers an insight into the rich and multi-layered approach of Judaism to texts, allowing readers to navigate their way, distinguishing between Torah text on the one hand and commentary, midrash and legend on the other.

The third layer appears as margin boxes that provide further commentary, historical background and source material. This material outlines the difficult or thorny issues in the text and suggests how these issues have been dealt with by traditional and contemporary commentators. It is designed for older family members, teenagers and adults, and enriches parents' ability to guide their children through the Torah text.

Separate margin boxes signposted by a **?** symbol contain questions for children and parents to discuss.

The material in the second and third layers reflects a multitude of voices: not all voices express my personal view but have been included to reveal the richness of different ways of looking at and understanding the text. At the end of each parasha the story is drawn together with its meaning for our own lives.

Stories to challenge and stretch your thinking

Current children's education often focuses on developing the processes of thinking, with curriculum units on philosophy for children and values clarification, so that in their secular studies we expect children to develop these sophisticated thinking skills. It is a great pity that, in contrast, Bible stories are often taught in a way that is more simplistic, didactic and uni-dimensional. The irony is that the Genesis stories, and the commentaries about them, reflect exactly the sort of sophisticated thinking skills we want to impart.

Michael Rosenak, in his book *Commandments and Concerns – Jewish Religious Education in Secular Society* writes that: "It was often the case in the past that students felt that 'learning Torah' involved a suppression of their reasoning power… students must be challenged to apply themselves fully, with reason and feeling, to comprehending the text." Indeed the stories and commentaries embody the idea that there are many different ways to think about a problem or a story and often deal with issues of philosophy, morality, relationships. So the story of creation raises questions about our relationship to the environment; the creation of Adam and Eve invites us to consider the relationship between the sexes; and the story of Noah makes us reflect about what it means to be a good person. In the book I have included these issues for parents and children to talk about, including questions of philosophy, morality, relationships between people, science.

Engaging personally with the Torah text

Any person who wants to get a real taste of the Torah needs to engage with the text in a personal way. You need to find your own path into the text, a path that allows you to be true to who you are, but includes a dedication to go beyond the surface. It is through this interpretive process, through personally wrestling with the text, that the Torah retains its vitality and wonder.

I believe that all retelling of Torah is interpretation. There are so many commentaries that influence our understanding of the text; one cannot retell and teach them all. There is a choosing, a selection, an editing, and that very choosing is interpretation – a choice to focus on one understanding of the text and ignore another. Interpretation forms reality. We live in a time when religious interpretation is used as an excuse for coercion, hatred, violence and bloodshed. It is our responsibility to be mindful of what interpretation of our texts, culture and religion we want to pass on to our children. For this will be their reality.

God's gender

God's gender is a tricky issue that needs to be negotiated when retelling the Bible stories. In most versions of the Bible, God is understood and translated in masculine terms. However in the Torah God has numerous names, some of which suggest masculine, some feminine and others genderless qualities. One of the most frequently used names of God in the Torah, *Elohim*, is actually a plural noun and can be seen to encompass both the masculine and the feminine. The other word used for God is made up of the four Hebrew letters *Yud, Hay, Vav, Hay – YHVH*, referred to as "Hashem". These are the first letters of the words *Yihiye, Hove, VeHaya* – "the one who was, is and will be." This name of God is a word without gender. YHVH is not a noun; it is God as a verb. Similarly another name for God, 'Eyn Sof' – 'Without End', is abstract and genderless.

Judaism recognises the feminine aspect of God as embodied in a further name for God, *Shechinah* – 'the one who dwells within.' *Shechina* is a central metaphor of feminine divininity in Jewish Midrashic and mystical texts from the first millennium C.E. onwards. However, the feminine aspect of God is generally less accessible.

I did not want to limit my expression of God to a masculine aspect. One possibility might have been to alternate the use of the masculine and feminine pronouns: God as He/She, however I felt this approach would be confusing. Instead I have chosen to express God in genderless terms, omitting any pronoun. It is hoped that in this way God is conveyed in more abstract terms: not as male or female but rather as an energy pervading the world.

How to use this book

It is my hope that families read this book together and use it as a starting point to enjoy the richness of the text and commentaries, discuss the stories, ask questions, delve deeper and discover new meanings. As such it offers a way for families to connect around the Genesis stories, showing how these stories reflect our own struggles and dilemmas.

Parents of younger children will probably read only the first layer, the retelling of the actual story, to their children.

Other family members (older children, parents, grandparents) are encouraged to read the first two layers together. You could perhaps share the reading, with one person reading the first layer out loud and the other responding with the second layer. The Torah text and commentaries often raise interesting and challenging issues to discuss. Questions in the second layer and in the sign-posted margin boxes stimulate conversation. Asking your own questions and discussing what interests or worries you in the story, reflects the authentic Jewish way of reading the text.

In this way the Torah stories retain their vitality and relevance and reading them is lively and interactive. This process of learning the text together is reminiscent of traditional Jewish chevruta learning, studying the text in pairs in the *beit midrash*, the study house, as existed for hundreds of years and continues today.

The stories and commentaries are rich and full with ideas, the issues raised are often complex. You may find that reading a few pages at a time is enough. Or you may choose to focus on the commentaries of only one genre such as Sages of Old, or explore a particular issue on one reading, and then come back to other commentaries and issues on a subsequent reading.

The third layer in the margin boxes provides further material for teenagers and adults, and expands parents' knowledge in discussing the text with their children. The second and third layers together provide resource material for children and adults wishing to prepare a *devar Torah* for the Shabbat table, a bar or bat mitzvah, or any other occasion. The references to all source material are given in the endnotes so readers can follow up on any of the commentaries cited in Sages of Old, Scholars of our Time, Midrash, in the margin boxes, etc.

Why this book?

Working on this book has been a daunting and at times overwhelming task. I only hope I have done it a measure of justice. I realize of course that this book captures but a glimmer of the depth, the possibilities and permutations existing in the original Torah text and commentaries, just a few of the possible seventy faces. But it is a beginning.

My impetus for retelling these stories came from my own children. When I looked for Genesis stories to read to them, I found myself stuck. While a lot of fascinating commentaries on Genesis have been written over the last decades this sort of material has not filtered into the Genesis stories written for children and the family. Many of the Genesis books available also did not include rabbinic commentary, Midrash and Legend, or differentiate them from the actual Torah text. I wanted my children to be exposed to the richness, poetry and contemporary relevance of the stories. By incorporating the multiple layers I was able to add depth and magic to the stories, inviting children to own the stories and engage with them and their heroes.

Furthermore, with these stories I wanted to give my children, and children everywhere, a taste of the richness of the Jewish tradition. I hoped to bring to light some of the images, archetypes and metaphors buried in our sources – such as the vivid image of the splinters of primal light scattered throughout the world; or the archetype of *Chesed* (lovingkindness), embodied by Abraham, as a way of being in the world; or the *Lech Lecha*, the journey of Abraham and Sarah in the desert, as a metaphor for a journey to find ourselves. I wanted these stories, with their sense of mystery and wonder, their telling of things sacred, to seep into the minds and imaginations of our children, a rich resource to be drawn upon as they grow up.

FOR KIDS – HOW TO SEE SEVENTY FACES

The first book of the Torah, the Book of Genesis, tells the story of how the world began, how the first man and woman were created and how the first generations of people lived. It tells us about the forefathers and foremothers of the Jewish people – Abraham and Sarah, Isaac and Rebecca, Jacob and Rachel and Leah.

The Torah is a very special book. An ancient saying tells that the Torah is like a person with seventy different faces, so that each time you look at the Torah from a new direction, you see another face. Each face gives you a different understanding of the story. The idea that the Torah has seventy faces reminds us that life, too, has many sides and meanings. You can look at the same thing from various viewpoints and see it differently – which means that you understand it differently too.

Some of the different faces of the Torah are easy to see and understand; others are hidden, like secrets we need to discover. The Torah is like a never-ending pass-the-parcel game: each time you unwrap a layer of paper, there is another layer underneath ready to be unwrapped.

How can we discover some of the seventy faces of the Torah? Luckily for us, people have been studying the Torah for thousands of years and writing their thoughts and ideas in many books of commentary. I have collected many of these commentaries, so you can see the different faces in this book.

Like the Book of Genesis this book is divided into twelve parashiot. A parasha is like a chapter or story - we read a parasha each week in synagogue. Each page of the book is designed to show how you can understand Torah. On the top of the page the actual story from the Torah is told. Then just underneath it you can read the commentaries and discover different meanings and ways of understanding the story. These meanings come from many sources:

Sages of Old – wise and famous Rabbis who lived hundreds of years ago

Scholars of our Time – women and men who study the Torah today and write books about how it is relevant for us in the twenty-first century

Midrash – collections of stories written by people who studied the Torah in the *beit midrash*, study houses, over many centuries

Legends – fables and magical tales which grew up as the Torah was passed down over the generations

Kabbalah – books written by Jewish mystics who see the Torah as a way of understanding God

If you want to know exactly which books the commentaries come from you can find out in the endnotes at the end of the book.

These commentaries are not the only way to understand the Torah. Another way to discover some of the faces of the Torah is to read the stories quietly and deeply yourself. Then you may discover that sometimes the Torah is like a mirror – when you look into it, you see a reflection of yourself.

I hope you have fun on your journey of discovery through the first book of the Torah, the Book of Genesis.

בראשית

BERESHIT

The seven days of creation

Intolerable chaos: The words tohu vavohu do not appear anywhere else in the Torah and so commentators struggle to understand exactly what they mean." "Tohu" would describe a chaotic condition which would give us the impression of everything being mixed up, and nothing consolidated separately. More difficult is "vohu" which we only find elsewhere in "vay," an expression of pain in Rabbinic Hebrew...vohu would then designate the chaotic condition as being intolerable, full of contradiction and struggle."
R. Samson Raphael Hirsch

? Have you ever tried to create something – write a story, build a cubby house, paint a picture? Sometimes in the beginning there can be a feeling of *tohu vavohu* – chaos, formlessness. Everything is a mess, on the table, in your mind, and you are not quite sure how things will work out. And slowly out of the chaos comes a way of ordering things, and creation begins.

? Did you try saying *tohu vavohu* out loudly and slowly? What does it sound like to you? (To me it sounds like being inside a great swirling, whirling wind.)

Ch.1: 1 – 2 At the beginning God created the heaven and the earth. And the earth was *tohu vavohu* – nothingness and chaos, and the world was empty and dark. The spirit of God moved upon the waters like a wind blowing over a deep dark sea.

The Torah begins with the Hebrew word *Bereshit* – at the beginning. *Bereshit* begins with the Hebrew letter *Bet*. Sages of Old tell that the letter *Bet* is the right letter to start the Torah because the shape of the letter itself tells us about creation. The letter *Bet* is closed on three sides, above, below and behind – it opens up in one direction only, the direction from which the words flow. In the same way our knowledge about the creation of the world is closed on three sides – we do not know what existed before or above or below the creation of the world. These are a mystery.

In the beginning of God's creation of the world there was *tohu vavohu*. *Tohu vavohu* are special Hebrew words that cannot really be translated – they describe nothingness, formlessness, chaos. Try saying *tohu vavohu* out loud slowly and you will see that it is an onomatopoeic word – it sounds like what it means .

God's creation is a process of bringing order to chaos, dividing and naming the elements of the world.

Ch.1: 3 – 5   And God said, "Let there be light" and light shone, and God saw that it was good. God divided the light from the darkness and called the light Day and the dark Night. And there was evening and there was morning, the first day.

The first order God brings is dividing the light from the dark, the day from the night – the creation of time. A Scholar of our Time explains that the world needs both light and darkness. The light awakens everything to life and growth, the darkness allows for rest and sleep. If there was only light continually we could not bear it. After the long hours of daylight, we are tired, ready to rest in the darkness "sheltered under the motherly wing of night."

Everything grows at first in darkness, the baby in the mother's womb, the seed of the plant in the soil. And then growth continues in the light, as the baby is born and the leaves and flowers blossom in the light.

Many stories are told about the light that was created on the first day. Sages of Old tell that this newly created light was so bright you could see from one end of the world to the other. With this light you could see everything happening everywhere. But God saw that this light was too bright for people so God hid the bright light away to be revealed only at the end of days.

Kabbalah teaches that this light, which contained the powerful energy of creation, was held together in an enormous bowl. But the energy of the light was so strong that the bowl shattered and broke. As the light fell to earth, it separated into many little splinters. These splinters of light still containing the sparks of positive creative energy, of goodness, are scattered all over the world, through different countries and peoples. They may be hidden in the long work hours of doctors and nurses who look after sick children, in the sweat of men and women who plant trees to grow forests, in the Hebrew songs and prayers for peace. Some people spend their lives searching for these sparks; imagine travelling the world to find them! According to Kabbalah, if we gather up all the sparks we will be helping to fix the world.

Mystical light: Mystical ideas about the light of creation are based on Kabbalistic concepts developed by Rabbi Isaac Luria in the sixteenth century. Lurianic Kabbalah, as it was called, involves a dramatic explanation of the world's creation drawn in a mystical yet sharply visual imagery.

A broken vessel: According to Lurianic Kabbalah the light of creation was contained in a vessel. The vessel was broken, its "outer husks or shell" were shattered, and the inner light (the creative life – energy) was scattered in two directions. Some of this light, called holy sparks, returned to its source, to God. But the other sparks, entangled with the shattered husks, called klipot, fell down to earth and are scattered all over the world. The sparks yearn to return to their source. The process of "lifting the sparks" which involves bringing about a tikkun or repair of the world, is the task of humanity.

Tikkun Olam – Repairing the world: This concept of the scattered sparks provides a beautiful image of the richness existing across different peoples and encourages one to be sensitive and respectful of the beauty in other cultures It gives a purpose to the scattering of the Jews across the world. They are to go everywhere to gather the sparks, the positive creative energy and thereby help to bring about tikkun olam – repairing the world.

? How does light make you feel? And darkness?

? Jewish people have been involved in fixing the world (*tikkun olam* in Hebrew) in many different ways: fighting racism, reducing poverty and working for the environment. Who inspires you to be involved in fixing the world?

Beyond the singular: The Talmud explains that shamayim, the Hebrew word for sky, is a compound of sham mayim, "the waters are there". Shamayim is a word in plural form (the – im suffix denoting plural) similar to words like panim (face) and mayim (water). These words exist in the plural because the concepts are beyond the singular: a face has the duality of two profiles, water is made of multiple drops, sky is a vast expanse.

The dark ages: There is a fascinating parallel between the description of the world during the time of the flood (chapter 6) and the state of the world before creation (chapter 1). In both, the world was dark – during the year of the flood the sun and moon did not shine – and deep waters covered the earth.

Ch.1: 6 – 8   Deep waters still covered the earth to an endless height. There was just water and water as far and as high as you could see. Then God said, "Let there be sky between the waters." God spread out a sky, and it separated the waters below the sky from the waters above. And God called the sky Heaven. And there was evening and there was morning, the second day.

On the first day of creation God divided the day from the night and so created time. On the second day God divided the waters above from the waters below, and so created space.

Creation begins simply with God's words, "Let there light," "Let there be sky." As God says, so it becomes – words have the power to create reality. Sages of Old explain that God speaks ten statements that cause creation and bring the world into being.

A Midrash tells that when the waters below were separated from the waters above, the waters below wept and cried, "But we want to be close to God above!"

The Sages of Old show how special the Hebrew word for sky *shamayim* is. Inside the word *shamayim* is the Hebrew word for water *mayim* – the Hebrew language shows how deeply connected water and sky really are. There is water above the sky in clouds, and water below the sky in the seas. The water above the sky is actually evaporated water. When it rains this water in the clouds falls through the sky to join the water in the seas below. A Scholar of our Time describes the movement of water in the world; "this great cycle and exchange – that the ocean surrounds the earth, all water rushes to the sea, rises from the ocean to the clouds above and thence pours down again."

It is the sky that keeps the perfect balance between the waters above and the waters below. Can you imagine what would happen if there were no sky to keep the balance? That balance has been broken once, as we shall see in the next chapter, when God made the flood. Then the waters above the sky poured down and the waters below the sky swelled up. There was *tohu vavohu* and deep waters covered the earth again, as in the very beginning. You'll have to wait till the next chapter to see what happened.

Water wheel : "To this vault henceforth the earth sends up its vapour which as clouds from above absorb the water and give it back to the thirsty earth and its thirsty creatures... the changing wheel of giving and receiving.."

? Do you know about the water cycle – from clouds to rain to sea to evaporation and back to the clouds? Could you draw a picture of the cycle of water?

Jewish mean time: Just as in Judaism the concept of a day is different (extending from evening to evening), so Judaism has a different approach to time in general, and to sacred time in particular. Time is one of the underpinning principles in Jewish life. This is reflected in the importance of Shabbat and the festivals as an opportunity to join with community and connect with God. For Jews, sacred time can be seen as more important than sacred place. Over the centuries sacred places changed, synagogues and temples were destroyed but Jewish people still observed and celebrated sacred time, the holy days and festivals.

Trees and ourselves: "For trees have a double function, to produce fruit for man, and to carry on the species by the seed hidden in the fruit.... That is why the Torah gives the warning; although fruit trees serve for your enjoyment, do not forget that the fruit has a duty also to its own species.... Do not allow your longing for the fruit to lead to denigrating the tree for its species." R. Samson Raphael Hirsch's words from the nineteenth century have a contemporary environmental relevance.

? Is it tomorrow yet? In our everyday lives we wake up to a new day. But in Judaism a new day starts when it gets dark. How is a day different when it goes from evening till evening as compared to beginning in the morning?

Ch.1: 9 – 13 Next, God gathered together all the waters below the sky in one place and named those waters Seas, and the dry land that appeared was called Earth. The waters rolled away and the mountains and rocks and deserts could be seen. And God said, "Let the earth grow grass and plants and fruit trees of all kinds." So the earth grew green and lush with many different plants and flowers and trees and forests. The plants grew seeds and the wind blew the seeds, spreading green life all over the earth. And God saw that it was good. And there was evening and there was morning, the third day.

A Scholar of our Time explains that when the seas were created, God told the water not to stay in one place but to break into the dry land to create lakes and rivers and streams. So the seas and the rivers divide the land up into separate continents and countries.

You will realize, as you read more and more of the Torah, that the Torah's language is very special. Each word, and the specific order of words in a sentence exist for a reason and have meaning and importance. At the end of the description of each day of creation the same words "And there was evening and there was morning" are repeated, giving the story a rhythm like a poem. But why is evening mentioned first?

The Sages of Old explain that in Judaism each new day begins at evening time, when it becomes dark enough to see three stars shining in the sky. Also the order of evening and then morning is similar to the order of creation. Creation moves from darkness to light, just as the new day in Judaism moves from darkness in the evening to light in the morning. The Torah's language, "And there was evening and there was morning" also suggests that evening and morning exist at the same time. This is in fact true. When there is evening in one part of the world, there is morning in another.

Ch.1: 14 – 19 Then God said, "There shall be lights in the sky to divide between the day and the night." God made two large lights, the greater light to rule the day, the sun, and the smaller light to rule the night, the moon, together with the stars. The sun and the moon are signs for counting the days and the seasons and the years. And God saw that it was good. And there was evening and there was morning, the fourth day.

Seeing the light: Medieval commentators noted a contradiction between the concept that light was created on the first day, and yet the sun and the moon, which radiate and reflect light, were created on the fourth day. They solved the problem by saying light itself was created on the first day and was all pervading, filling the entire universe. The sun and moon serve as receptacles to contain the light. Some commentators even explain that darkness at night covers the light, and the moon and stars are like holes or windows cut into the dark expanse to let in the light.

At first the Torah writes that God made "two large lights" and then the Torah describes a greater light, the sun, and a smaller light, the moon. A story from Midrash explains why the description changes from "two great lights" to a "greater light" and a "smaller light." Midrash relates that when God first created the sun and the moon they were the same size "two large lights". But the moon complained: "There cannot be two rulers in the sky – we cannot both rule if we are the same size. One should be larger than the other." The moon wanted to be bigger than the sun. But instead, God told the moon, "Make yourself smaller. Also you shall not be alone in the sky, you shall have the many stars to accompany you." The moon became not just smaller but able to wax and wane; so that when it is big, it seems as big as the sun, but then it dwindles and disappears altogether, leaving the sun ruling alone in the sky.

? What's the time? The Torah says that the sun and the moon are signs for counting the days, seasons and years. How do we measure time with the sun? With the moon? Could you measure time without the sun and the moon?

Kabbalah teaches that the moon was sad, so God decided to make it special in another way. The sun shines on the outside of things and we see their colour, shape and size. But the light of the moon is different: its light shines through to the inside of things – we can see past their outside to their heart and how they feel.

Scholars of our Time have noted that from earth, the sun and the moon appear to be of equal size, – although the sun is really much larger, it is so much further away than the moon that it appears the same size. When there is a total solar eclipse we see how the moon perfectly covers the sun, so that only the outer rays of the sun are visible. Perhaps the story above tries to explain this contradiction – that although the sun is actually much bigger than the moon from earth they appear the same size.

Leviathan: the great sea monster: Some of the creatures described in Jewish legends exist in the myths and folklore of other cultures. For example in the Babylonian creation story, Emuna Elish, the god of the sea was a great watery serpent which had to be vanquished by a more beneficient power before the world could come into being. Remnants of this serpent remain in Bereshit in the shape of the leviathan. However, Bereshit states clearly that "God created the great sea – monsters," as if to contradict any idea that these monsters had any part to play in creation.

Legendary ziz: "It once happened that travellers on a vessel noticed a bird. As he stood in the water, it merely covered his feet and his head knocked against the sky. The onlookers thought the water could not have any depth at that point, and they prepared to take a bath there. A heavenly voice warned them; "Alight not here. Once a carpenter's axe slipped from his hand at this spot and it took seven years to touch bottom." The bird that the travellers saw was none other than the ziz."
Louis Ginzberg

? Can you imagine an unusual legendary bird or fish that was created on the fifth day but no longer exists? What would it be like?

Ch.1: 20 – 23   Now God looked at the earth and saw that it was empty. So God said, "Let the waters teem with swarms of living creatures." And the seas became filled with whales and dolphins and turtles and sharks and jellyfish, and the rivers and lakes became filled with salmon and frogs and eels. Then God turned to the sky and said, "Let the sky be filled with winged creatures that will fly about over the land and across the expanse of the sky." And the sky was filled with the fluttering of the wings of birds as they flew through the air: sparrows and pigeons and doves and eagles and flamingos and peacocks and kookaburras and owls. And God blessed them all, saying, "Fish, be fruitful and become many. Fill the waters of the seas; and birds, fill the skies." And God saw that it was good. And there was evening and there was morning, the fifth day.

Many strange and wonderful birds and fish were created on the fifth day. Some of these creatures no longer exist and we have only legends to tell us about them. Legends tell that of all the winged creatures flying through the sky, a bird called the ziz was the king of the birds. The ziz was so enormous that when its ankles rested on the earth, its head reached to the sky. Its wings were so huge that, when unfurled, they darkened the sun.

Although the ziz was the biggest bird, the phoenix was perhaps the most special bird. It had the gift of everlasting life. When it had lived a thousand years its body shrank, and its feathers dropped off until it was as small as an egg. This was the nucleus, the beginning of the new phoenix.

Of the sea creatures the leviathan was the most amazing. The leviathan was longer than a hundred kilometres with fins that flashed with a brilliant flame. It was so big that when it was thirsty the leviathan drank all the water flowing from the river Jordan into the sea.

Ch.1: 24 – 25 Next God said, "Let the earth bring forth living creatures, all kinds of animals and creeping things, beasts great and small." And so, lions and monkeys and caterpillars and rabbits and horses and lizards and bears and all the many other different animals walked and crawled and ran across the earth that was their home. And God saw that it was good.

If you look closely inside the order of creation, a pattern unfolds. Creation moves from very simple to very complex organisms. First God created dark and light, then sea and land, then fish and birds, then animals, and, lastly, the most complex organisms of all, people. If you were in charge of creating the world, in what order would you create things?

The Sages of Old trace another pattern in the order of creation. This pattern shows a balance between things created in the upper world and things created in the lower world – for God wanted peace between the upper and lower worlds. So on the first day God created heaven in the upper world and earth in the lower world. On the second day God created the sky in the upper world. On the third day God created the dry land and vegetation in the lower world. On the fourth day God created the sun, moon and stars in the upper world. On the fifth day God created the fish in the lower world. On the sixth day God created humans, using both the soil of the earth from the lower world and the breath of God from the upper world. And so there is a balance between the upper and lower worlds.

Uncompleted: "The Lord created the world in a state of beginning. The universe is always in an uncompleted state, in the form of its beginning. It is not like a vessel at which the master works to finish it: it requires continuous labor and renewal by creative forces. Should these cease for only a second, the universe would return to primeval chaos." R. Simchah Bunem

Even the gnats preceeded you: Why were people created last? One Midrash explains that while "All things were created on your behalf," if people become too proud they are reminded that "Even gnats preceded you in the order of creation." This dichotomy between a need to remind ourselves of our special worth, on one hand, and our humility on the other, is a recurrent theme in Jewish thought.

Ongoing pattern of creation: "Being is better than nothingness, order superior to chaos, and man's existence – with all its difficulties – a blessing. But creation is never called perfect: it will in fact be man's task to assist the Creator in perfecting His creation, to become His co-worker." Gunther Plaut

More than one God? Rabbinic commentators worried that the use of the plural ran the risk of suggesting a plurality of gods. A Midrash tells that when Moshe wrote down the Torah and came to the verse, "Let us make people," he queried God: "Sovereign of the Universe! why do you thus furnish an excuse to the heretics for maintaining that there is more than one God?" "Write," God replied. "Whoever wishes to err will err. Let them rather learn from their Creator that when I came to create people, I took counsel with the angels."

Translators' problem: The Talmud records that when King Ptolemy assembled seventy-two elders and placed them in seventy-two separate rooms, ordering them to translate the Torah, God prompted each one of them and instead of writing "Let us make man" they all wrote "I will make man." Thus Ptolemy would not have a pretext to claim that the Torah recognized the existence of a plurality of creators.

Putting it to the vote: Like the angels, the school of Shammai and the school of Hillel also argued about whether people should have been created, The school of Hillel argued for people and the school of Shammai against. They finally voted, and decided that it would have been better for people not to have been created, but seeing they had been created, people should act with conscience.

? Are there some projects you work on, or decisions you make, where you like to get advice from other people?

? Which angels do you agree with? Is the world better off with people in it or without people?

Ch.1: 26 Now that God had created the land and the sea, the sun and the moon, the fish, birds and animals, God said, "Let us make people in our image, like us."

Why does God say, in the plural, "Let us make people"? What does God mean by "us"? Sages of Old and the Midrash help us understand why God said "us" instead of "me."

Sages of Old explain that the creation of people was so special that, for the first time, God involved the angels as well, asking them for their advice about creating people. The Sages of Old explain that the Torah is teaching us that it is good to take advice from others, especially when you are working on important projects and decisions.

Midrash tells of an argument between the angels as to whether God should create people or not. God's plan was to create people who would choose their own path in life. The angel of Justice and the angel of Love agreed with God: "Let people be created because they will do justice and be loving." But the angel of Truth and the angel of Peace disagreed: "Don't create people," they said, "People will bring lies and fighting into the world, and the world will not be peaceful anymore." Listening to the angels of Justice and Love, God began gathering soil from the earth to make the first person.

Ch.2: 7 God formed the first person, Adam, from the soil of the earth, the *adama*. Then God created Adam's soul, the *neshama*, by breathing the breath, the *neshima*, of life into Adam's nostrils.

And so a person is made from both the earth below and the breath of God above. We are stuck on the ground but we also try to fly like the angels! In the pattern of creation people are the link between the earth below and God above, a central pillar joining the two worlds.

A Sage of Old teaches that the soil, the adama for making Adam was gathered from all four corners of the earth, so that when a person dies they can be buried in any part of the earth and returned again to the adama from which they were formed.

Midrash tells that when Adam's soul was created, all the souls of all the people who will ever live were created too. This is how the Midrash explains it: all the souls are stored up in heaven – the right soul must be drawn down for each person. Before a baby is born an angel carries it to God and God decides what kind of soul is needed, what kind of person that baby shall become – female or male, strong or weak, beautiful or ugly, rich or poor. But the person alone decides if he or she will become good or bad. Then all day from morning till evening the angel carries the soul through the whole world, showing where the person with that soul will live and die.

In the evening, the angel takes the soul back to the baby in the mother's womb. Two angels watch over the soul during all the nine months of pregnancy, holding up a special light, like the light that was created on the first day, so the soul can see from one end of the world to the other. When it is time for the baby to be born, the angel Gabriel pinches the baby above the upper lip, leaving the little triangular mark we all have. Immediately the baby forgets everything its soul has seen and learnt. Life is then a relearning of the soul's wisdom.

Body and soul: In the traditional Jewish view, the soul, which was breathed into Adam by God, is that element which turns matter into a living entity. The soul is considered to have a separate existence from the body. The soul pre-exists the body; its introduction into the human embryo is God's part in the ever-renewed creation of human life. During sleep the soul leaves the body temporarily and draws spiritual nourishment from on high. In death the soul departs from the body, though it hovers around the body for three days, hoping to return to it.

Three souls each: There are three different Hebrew words for soul – nefesh, which means life or self, ruach which means wind and neshama which means breath. Medieval Jewish philosophers believed there were three aspects to the human soul, or even three different souls within a person from nefesh, the lowest soul which people have in common with animals, to neshama the soul with which people communicate with God.

? Why do you think the Hebrew word for soul *neshama* and the Hebrew word for breath *neshima* are so similar?

Adam, the species: There is agreement amongst the rabbinic commentators that the term "Adam" signifies not a specific individual but humankind as a whole, both male and female.

The dualty of Adam: Rashi and a range of other commentators agree that the first Adam created was both male and female, thereby suggesting an egalitarian version of the creation of man and woman. As one Midrash tells man was created originally with two faces (panim) – the word panim also denotes outlooks, facets, perspectives. The original Adam contained a duality that was later separated into male and female, each with its own perspective.

In God's image: "The idea of our being made in God's image is the fundamental paradox of the creation story – its most mysterious and empowering assertion. God is without form, without gender... Being created in the image of an infinite God means that our spiritual potential for growth and transformation is limitless... If we define ourselves as being made in the image of God, no-one else can ever define us even to ourselves." Naomi Rosenblatt

Human dignity: "Above all demarcations of race and nations, castes and classes, oppressors and servants, givers and receivers, above all delineations even of gifts and talents stands one certainty: Man. Whoever bears this image is created and called to be a revelation of human dignity." Leo Baeck

? Do you think Adam was created as an adult or a child? Did Adam have a belly button? (Remember what a belly button actually is!)

Ch.1: 27 So God created Adam, in the image of God; male and female God created them.

The Torah says that Adam, the first person created, was both male and female. But how could God create a person who was both male and female?

Many Sages of Old say that the first Adam was actually a male and female together, a man and a woman joined back to back – the woman's face looking out one way, the man's face looking the other way. If Adam was to be created in God's image, then God had to include both the male and the female aspects.

What does it mean that Adam, the first person, was created in God's image? Being created in God's image is awesome, it emphasizes the specialness of people in all of creation – the holiness and dignity of all people, no matter what their race, nation or religion. And even though all people are created in God's image each person is unique. Since creation no other person was ever exactly like you, or ever will be.

Ch.1: 28 – 30 And God blessed Adam and said, "Grow and have many children and fill the earth with people. And rule over the earth and take care of it: the fish of the sea, the birds of the air and all the animals that walk over the land." And God also said, "I give you all the plants of the earth and the fruits of the trees to be your food. And the animals, birds and fish shall also eat plants and grasses as their food."

The Torah tells that God created people to rule over the earth and take care of it and its creatures. Scholars of our Time explain that the role of people is to help God in looking after creation, to be God's co-workers in the process of creation. The Torah gives us many laws about how to look after the environment – such as not cutting down trees and letting the earth rest from farming every seven years. These laws remind us that, according to the Torah, land does not really belong to people, all land belongs to God.

In the beginning, God gave Adam "all the plants of the earth and the fruits of the trees to be your food." People did not eat meat, and all the animals were herbivores, eating only grass and plants. So people and animals lived in peace together, not hunting each other for food, but side by side on the earth. It was only later that God allowed people and animals to eat meat – after the time of Noah and the flood. We shall read about this in the next parasha.

Earth and earthling: "Perhaps the most profound Jewish statement about the relationship between human beings and the earth is bound up in two words in Hebrew…Adam and Adamah, Earthling and Earth… The two words are connected to teach us that human beings and the earth are intertwined." Arthur Waskow

Rule over the earth: "To claim that this verse provides justification for the exploitation of the environment, leading to the poisoning of the atmosphere, the pollution of our water, and the spoilation of natural resources is … a complete distortion of the truth. On the contrary the Hebrew Bible and Jewish interpreters prohibit such exploitation. Judaism goes much further and insists that man has an obligation not only to conserve the world of nature but to enhance it because man is the copartner of God in the work of creation." Robert Gordis

Environmental Judaism: The Torah contains various laws about looking after the environment. Rabbis extended these prohibitions and they forbade destruction of any objects beneficial to people, including wasting food or fuel. Some modern groups argue that ecological principles can be derived from Judaism. Rabbi Zalman Schachter-Shalomi has suggested we should add a new code of eco-kosher practices such as forbidding foods grown using earth – destroying pesticides.

Side by side: Although many translations of the Bible state that God took one of Adam's ribs to create a woman, the rabbinic commentators are nearly unanimous in translating the Hebrew word *tzela* as "side," a more egalitarian interpretation. Indeed the other place in the Torah where the word *tzela* is used is "The second side *(tzela)* of the tabernacle." (Exodus 26:20) Judith Antonelli, Jewish Orthodox feminist, writes that Eve's creation from Adam's rib has been used in Christian, not Jewish thought, to justify chauvinism and subordination of women.

Alone, not lonely: Why did God create Adam alone first? Rabbi Soloveitchik answers that the state of *levado* – that awareness of being alone – is responsible for the uniqueness of human beings. "Social man is superficial: he imitates, he emulates. Lonely man is profound: he creates, he is original."

"A helpmate opposite him": If he merits, she will be a helpmate; if not, she will oppose him." Rashi

? In what ways do you think *ezer kenegdo* – " a helpmate standing opposite" is a good description of the relationship between a husband and wife?

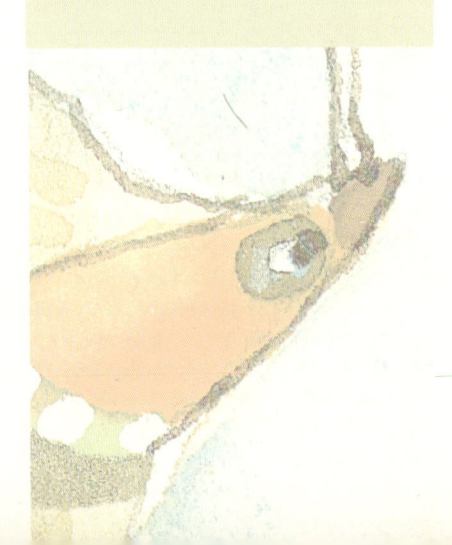

Ch.2: 19 – 22 God brought all the creatures to Adam to be named, and Adam gave a different name to each bird, fish and animal. Adam saw that each creature had a partner, there was a male and female of each kind, but Adam found no partner. God, too, saw that Adam was lonely and needed a partner to talk to, to play and grow with, to love. So God made Adam fall into a deep, deep sleep. While Adam was sleeping God divided off a side from Adam and built it into a woman.

Why did God create Adam alone in the first place? Sages of Old explain that Adam was created alone and single for the sake of peace among people, so no person could say to another "My father was greater than yours." For all people come from the same beginning.

The Sages of Old explain that Adam had been a man and a woman, back to back and together, but now God divided the male and female halves (as God had divided the light and dark, and then the sea and land) to create a separate man and a separate woman.

There is another way of telling the story of the creation of the first man and woman. Other Sages of Old say that the first Adam was a man, and God later created woman by separating off Adam's rib and forming it into a woman. These two stories give quite different ways of understanding the creation of man and woman, and the relationship between them. Which story do you like better? Why?

The Sages of Old explain that the Hebrew word for the partner God makes for Adam is *ezer kenegdo*, which is translated as "a helpmate standing opposite him." What sort of a helpmate is one who stands opposite? The Sages of Old explain that a true partnership between a man and a woman involves two things: being a helpmate – sharing common dreams and working together, and standing opposite – remaining separate individuals who are open to each other's differences.

Ch.2: 23 And the man was still called Adam, meaning "from the earth" and the woman was called Eve – Hava in Hebrew – meaning "the mother of life." And when Adam saw Eve he said, "This woman was once a part of me, of my bone and my body." So it is that when a man grows up he will leave his mother and father to find his woman partner and be united with her, to live and grow and love with her. And God saw all that had been created and behold, it was very good. And there was evening and there was morning, the sixth day.

And so the man and the woman who had once been joined back to back were separated. But when a woman and a man love each other and form a partnership, it is as though they have been reunited. They are quite different from each other, yet in their togetherness there is a balance, a balance that is based on love and equality.

Eve and Isha: "...the two names that were given to Eve, to signify her two roles: Eve (Hava, "life-giver") signifies her sexual, procreative function, while Isha – "woman" – signifies her intellectual, spiritual role, parallel to that of man." Avivah Zornberg

Women's beginning: "Some feminists have problems with the way the Bible describes the creation of women – from the side of man and as his helper. I frankly don't see any problem with women's beginning in Eden. Man is created from dust in a single verse. Woman is fashioned from flesh and bone over the course of six verses. ... Woman's absence from Eden clearly signals its incompleteness to God." Naomi Rosenblatt

Three in a marriage: The Hebrew words for man (ish) and woman (isha) are very similar. Both contain the letters Aleph and Shin (which spell 'fire'), with the addition of the Yud in the man and the Heh in the woman. Yudheh is another name for God. This teaches us that where there is sacredness in the union of the man and the woman, it is a healthy relationship, but where sacredness is absent, fire remains, with the potential for destruction.

A woman reveals: "A woman has a mystical capacity to open up and reveal the hidden soul of a man. Through her spirit she can bring to the soul of a man a deeper dimension of suffering and joy that opens up the wellsprings of his inner being....".
R. Abraham Kook

Shabbat keeps us alive: "More than Israel has kept the Shabbat, the Shabbat has kept Israel."
The Talmud

Sacred time: "The weekly choice to dedicate one day not to the shopping mall, not to the television or telephone or computer, not to the consciousness of the market place, opens up the possibility for sacred time in which the call of God can be heard."
Michael Lerner

Hope for progress: "To set apart one day a week for freedom, a day on which we would not use the instruments which have been so easily turned into weapons of destruction, a day for being with ourselves.... a day on which we stop worshipping the idols of technical civilization, a day on which we use no money, a day of armistice in the economic struggle with our fellow man and the forces of nature – is there any institution that holds out a greater hope for human progress than the Sabbath?"
Abraham Joshua Heschel

True rest: "Shabbat may still be the most important religious form that Judaism has to give to humanity. In our age of ever increasing pace and demand, the need for a day of true rest is all the greater."
Arthur Green

? In what ways does your family – or would you like your family, – to make Shabbat a special time in your home?

Ch.2: 1 – 3 Thus the heaven and the earth were completed. By the seventh day, God finished all the work of creation and God rested. God blessed the seventh day and made it holy.

On the seventh day God made nothing new; it was the day of rest and celebration. Ever since, there are people who make nothing new on every seventh day, but joyously celebrate what already is. The seventh holy day is the Shabbat. Every day of the week we work and are busy. On Shabbat we can just be at peace, with ourselves, with our family. Shabbat begins on Friday evening. The house has been cleaned, the table set with fresh table cloth and flowers, challah and wine. The Shabbat candles are lit and there is a magical moment in the home.

A Scholar of our Time writes "When all work is brought to a standstill, the candles are lit. Just as creation began with the words, 'Let there be light' – so does the celebration of creation begin with the kindling of lights."

Finding the Balance

And so the world was created with harmony and balance. There was balance between the light and the dark, the sea and the land, the sun and the moon. And all the living things on the earth lived together in peace – the plants and the fish and the birds and the animals and the people.

But today the world has lost that harmony and balance. People have not looked after the earth properly. Parts of the earth and its oceans have been spoiled. The forests have been cut down, the seas and lakes have been dirtied. Birds and fish and animals cannot live in them anymore. People and animals no longer live side by side. And people do not live in harmony with each other. There is hatred and intolerance, stealing and war.

Perhaps the angels who told God not to create people were right after all. But then people are the only ones who can fix the world, putting back the balance and harmony that were there in the beginning. An ancient phrase calls this *tikkun olam*, fixing the world. Maybe seeking out and gathering up the scattered sparks of goodness will help fix the world. It may be the most important thing we can do in our lives.

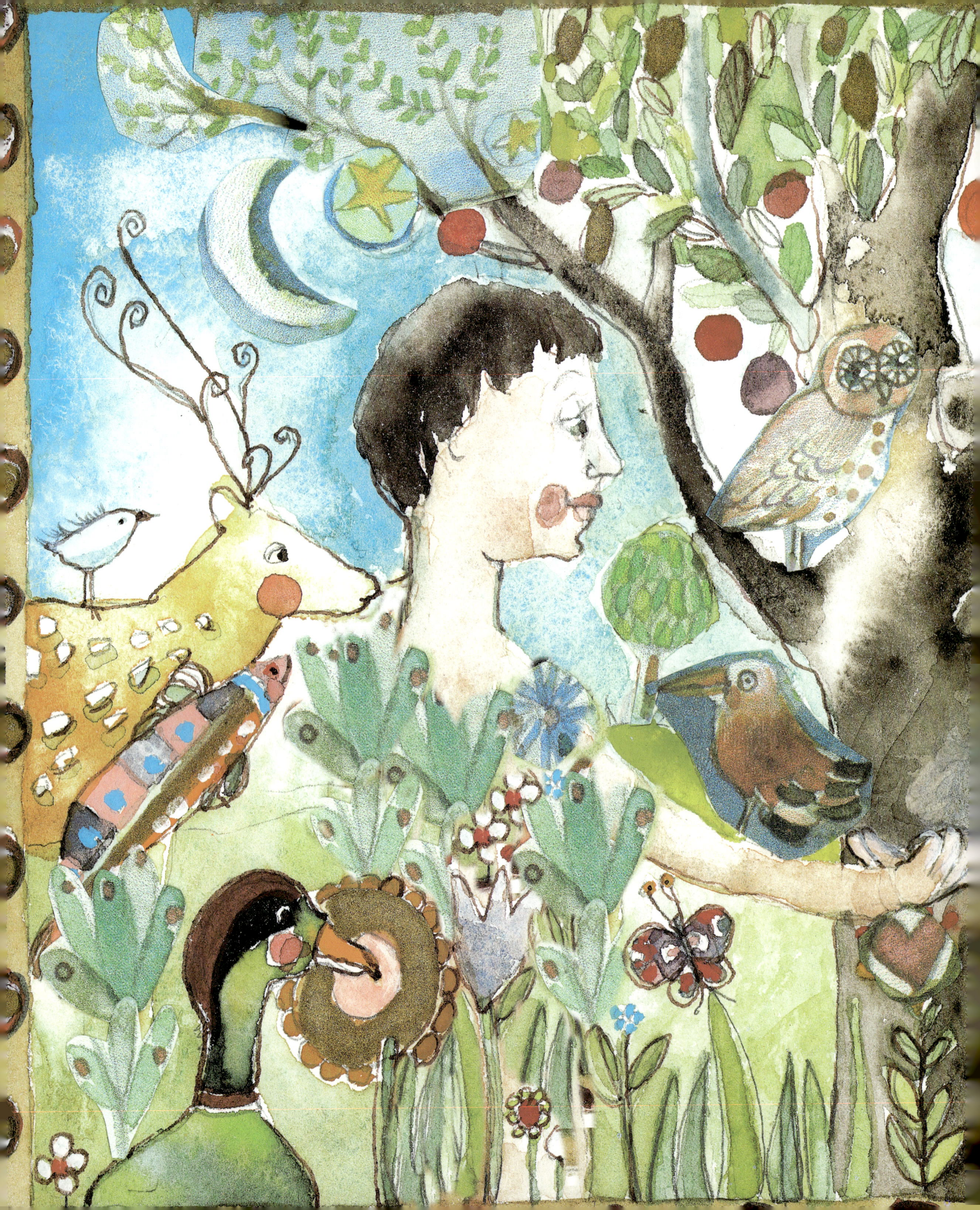

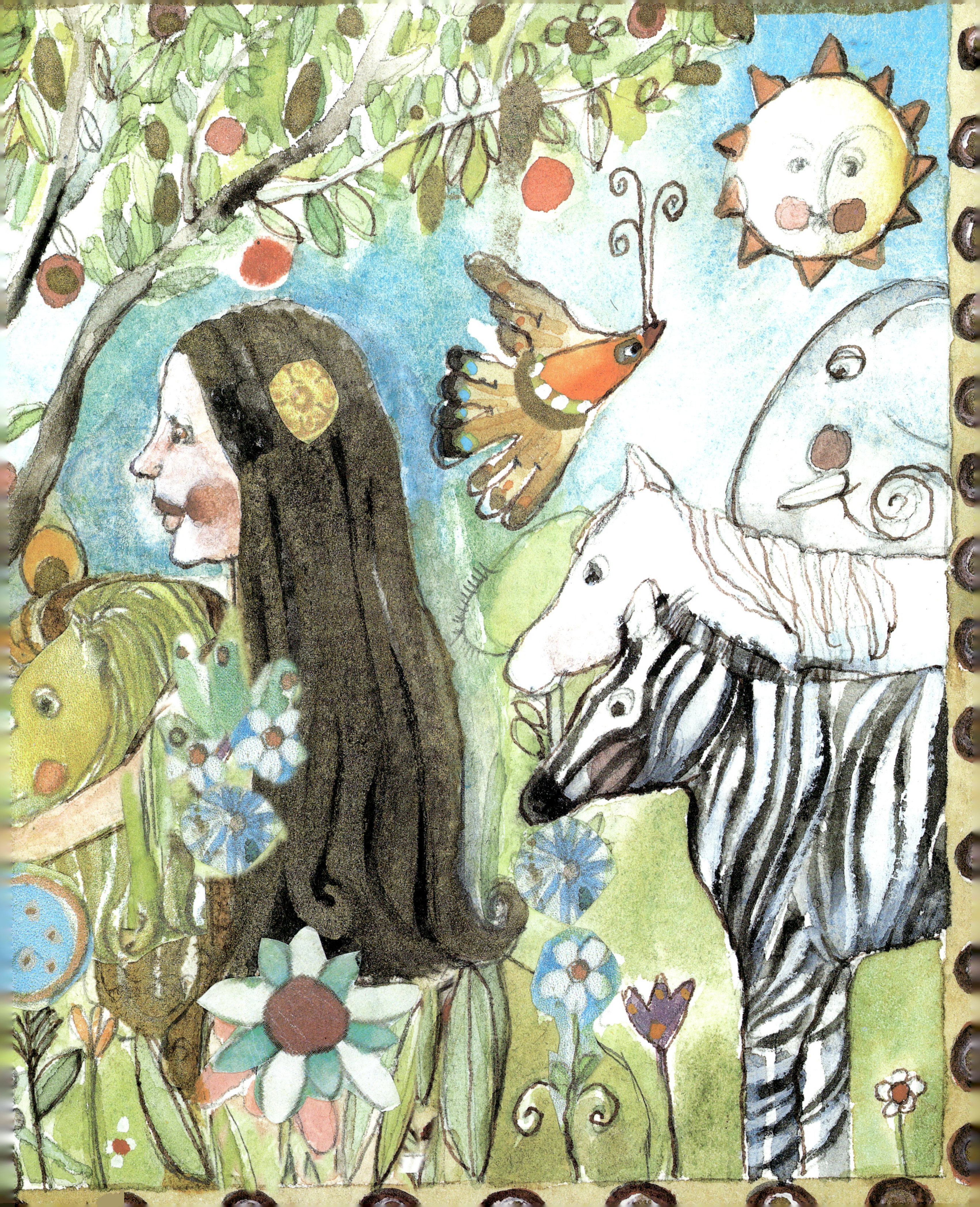

35

נח

NOAH
Noah and the flood

Moral relativity: What does it mean to be righteous? Does it mean to follow all the laws and mitzvot, keeping to "the letter of the law"? Or does it mean to go beyond living your own good life and be involved in the world beyond? Does one's sense of morality need to be viewed relative to the generation in which one lives?

Comfort zone: The word noah means "comfort." Noah was to bring comfort to the world, and humankind was saved through him. But Noah has been criticised because he remained within his own comfort zone. He did as God commanded him, but he didn't extend himself beyond. He didn't move out of his comfort zone to plead with God not to destroy the rest of humanity. Noah looked after himself and his family but he didn't reach out to save others.

Noah's three sons: According to traditional rabbinic commentary, the three sons of Noah are the ancestors of the new world of human beings. The name of each son discloses the different approaches of each to life, and the peoples they would father. Shem, coming from the Hebrew word for name, suggests one who is cognitive. Cham, coming from the Hebrew word for heat, suggests one who is emotional and Yefet, coming from the Hebrew word for beauty, suggests one who seeks beauty.

? What do you think makes someone a good person?

Ch.6: 5 – 10 **Ten generations passed from the time of Adam and Eve. In the beginning Adam and Eve were created from both the breath of God above and the earth below and placed in the world to take care of it. But over the generations people had forgotten to live peacefully in the world and had become evil.**

It was into this generation that Noah was born. Noah was a righteous man, perfect in his generation. Noah and his wife had three sons Shem, Ham and Yafet.

The Torah tells how in the ten generations from Adam to Noah people forgot their place in creation as the link between the earth below and God above. People were created with free will, to choose to do good or evil. However over time people had chosen only evil, they were cruel, selfish and violent, they stole and killed. Amongst such people only Noah stood out as a good and moral person. But why does the Torah write: "… Noah was a righteous man, perfect in his generation"? Why isn't it simply written: "Noah was a righteous man"? What does his generation have to do with it?

The Sages of Old explained this phrase "perfect in his generation" in two ways. It can be understood as a compliment to Noah. Noah managed to remain a righteous man even when all the people around him were selfish and cruel. It is difficult to remain a moral person when all around you are not. Noah had the courage not to be influenced by people around him, but to stick to his own path.

On the other hand, the Sages of Old also understood "perfect in his generation" as a criticism of Noah. Noah stood out as a righteous man in that generation of evil people, but had he lived in a different generation of good people, such as the generation of Abraham, he would not have stood out as any more righteous than the others. These are two quite different ways of understanding the phrase "perfect in his generation." When you read the story I wonder which you will agree with?

Throughout the story of Noah, there is a question lurking beneath the surface: "How righteous a man was Noah? Was he a perfectly righteous man, or was he a fairly good man who could have done better?"

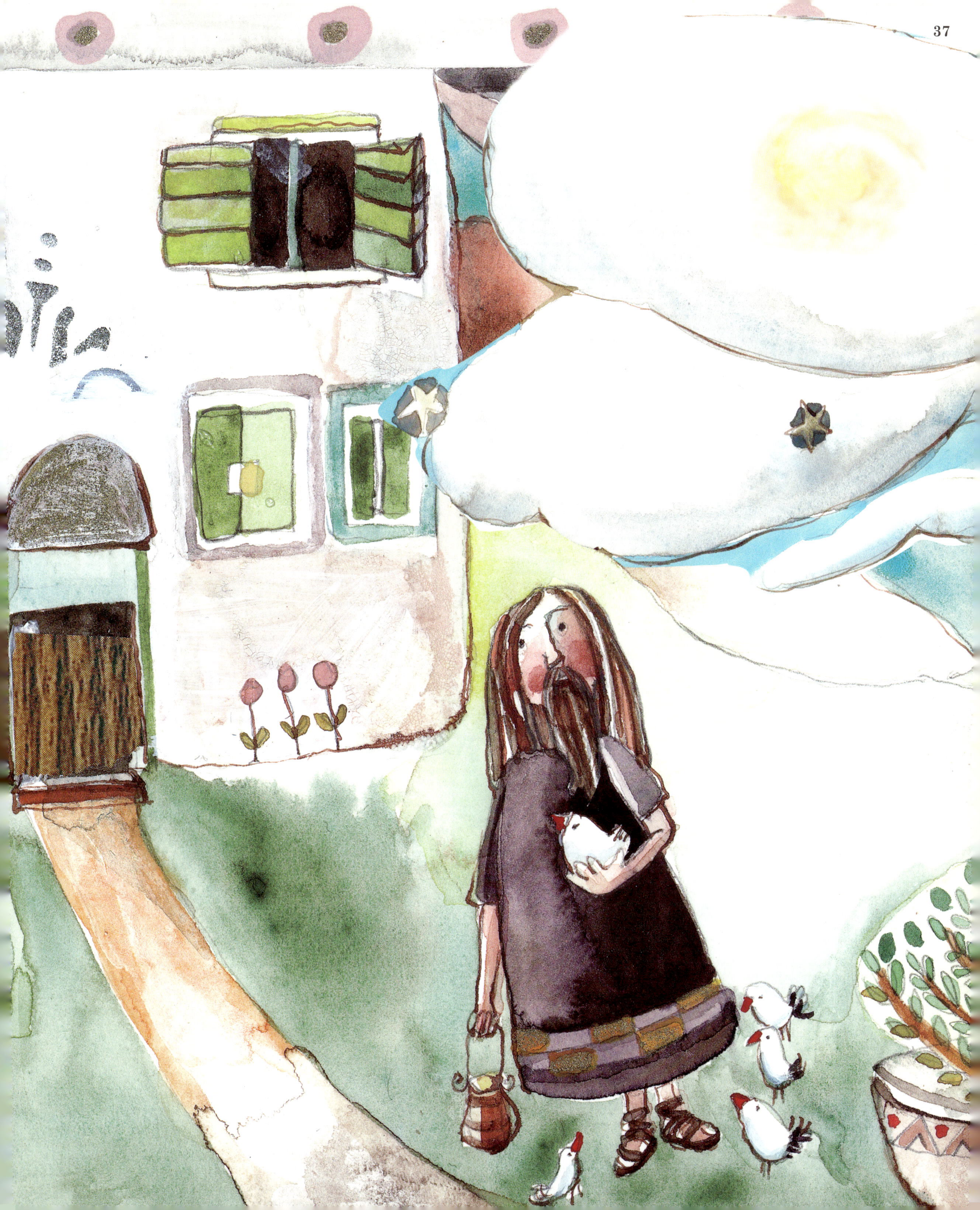

Spoiled world: "Without a guiding vision for their lives, humans ran amok, choosing brutish violence over peaceful coexistence. The strong preyed on the weak, men violated women and humankind despoiled the earth that God had commanded them to protect." Naomi Rosenblatt

Struggling with the text: Although the story of Noah and the flood has often been retold for children in pretty picture books with cute animals marching two by two to the ark, the biblical story actually contains some disturbing and challenging elements. It connects us with the text and tradition to understand that many great Jewish scholars, today and in the past, have struggled with these very issues.

The ruin of human wickedness: "...in biblical theology human wickedness, the inhumanity of man to man, undermines the very foundations of society. The pillars. upon which rest the permanence of all earthly relationships, totter and collapse, bringing ruin and disaster to mankind." Nahum Sarna

? Do you remember what God's hope for people was when humans were first created? (You can look back at the sixth day of Creation to be reminded.) There is an enormous gap between God's hope for humans and the way they were actually behaving at the time of Noah.

Ch.6: 11 – 13   God saw that, apart from Noah and his family, the wickedness of humankind was great upon the earth and all the thoughts and feelings of people were only evil. The world had become spoiled and the earth was filled with cruelty, violence and robbery. God's heart was saddened and God regretted having made humankind on the earth. So God said, "I will wipe out humankind and all living creatures from the face of the earth. From humans to animals to creeping things to the birds of the sky, for I regret having made them."

God was very disappointed with the way humankind was behaving. This was not at all what God had planned and expected when the decision to create people was made. So God decided to wipe out all creation and start again with a new beginning. Some Sages of Old and Scholars of our Time worry that this story raises some difficult questions about God.

What do you think of God's decision to destroy all the people and animals? Although not every creature and person could have been evil, God decided to destroy them all. Many great Jewish scholars today and in the past have struggled with this issue. And so as we struggle with the same issue we are not alone but part of a long tradition.

One Scholar of our Time says that at the time of the flood God viewed humans as the centre of creation. If humankind failed then the creation of the whole world had failed and so God wanted to wipe it all out and start again. After the flood we shall see a major change in God's view of the place of humans in the world.

What do you think of God's decision to destroy all the people in the world, even the young children? The Sages of Old recognise that young children are not evil. But they argue that young children living with evil ways all around them will eventually learn evil too. Maybe we humans need to learn that if we do not stop the violence in the world we will all be affected by it. God regretted having made people when they could be so evil. God wanted to make a clean start to a new world. Noah and his family would be the start of a new generation of people.

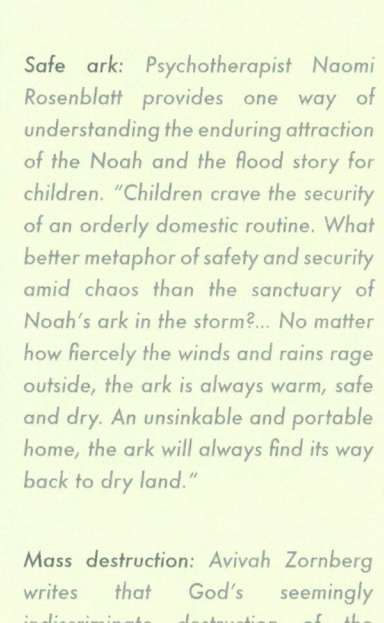

Safe ark: Psychotherapist Naomi Rosenblatt provides one way of understanding the enduring attraction of the Noah and the flood story for children. "Children crave the security of an orderly domestic routine. What better metaphor of safety and security amid chaos than the sanctuary of Noah's ark in the storm?... No matter how fiercely the winds and rains rage outside, the ark is always warm, safe and dry. An unsinkable and portable home, the ark will always find its way back to dry land."

Mass destruction: Avivah Zornberg writes that God's seemingly indiscriminate destruction of the entire world raises some difficult philosophical questions about God's dealings with humanity. "The Flood, then in its most radical imagery, becomes for all times a paradigm of the problem of God's dealings with man.... The Flood will never lose its potency to generate questions about shetef – about mass destruction and the relation of God to the individual."

A learning God: Lawyer Alan Dershowitz criticises God for "overreacting" with the flood, rather than displaying "a rational, proportional and individual response to evil." Dershowitz suggests that the God of Genesis is a learning God as well as a teaching God.... After the flood God gives people a code of laws to govern behaviour and control evil inclinations. These laws grow out of the experiences of both people and God, as people see the need for law, as a result of seeing the consequences of lawlessness.

Compare and contrast: The biblical commentators often compare different characters in Torah. So Rashi and others compare Noah with Abraham and Moshe, who found themselves in similar existential situations.

Standing apart: "At no time did a word of concern, of solicitude escape Noah's lips. It was as though he stood apart from the rest of the world. Noah was a righteous man: Noah deserves to be in the circle of the great. But there was a fatal flaw in Noah, and so he did not become the father of a new religion, a new faith, and a new community. He lacked compassion and, because he lacked compassion, he forfeited the far greater place in history that might have been accorded him." Morris Adler

? You will see that Noah is pretty quiet and doesn't say much throughout the story of the flood. What do you think Noah could have said to God and the people around him?

Ch.6: 8 But Noah found favour in God's eyes. And God said to Noah, "Humankind has become so evil and spoiled the earth, I am going to bring flood waters to wipe out all living creatures from the earth. But Noah, you and your family I will save."

God told Noah that all people and living creatures would be destroyed and only Noah and his family would be saved. What did Noah do? He remained a good and moral person. He built the ark exactly as God told him. But he didn't do more than that. He didn't argue with God not to destroy the rest of humankind. He didn't try to save the people around him.

The Sages of Old compare Noah, the hero of this story, with other biblical heroes. They compare Noah to Abraham, who, as we shall see in one of the next stories, argues with God not to destroy the people living in the city of Sodom. They compare Noah to Moses, who was also saved in an ark (or basket – *teva*.) But in Moses' time when God was angry with the Children of Israel for praying to the golden calf, Moses argued with God not to punish them severely. For this reason many Sages of Old and many Scholars of our Time believe that Noah was a good man who remained a kind person even when others around him were cruel. But he was not a great man. He didn't reach out beyond himself to save others. Lets wait till the end of the story and see what you think.

Ch.6: 14 And God said to Noah, "Build yourself an ark. Build it of wood and put tar on it inside and out. Make it with bottom, second and third decks, with many different rooms and a door on the side." Noah built the ark as God said.

God could have saved Noah in many different ways. Why do you think God chose an ark, giving Noah the job of building the enormous boat? The Midrash describes just how enormous the ark was; it was four hundred and fifty feet long, seventy feet wide and forty five feet high. It had three floors and three hundred different rooms. It took Noah and his family one hundred and twenty years to build the ark. The sound of sawing and hammering filled the air for a long, long time.

The Midrash explains that God gave Noah the job of building the ark because God hoped people would be curious and ask Noah why he was building such a big boat. Then Noah could explain that God was planning to bring a flood on the world because of their evil ways. God wanted to give people a chance to change their ways. But the people at that time were proud and cruel. They just laughed at Noah, calling him a crazy old man.

A Sage of Old tells that even once the rains started falling God hoped people would change their ways and be saved. Then God would make it a good rain, a rain of blessing. Only when the people did not change, the rain turned into a flood.

Time to change: A number of Midrashim express the theme of God giving people time to repent and change their ways. This concept is referred to in Ezekiel (33:11) – that God does not desire the death of the wicked but rather their repentance. Rashi explains that when God caused it to rain, it descended with mercy, so that in the event of the people repenting, the rain would be one of blessing. Only when they did not repent, it turned into a deluge.

The flood in other cultures: Many other Near Eastern cultures have a myth of a flood. Indeed, according to paleontologists about ten thousand years ago the sea rose as much as five hundred feet submerging many low-lying human settlements. The story most closely parallel to the biblical flood story is the Mesopotamian epic of Gilgamesh written in the third century B.C.E. In that epic a favoured man is chosen to survive the flood, he builds a boat and takes aboard animals of every species. However, significant differences exist between the two stories. The Epic of Gilgamesh has no moral underpinnings or causality – the flood occurs because men disturb the sleep of the gods. In contrast the biblical flood story is about God's design for a moral world conflicting with the human potential for violence and self-destruction.

Floating prison: Avivah Zornberg describes the prison-like quality of the ark. "Noah came into the ark . And God shut him in – an ambiguous slam of the door, protecting, imprisoning. Claustrophobia sets in as we read of all the animal flesh, male and female, enclosed with Noah, for twelve months." In some senses Noah's experience in the ark was a punishment for not having reached out to save others, at the same time it was also a remedying of that behaviour by imposing upon him the care of all the animals.

Legendary: Jewish legends add fascinating and quirky detail to the story. As legends tell of many strange creatures that were created on the sixth day, so these creatures enter the ark. "Two creatures of a most peculiar kind also found refuge in the ark. Among the beings that came to Noah there was Falsehood asking for shelter. He was denied admission, because he had no companion, and Noah was taking in the animals only by pairs. Falsehood went off to seek a partner, and he met Misfortune… The pair were then accepted in the ark." Louis Ginzberg

Ch.6:18 – 22 **When the ark was completed God said to Noah, "Go into the ark, you, your sons, your wife and your sons' wives with you. And take with you two of every animal, a male and female of each kind, into the ark. Take two of each of the birds and the beasts and everything that creeps on the ground into the ark to keep alive with you. And also gather together all kinds of food, fruits, vegetables, seeds and herbs that will be food for you and the animals." Noah did as God said and God shut them into the ark.**

Legends tell that the animals came to the ark of their own accord. Thousands of beasts, reptiles, birds and creeping things made their way to the ark. Noah, his wife Na'ama and their family stared in wonder at the beauty and variety of all the creatures in the world. Legends also tell about some strange creatures entering the ark. One enormous animal, the Re'em, could not fit into the ark so Noah tied it to the back and it swam behind! Also a giant called Og pleaded to come on the ark, promising he would serve Noah all his life. Noah agreed but he could not make space for the giant, so Og sat safely on top of the ark and Noah gave him his food through a hole in the roof!

Why do you think the Torah writes: "God shut them into the ark"? Surely Noah could have closed the ark door himself. A Scholar of our Time explains that the ark saves Noah but in some ways the closed space of the ark is also a prison. God shuts Noah into the enclosure of the ark for a full year and during those twelve months Noah must devote himself to caring for all the animals.

Ch.7: 11 – 12, 18 – 23 And so the flood began. The rains poured down for forty days and forty nights. The windows of the heavens opened from above, and from below water burst forth from the springs under the earth. The level of the water increased and the waves loomed up to the sky. The floods rose higher and higher, covering the peaks of even the greatest mountains. And all the people and all the creatures on the earth drowned. But the ark glided safely across the vast expanse of waters.

During the time of the flood water covered the entire earth, the world was full of darkness and water, just as it was when God began to create the world. Scholars of our Time describe the flood as though God was "unmaking" the world – creation was unravelling, like a movie playing backwards. Imagine the movie rewinding to the beginning of the first day when the world was tohu vavohu – a dark and watery chaos. It was on the second day of creation that God spread out the sky to separate and balance the waters below the sky from the waters above. Now God removed that balance; the waters above the sky poured down and the waters below the sky swirled up, and the world became a chaos again as it was in the very beginning.

Why do you think God chose to destroy all living creatures with water, the very substance that all life needs to survive? A Scholar of our Time describes how God created the first person by moulding together soil and water. Then in the flood God destroyed people by completely covering them with water so they would dissolve. It is as though God is saying, "I can bring life with water and I can also bring death with water."

Creation unravelling: There is a poetic beauty in the description of the flood as creation unravelling. Nahum Sarna points out these echoes of the creation story: "The world is covered in darkness and returns to a time before the organisation of time through the sun, moon and the seasons. The separation of seas and dry land is undone as waters cover the earth, and the world returns to a time before the organization of space. The flood is brought about by the reuniting of the two halves of water that were separated in the beginning. Noah is the first man to be born after the death of Adam and he becomes a second Adam, the second father of humanity. Like Adam, he lives in harmony with the animals and receives the divine blessing: "Be fruitful and multiply."

? If you were making a movie of the flood, how would you make it?

Bridge to a new world: The ark was a bridge between the old world and the new, an enclosed space where Noah has to learn to care for others and so experience a responsibility for others that is the model for the post flood world. "The ark had to be more than a protection against the raging elements without; it had to enclose within it a disparate collection of thousands of creatures led and cared for by Noah and his family, forcing them together, imposing upon them an awesome regime of selflessness that allowed not a free moment for self-indulgence. For Noah personally this was a vital lesson." R. David Cohen

Learning to care: "So Noah and his family became caretakers for all surviving animal life, labouring, trudging, serving, so that when the progenitors of humanity emerged from the ark to rebuild the deluged remains of the earth, they would do it with a reborn awareness of the role of man as a caring, unselfish being." R. Mordechai Gifter.

? Do you have pets or other animals that rely on you for food and shelter? What does looking after animals teach you about looking after people?

Ch.6: 24 When the rains finally stopped, the waters remained on the earth one hundred and fifty days. Only after a year did the waters subside. And Noah and all the animals remained shut in the ark, tossed about on the flooding seas all that time.

Can you imagine what it would be like to live for a year closed up in an ark with thousands of animals? During all that year Noah and his family had to look after and feed all the animals. Legends tell how it was not an easy job; there were so many different animals and Noah had to find the right food for each of them and keep their areas clean. The day animals had to be fed by day and the night animals by night. When the flood tossed the ark from side to side, all the animals were shaken up like lentils in a pot. The lions roared, the wolves howled, the monkeys screeched. One day when Noah was late feeding the lion, the angry lion growled and bit him but still Noah continued to take care of it.

Why do you think God gave Noah the job of looking after so many animals? Scholars of our Time explain that in the ark Noah had to learn to care for others. Before, he had looked after himself and his family but he hadn't gone beyond that to save other people from the flood. For Noah and his family the time in the ark was a time of learning to care for all the creatures of the world. When the flood ended Noah and his family came out of the ark with a new understanding of their place in the world. The long journey in the ark, lasting a whole year, was a bridge between the old world, where people had not looked after one another, to a new world of creation. Whilst one world was being destroyed, God was busy creating a new world.

Ch.7: 1 – 4 God remembered Noah and all the creatures in the ark, and God caused a spirit of comfort to pass over the earth, and the waters were calmed. The windows of the heavens were closed and the springs of the deep were closed, and the rain stopped. The level of the waters lowered and returned to their place in the seas and the lakes. Finally the ark stopped moving and came to rest upon the mountains of Ararat.

Maths counts: Traditional commentators studied the Torah text thoroughly from a wide range of perspectives – existentially, morally and even mathematically! Rashi calculated the rate at which the flood waters lowered: 15 cubits divided by 60 days = .25, so the waters lowered by ¼ cubit a day.

A renewed creation: There is a parallel between the sequence of events after the flood and the first days of creation – the spirit of God moving over the waters, the separation of the waters above and below, the separation of water and land. These parallels highlight the concept that the world after the flood was a renewed creation.

When God stops the waters of the flood it is as though the story or the movie of the world rewinds back to the beginning and starts again. So after the flood the spirit of God moved over the waters as on the very first day of creation. Then God separated the waters below the sky from the waters above, as on the second day of creation. And then God gathered together all the waters below the sky in one place, in the seas, as on the third day.

The Sages of Old tell us that there were fifteen cubits of water (a cubit is about forty centimetres) above the peaks of the mountains, and it took sixty days for the water level to lower to expose the peak of Mt Ararat. Can you work out how much the waters subsided each day until the ark rested on Mt Ararat?

Freedom is sweet: The olive leaf is bitter. Rashi and R. Samson Raphael Hirsch explain the dove's presentation of the olive leaf to Noah as carrying a message "Better that my food be bitter but from God than sweet as honey but dependant on human beings." For a full year the dove had not had the opportunity to find its own food. These commentators describe how even the bitterest food eaten in freedom is preferable to the sweetest food in confinement.

? Imagine flying with the dove over the flooded land. What did the dove see? How did the dove feel when she could find no place to land and had to return to the ark?

Ch8: 6 – 12   Noah opened the window of the ark, but he could see no land. "I will send out a bird to find dry land," said Noah. So he sent the dove to see if the waters had subsided. The dove was gone a long time. She found no land and when she finally came back she flew into Noah's hand and lay very still, exhausted.

Seven days later Noah again sent out the dove. That evening the dove flew back holding the leaf of an olive tree in her beak. Seeing the olive leaf Noah rejoiced because he knew dry land was near. Noah waited another seven days and sent the dove again. This time the dove did not return and Noah knew that she had found a warm, dry place to build her nest.

Why did the dove return holding the leaf of an olive tree? Why wasn't it the leaf of an oak tree or an apple tree? A Scholar of our Time explains that the olive tree is known to be a very strong tree that lives for up to a thousand years. It is a symbol of strength, long life and peace, as though God is promising Noah these blessings for the future. Today the olive branch is a worldwide symbol of peace. It is also part of the official emblem of Israel.

Ch 8: 15 – 20 Noah opened the door of the ark and looked out and saw dry land. Then God said, "Go forth from the ark, Noah, you and all your family. And let out every living creature and they shall roam on the earth and multiply and be many."

So all the animals left the ark, the beasts, the reptiles, the birds and the creeping things, and each went to their own special place in the world. Noah and his wife and their three sons and their wives left the ark. They built an altar to make an offering to God, as a way of giving thanks to God for saving them from the flood.

Let out – Hayetze: "Only give them the permission and they go out by themselves. The whole relief, the breathing freely again of those going out of the unnatural restriction of their stay in the ark, out into the free air again, is expressed in Hayetze."
R. Samson Raphael Hirsch

? If you were composing a blessing thanking God for saving you from danger, what would you say?

Midrash describes how after the flood the world was empty and bare – there were no trees or vegetation, just desolate land. Noah and his family had stored away seeds of all the trees and plants, and now they went to sow and plant all these seeds across the countries of the world, so that forests and jungles and fields would grow and color the bare world green.

A Scholar of our Time describes how the animals were all dazed after so long a journey at sea. After a year being rocked by the waves in the ark they were dizzy and not used to standing on dry land. Noah's sons and their wives gently led the animals out of the ark. The animals multiplied, each finding its own habitat, the polar bears and penguins in the snow and ice, and the giraffes and elephants in the grassy plains.

Noah made an offering as a way of thanking God for saving his family from the flood. There is a special blessing in Judaism, birkat hagomel, thanking God for saving one from danger. We say this blessing when we return from dangerous travel, recover from an illness or are saved from an earthquake or flood.

Part of the food chain: "There is a critical difference between viewing Man as just another species and seeing him as the purpose of Creation… Before the flood Man had transcended the animal – he was a steward of life, not wholly part of the food chain… His food was limited to the plant kingdom. After the Flood, he himself became a part of animal life, a predator and subject to predation."
R. Matis Weinberg

Lerner's vegetarianism: "The original injunctions to Adam and Eve prohibited the eating of meat. It was only after God's disillusionment with humans reached the level where S/He wanted to destroy almost the entire population, in the time of Noah, that God allowed people to eat animal flesh (presumably because the level of violence and insensitivity had become so high that channelling all this destructive energy into animal killing might at least preserve human beings)." The laws of Kashrut can be seen in this context. "Their hidden message from God is this: 'Okay, you can eat meat. But I'm going to make it such a hassle for you, and I'm going to restrict what you can eat so much, that you'll gradually come to realize that it would be easier to be a vegetarian.'" Michael Lerner

Ch9: 1 – 6 And God said to Noah and his family, "Be fruitful, have many children and fill the land. I give you all the animals and all the vegetation for you as your food. But you must not eat the flesh of an animal that is still alive. Also you may not take the life of any person; for any life taken I will require justice."

Before the flood people were vegetarians. Remember in the creation of the world God gave Adam all the vegetation to eat as food, but animal meat was not given to Adam as food. Now after the flood God allows people to eat meat. Sages of Old and Scholars of our Time give different reasons to explain this change. Which reason do you find most convincing?

A Sage of Old tells that when Noah and his family came out of the ark and saw the desolate world with no trees and plant life, they were scared they would not find enough to eat and might starve. So God allowed them to eat meat.

A Scholar of our Time explains that before the flood God saw people as being at the top of creation, and so people were not part of the food chain. But after the flood God no longer saw people at the top, rather as one species among many different species. And so people became part of the food chain. People eat animals and animals eat people.

A Sage of Old teaches that the fruit and vegetables in the Garden of Eden were as nourishing as meat. But after the flood, people had to eat meat to stay healthy.

A Scholar of our Time explains that God saw the violence and cruelty of the people living at the time of the flood. God saw that people yearned for meat and thought that if people were allowed to eat meat it might reduce their cruelty to each other.

Although people are now allowed to eat meat, the Torah gives restrictions on what meat we may eat and how we may eat it. Also the Torah has many laws that guide us about how to respect animals and be kind to them, even if we are not vegetarians. For example, you must always feed your animals, be they pets or work animals, before you sit down to eat your own evening meal. Many argue that the laws of kashrut are designed to make us respect the life of the animal, to make us aware that when we eat meat we are eating the flesh of a living creature and to minimize the cruelty involved. Some Jewish people have chosen to be vegetarians – they do not want to eat animal meat, and so they automatically keep kosher. At the same time as God allowed people to kill animals for meat, God gave clear laws prohibiting one person from killing another.

Temporary concession: R. Abraham Kook believed that the permission to eat meat was only a temporary concession. "A God who is merciful to his creatures would not institute an everlasting law permitting the killing of animals for food."

Jewish vegetarians: Where does Judaism stand today regarding vegetarianism? Many Jews, amongst them prominent thinkers and Rabbis have chosen to be vegetarians. Some argue that in Judaism, vegetarianism is repeatedly emphasized as the ideal. Not only at creation, but also after the giving of the Torah, attempts were made to make vegetarianism the norm. Others argue that the realities of meat production violate religious mandates to treat animals with compassion, protect the environment, conserve resources, feed hungry people and preserve human health.

Healthy chicken: Isaac Bashevis Singer was at a dinner and asked if he wanted fish or chicken. "Just vegetables," he answered. "Is it for your health?" he was asked. "No," he answered, "For the health of the chicken."

? What laws would you make to guide people to respect animals and be kind to them?

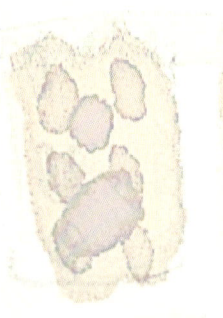

A change of view: R. Matis Weinberg elucidates the concept of a fundamental change in God's perception of people and the world before and after the flood. "Before the flood man encompassed the consciousness of the universe. If he failed, the failure was universal. But after the flood, it seems that suddenly the earth and its life-forms are viewed as significant in themselves, and Man is no more than another twig on the evolutionary bush."

A realistic view of humans: "At the end of the flood story God comes to a sobering realization about the human beings He created in His own image. Even the best of them will always embody a mixture of good and evil impulses... But Genesis resists pessimism by encouraging us to recognize evil in the world and in ourselves and to use our God-given free will to subdue it." Naomi Rosenblatt

Not a mirror image: "God separates His responsibility for creation from His response to the moral condition of humankind. Prior to the Flood, all of nature was doomed to destruction because God "regretted that He had made man on earth." Human corruption was sufficient reason to justify the destruction of all living things. After the Flood, however, God proclaims HIs awareness that although human beings are created in HIs image, they do not automatically embody all that God wishes them to be. God's reflections on them are, as it were, similar to a parent's realization that his child is not his mirror image but is a separate being with limitations, weaknesses and an independent will." R. David Hartman

? The Noahide laws are basic laws that all people must follow. What basic laws would you make for all people? Do you know what the seven Noahide laws are? If not you can look them up in the endnotes.

Ch8: 21, Ch9: 8 – 11 God blessed Noah and his family and said to them, "I establish my covenant with you and your children and your children's children. And with every living thing that is with you; the birds, the beasts and the creeping things. Never again shall I bring a flood to destroy the earth." And inwardly, God said, "I will not destroy the earth again because of humankind, because people's thoughts are evil from their youth."

God's covenant with Noah is the first covenant between God and humankind. It is a covenant between God and "The Children of Noah" – which includes all the nations of the earth. Together with this covenant God gave the Seven Noahide Laws that all the peoples of the world must keep.

However God's covenant is not only with people but with all the creatures of the world. At the beginning of this story God decided to bring the flood "because the thoughts and feelings of people are only evil." As God recognizes that people are only a part of all creation, so God promises not to destroy the whole world if people are evil.

A Scholar of our Time explains that before the flood God saw people as the centre of creation, so if people were evil the whole of creation had failed. Now God recognizes that people are just a part of the world, and so God will not destroy the entire world because of people's evil. God establishes the covenant not only with people but with all the creatures of the world. God has come to care for all of the earth; we are only a part of it – "only human."

Ch8: 22, Ch9: 12 – 17 Then out of the clouds, God made a rainbow appear that stretched across the sky. And God said, "This is my rainbow – a sign of the covenant between me and you and all living creatures, for all generations to come. When I bring clouds over the earth and the rainbow is in the clouds, it will be a reminder to you of my promise that never again shall water become a flood to destroy all life. While the earth remains, seedtime and harvest, cold and heat, summer and winter, day and night shall not cease. This is my promise of peace, peace between me and all living creatures."

The rainbow is the sign of the first covenant between God and creation. It is a sign that the rain we receive is necessary for life, and will not turn into a flood that destroys the world. Midrash tells that the rainbow's colors symbolize the variety in humankind. Just as there are many colors in the rainbow so there are many kinds of people – those who are good and those who are bad, all making up the rainbow of humanity.

Another way of seeing the rainbow is as an outer covering of God. Midrash compares God inside the rainbow to a fruit inside its peel. But unlike the fruit, we can never peel back the outer layer of the rainbow and see the inside of God.

Rainbow symbols: Some rabbinic commentators argue that the rainbow is a positive sign, reminding us of the covenant between God and humankind, and reassuring us that God will not destroy humankind again. Others interpret the rainbow as a sign with a stern message – when the rainbow appears it is to remind people that they have sinned and need to change their ways. So the rainbow is seen as a combination of justice and mercy. On the one hand it reminds us of humankind's sins and the punishment it suffered for them (justice) and on the other hand it signifies the promise not to destroy humankind again (mercy).

God in a rainbow: The rainbow's combination of justice and mercy is a reflection of God who is seen to combine the attributes of justice and mercy. Indeed the commentators draw a comparison between God and the rainbow, seeing the rainbow as an appearance of a form of God's image. "This is something which resembles Me, as it states: 'The rainbow which is in the cloud.'"

Umbrella of trust: "The rainbow of peace hung in the sky, a prism for the light of heaven to shine through. This protective shield against the devestating floodwaters of the clouds was a symbol of a covenant of everlasting life between God and His creation. This umbrella of trust was God's unconditional vow to preserve the earth." Naomi Rosenblatt

? How do you feel when you see a rainbow?

Stepping outside the ark

So what do you think about Noah? Do you think he was a perfectly righteous man, or a good man who could have done better? Would you interpret "Noah was a righteous man, perfect in his generation" as a criticism of Noah or a compliment?

Noah's behaviour in the beginning of the story has been described as a *tzaddik im peltz*, which is Yiddish for a holy man in a fur coat. Why is Noah compared to a holy man in a fur coat? In a cold room there are two ways to warm oneself. One is to build a fire, and then everyone in the room warms up. The other way is to put on a fur coat – then the wearer of the fur coat is warm but everyone else stays cold. Noah was wrapped up in the warmth of his own righteousness, but was not really worried about the cold of others. But through the story Noah changed. During his journey in the ark Noah learnt to care for others, he had to look after all the thousands of animals. He had to take off his fur coat and get to work – feeding the animals and cleaning out their areas.

So what does the story of Noah have to say about what it means to be a righteous person? Like Noah, we in our own lives try to create an ark of safety and peace around ourselves. We try to create that ark in our family and our home. At times when the world feels difficult and complicated we withdraw and hide away from it in the safety of our family and home. But the story of Noah teaches us that living our own good life in our ark of comfort is not enough. To be a truly righteous person we have to step outside our ark of comfort and help to fix the world beyond.

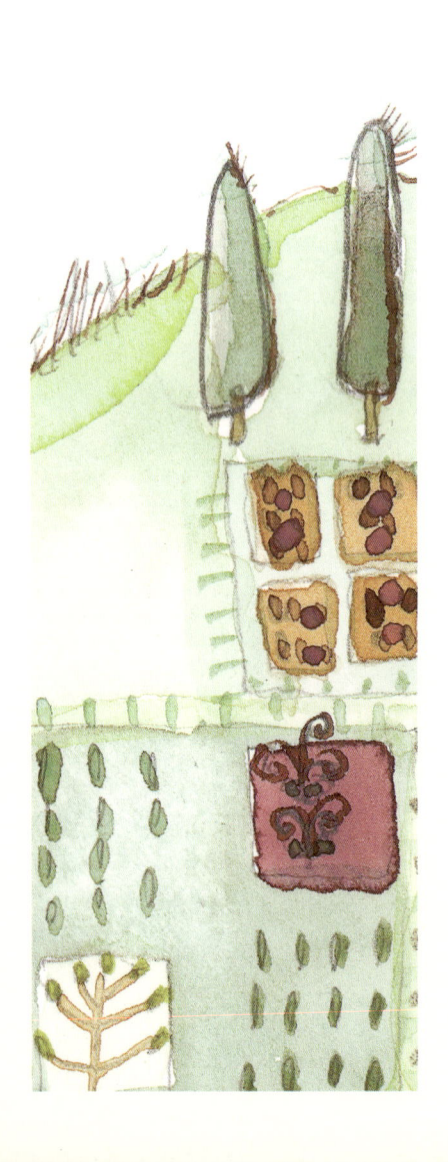

53

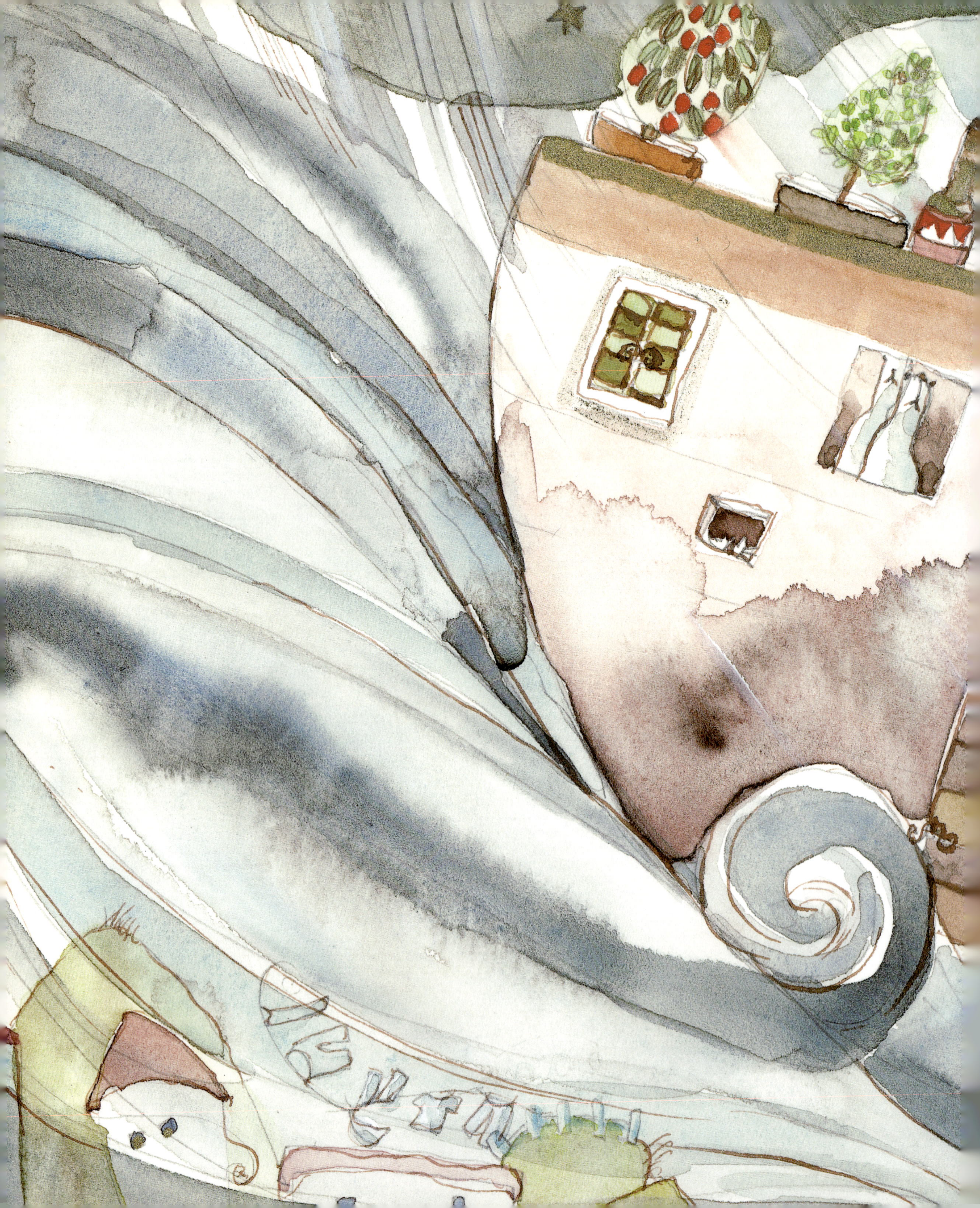

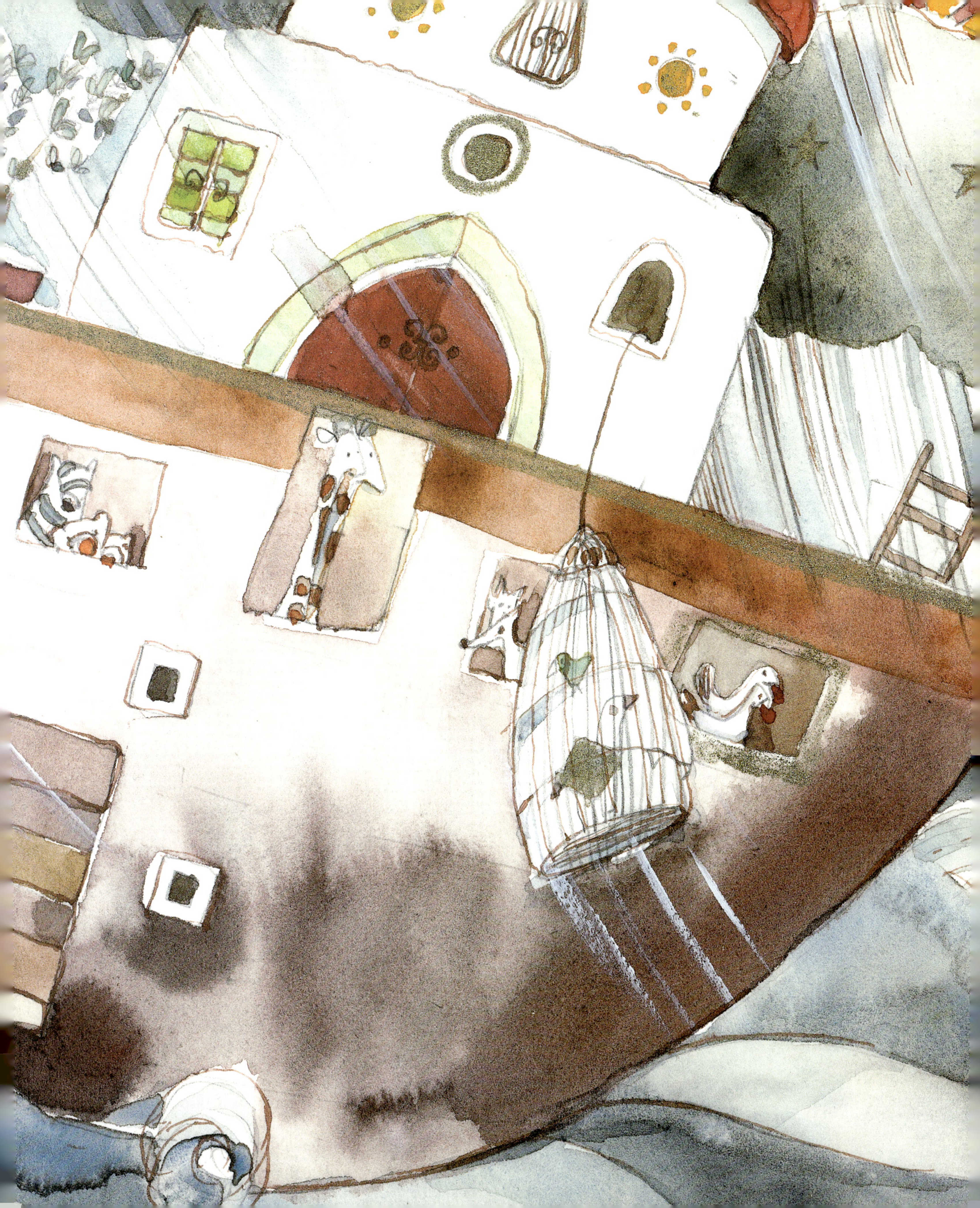

לך לך

LECH LECHA

God calls Abraham "Go forth"

Filling the gap: The Sages and Midrash are acutely aware of the immense gap in the Torah text, which tells us little about Abram's life before God spoke to him, and nothing about why Abram was chosen. They describe the idol – worshipping family and community around him, and so Abram's belief in God and his understanding of the world are seen as a radical departure from all that had gone before. "Abram had no teacher, no one to instruct him in anything. He was submerged in Ur Casdim, among idolaters. HIs father and mother and the entire population worshipped idols...But his mind was busily working and reflecting until he attained the way of truth, and knew that there was one God." Rambam

Infertility and rootlessness: "The barrenness of Sarai evokes the other meaning of the word akara: the couple is uprooted, the ground cut from under their feet...(as) akarim they recognize the sterility of the place that nurtured them" Avivah Zornberg

Ch.11: 26 – 30 After the flood came ten generations. People lived to be very old in those days. Shelah lived four hundred and thirty-three years and had many sons and daughters. Peleg lived two hundred and thirty-nine years and also had many sons and daughters. Then a man called Terach married Amatlai and they had three sons. One of these sons, Abram, was very special. Abram married Sarai. But Sarai was barren: although they wanted to have a child, Sarai could not become pregnant. And so it was just the two of them, Abram and Sarai.

Ten generations passed from the time of Adam and Eve until the time of Noah. And ten generations passed again from the time of Noah until the time of Abram and Sarai. The Torah tells us quickly about generations of people who lived long lives and had many children. Then the Torah slows down when it comes to Abram and Sarai. Their story is important and the Torah wants to tell us about it in detail. With Abram and Sarai there is a stop to the flow of generations – Abram and Sarai could not have children because Sarai was barren.

A Scholar of our Time explains how the Hebrew word for "barren," *akara*, is very like the Hebrew word *akur*, "uprooted" or "without roots." When you don't have children your roots in any place may not be as strong. Children give you roots, they give you a reason to stay in one place. Perhaps because they didn't have children, Abram and Sarai could go on their long journey.

The Torah does not tell us about Abram and Sarai's lives before God first spoke to Abram. We know that Abram must have been special (since God chose him to be the forefather of the Jewish people) and the Midrash helps us understand why. Midrash tells that Abram lived in Ur Casdim, a big town where all the people worshipped idols. Abram's own father Terach made idols and sold them. But when Abram was very young he realized that an idol could not be God. One day Terach left Abram in charge of selling the idols. A woman came with a bowl of figs and said, "Here, offer these to the gods." After she left, Abram took a stick, smashed all the idols and placed the stick in the hand of the last remaining idol, the biggest one. When his father came back and asked, "Who did this to the gods?" Abram answered: "A woman came with a bowl of figs. When I offered it to the idols, one idol said 'I will eat first' and another said 'No, I will eat first'. Then the biggest one jumped up and smashed all the others." Terach said, "Are you making fun of me? There is no life and power in these idols to do such things." So Abram replied: "Then why do you pray to them? Let your ears hear what your mouth is saying!"

Once Abram understood that an idol cannot be a God he tried to work out who God really was. Another Midrash tells that when Abram was a young boy he looked up at the stars one night. He saw their beauty and said to himself, "These must be the gods." But the dawn came and as the sun rose the stars faded. Abram exclaimed, "I will pray to the sun. The sun must be God." But then the sun set and the moon rose, and it too faded as morning came. Finally Abram said to himself, "All these are not God. There must be one who is the maker of the sun, the moon and the stars."

And so from a young age Abram realized there must be a real God. A God who had created the world. A God who set nature on her course – so that trees know to flower in spring and lose their leaves in autumn. Abram realised that this God would not be something we can see, it does not have a shape or a colour, it is neither male nor female. In the Torah this God has many many names: *Ribono shel olam* (Master of the universe), *Eyn sof* (The never-ending one), *Shechina* (The one who dwells within), *El olam* (God the everlasting one). Abram and Sarai taught the people around them about this God, an invisible God whom we need to find and to know.

Abram the rebel: Abram's early struggle is a difficult one. Unable to accept the religious and political system in which he grew up, he is placed in conflict with his father and with the ruler of the land. The Midrash tells that after Abram rejected the idol-worship that was his father's livelihood, Terach handed him over to the ruler Nimrod. Nimrod was enraged at Abram, who was rejecting the idol-worship that was central to the established order of the kingdom, and threw Abram into a fiery furnace, an example to all other potential rebels. But Abram was saved, and emerged from the fire unscathed.

Abram the iconoclast: "Abram was a leader of a world movement to stamp out the gods... A monotheist philosher who relentlessly cut away the cobwebs of superstition and delusions, an uncompromising iconoclast. A genius and prodigy who single-handedly escaped from (and helped to overturn) the intellectual assumptions of an entire civilization."
R. Matis Weinberg

? Like Abram, many people have wondered about who or what God is. How do you imagine God to be? If you could make up the best name for God, what would it be?

Self transformation: "The imperative of transformation is the driving force for Lech lecha.... To leave one's place is ultimately to seek to become the other... An act of radical discontinuity is depicted in the Torah as the essential basis for all continuity: for that act of birth that will engender the body and the soul of a new nation." Avivah Zornberg

"Go for yourself": is how Rashi interprets the call to Lech lecha, " go from your land, for your good, for your benefit."

Left behind : "All changes, even the most longed for, are melancholy. For what we leave behind is a part of ourselves. We must die to one life before we can enter another." Anatole France

Abraham the patriarch: Michael Rosenak writes about Abraham as the archetypal father and asks – in what way do we see Abraham as a role model, a mentor, a hero? "Looking at the newborn child, we ask: what would we wish this child to think of when he thinks of Abraham? With what can we ourselves identify?"

Ch.12: 1 Then one day God spoke to Abram, and said, "*Lech lecha* – Go forth, go for yourself, – from your land, from your birthplace and from your father's house, to the land that I will show you."

So begins God's great call to Abram, to go forth and leave everyting he knew behind. Why does God say "Go for yourself"? The Sages of Old explain that this journey will be for Abram; through this journey Abram will change and grow to be a great man. And why does God tell Abram to leave everything in a back to front order? You would think that first you need to leave your father's house, then your birthplace or town, then your land. A Scholar of our Time explains that Abram's leaving was not just a moving away to another place but a leaving of things important in his heart. When that is the case, it is hardest to leave your parents' home, and next the town where you grew up, and finally your land. God told Abram to go from his father's house last, as it was the hardest to leave behind.

So when Abram was forty years old, he had to leave everything he had ever known: his country, his way of life at his father's house, all the people and places he had grown up with. He had to start a journey away from all the things familiar to him and go out into the desert, towards the unknown. It was in the desert that Abram was going to change, and grow to become a great person. Sometimes, it is only when we journey away from the things we know that we can learn new things about ourselves and the world.

Spiritual withdrawal: Various traditional commentators have discussed the inverted order in God's command to Abram – country, birthplace, father's house – suggesting that what is being referred to is a spiritual rather than a physical withdrawal, beginning with the periphery and ending with the inner core. Abram was being asked to leave behind the dominant ideas and religion of his father's house.

Lech lecha: Lech (go, walk) involves an outward movement. The word lecha (for, to yourself) is an inwards movement. Lech lecha is movement both outwards and inwards at the same time.

Journeys: "All journeys have secret destinations of which the traveller is unaware." Martin Buber

? If you were going on a journey to learn and grow, where would you go? What would you take with you?

Kabbalistic patriarchs and matriarchs: According to the Kabbalah, each of the matriarchs and patriarchs of the Jewish people represents a different fundamental and primary attribute of life and of God. The ten fundamental attributes of God, called sefirot, are: Keter (Crown), Chochmah (Wisdom), Binah (Undertanding), Chesed (Lovingkindness), Gevurah (Power), Tiferet (Beauty), Netzach (Eternity), Hod (Splendour), Yesod (Foundation), Malchut (Kingdom).

Abraham's Chesed: Abraham represents the sefira of Chesed – lovingkindness, expansive compassion and generosity. Rashi notes that Chesed underlies God's motivation to create the world. As the basic undercurrent of creation, the flow of Chesed propels us towards connection and unity. For example Abraham expressed Chesed in his generous hospitality to wayfarers who knew they were welcome at any time in his tent city in the desert.

"What does it mean to bless and be blessed? It means, first of all, to be aware of each act we do. To our awareness of each act we add joy. We begin to see how simple things such as eating or drinking, helping a friend, providing hospitality, visiting a scholar or forgiving an enemy are, in turn, blessed by God. And so our consciousness is elevated so that we ourselves feel blessed by joy, wonder, splendour and peace." Avram Davis

Feeling blessed: "A blessing is the unconditional love that a parent can confer on a child... a way for the parent to envelop the child with a sense of safety and care... we need this feeling of being blessed in order to go forth into the world with a sense of purpose and responsibility." Naomi Rosenblatt

? If you could choose a blessing for your life, what would it be? What blessing would you give to the world to make it a better place?

Ch.12: 2 – 3   And God also said to Abram, "I will make you into a great nation, I will bless you, and you will be able to bless others, all the families of the earth will be blessed through you."

God gives Abram some very special blessings: One of the blessings is that Abram will be the forefather of a great nation. Although Abram has no children God promises him that one day a whole nation will descend from him.

God also blesses Abram that he will be able to bless others. Scholars of our Time wonder what it means to bless and be blessed? They suggest that it means to be aware of each act we do and take time to appreciate who we are and what we have. When we bless people we give them our good wishes as a gift, offering them strength or comfort. So a blessing is a way of weaving sacredness into our lives.

Even more, God blesses Abram that all the families of the earth will be blessed through him. Sages of Old explain that Abram will be the source of all blessing in the world. He will be the standard, the example by which other people bless themselves – so when a mother or father want to bless their son they will say "God make you like Abram."

Through Abram, God begins a relationship with one family, a relationship that will develop into the covenant between God and the Children of Israel. The relationship between God and Abram is one of the closest between God and any person in the Torah. Kabbalah helps us understand how Abram was a special man. According to Kabbalah each of the forefathers and foremothers represent a different important quality. Abram's quality is that of *Chesed* – lovingkindness, generosity and openness. We shall see Abram's *Chesed* in the next stories. God's blessing to Abram reflects this quality of *Chesed*. It started from Abram and opened out to include all the people in the world. It was a blessing that was open and wide, like the desert itself.

Ch.13: 14 – 17 Abram travelled with his wife Sarai and his nephew Lot, who was an orphan, and all the people who had learnt about God from Abram and Sarai travelled with them. They journeyed to the land of Canaan. It was in the land of Canaan that God appeared to Abram again and said, "Lift up your eyes and look out to the north, the south, the east and the west. All the land as far as you can see I will give to you and your children and your children's children to be their land forever."

Imagine Abram and Sarai travelling to the land of Canaan. One evening they pitched their tent under a large tree, near a stream where they could water their camels and sheep. As Abram gazed out over the rocky hills he heard a voice, "All the land as far as you can see I will give to you and your children."

According to God's promise the Land of Israel is an inheritance to the Jewish people forever. Forever means that even though the Jewish people may not always live in the land, they and the land of Israel will always be linked together. Even here God promised the land to Abram, but Abram never actually took possession of it in his lifetime.

Midrash tells that when God told Abram to look out to the north, south, east and west, a miracle happened. Abram was suddenly able to see the entire land without moving from the place where he stood.

Land of blessing: "The promised land is a spiritual domain, a realm of the future where Abraham's clan will dwell under God's everlasting protection and blessing." Naomi Rosenblatt

Israel in the Torah: This is one of a number of main texts on which the connection between the Jewish people and the land of Israel is based. Also in Genesis 15:18: "On that day God made a covenant with Abram, saying, 'To your descendants have I given this land, from the river of Egypt to the great river, the Euphrates.'" The Torah describes various geographical boundaries for the land of Israel.

Believing a promise: "As with the promised child, the promise of land confronts Abraham with a double test of faith. First, this land grant from God is post-dated until well after Abraham's death. Abraham has no guarantee that God will make good on his promise. And second, the land promised to his offspring is currently inhabited by a variety of tribes who worship other gods." Naomi Rosenblatt

God concepts: Jewish thought contains within it different concepts of God. Sometimes God is expressed in an anthropomorphic way, in human terms, as in this case where God takes Abram to look at the stars (God as the father figure, old man, judge). At other times, God is expressed in abstract terms, as in the concept of Eyn Sof, (The never-ending one) or God as embodied in the energy of the sefirot.

Beyond astrology: Rashi wrote that God's raising of Abram above the stars meant that Abram should abandon his astrological speculations, from which he believed he was not destined to have children. It is surprising to learn that Abram, the man who recognized God as the sole Creator, also practised astrology. However at that time the Sages believed that whilst God protects the people of Israel, the destinies of private individuals are influenced by the stars... although four things change that destiny – charity, prayer, change of name and change of conduct.

? Judaism and the Torah present different ways of imagining God. In this story God takes Abram outside to look at the stars and we imagine God like a parent showing a child the stars. How do you imagine God to be? Do you ever imagine God as an old man with a long white beard? A wise woman? An invisible energy in the world?

Ch.15: 3 – 5 Many years passed and Abram thought sadly to himself: What good is this promise of the land to me, when I have no children to pass it on to? Suddenly, God came to Abram and took him outside into the night, saying, "Look up at the night sky and count all the many stars if you can. So many shall be your children, and your children's children, and their children's children."

Midrash tells that when Abram looked up at the sky he saw a big star shining. "That star is you lighting up the world," said God. Then Abram saw two stars. "Those are you and your son," continued God. Then Abram saw three stars. "You and your son and your grandson," God said. When Abram looked up at the sky again there were twelve stars. "There will be twelve tribes," explained God. Then the whole sky from one end to the other was covered with stars. "So many will your descendants be, too many to count," promised God.

The Sages of Old tell that God took Abram not only outside but out of our world altogether and up into space. God raised Abram above the stars to gaze at their huge number. Imagine God with Abram, both of them gazing at the dark night sky filled with stars, sealing a promise.

Ch.16: 1 – 3 But year after year after year passed, ten years while Abram and Sarai were living in the land of Canaan, and still Sarai had not become pregnant. Sarai was getting older and older, and she felt very sad thinking that she would never have a child. Sarai had a maidservant called Hagar, and one day she said to Abram, "I will give you my servant Hagar as a wife, perhaps you will have a child through her." Abram listened to the voice of Sarai.

Remember, the story of Abram and Sarai began by telling us that Sarai was barren. In biblical times having children was seen as the main role of women. A woman who could not have children was not fulfilling her role in life. So Sarai might have felt very bad about herself, that her life without children was empty and meaningless.

One of the most painful things for a woman is to want a child but be unable to have one. Sarai wanted a child so much she was willing for her husband to try and have a child with another woman. The Sages of Old explain that in those times, if you gave your servant to your husband and she had a child, that child would be considered your own.

Into her own hands: Did Sarai's behaviour, giving Hagar to Abram so that he might have a child with her, mean that she did not trust in God's promise to Abram that he would have a son? Or maybe Sarai lost hope that she would be the mother of this son?

Barrenness: "The theme of the barren woman is a major theme in the Tanach, especially though not exclusively in Genesis. This is extraordinary in a book whose major subject is the passing on of the covenant with God within a family. A book that deals with children as the vehicle of transmission for the divine promise is full of women who have major difficulties in conceiving." Noam Zion and Steve Israel

Good intentions but: How carefully we need to weigh the consequences of our well intentioned acts! "We like to imagine we are equal to any commitment we take on... (but sometimes)... our altruistic impulses collide with our human limitations... Sarah makes the critical error of underestimating her susceptibility to that most agonizing of human emotions: jealousy." Naomi Rosenblatt

Claiming a child: "The custom of an infertile wife providing her husband with a concubine in order to bear children is well documented in the ancient Near East... In Sarai's case, it is unclear whether she had fully despaired of ever having children of her own or whether her action reflects the widespread popular belief that a woman who is unable to conceive may become fertile by adopting a child." Nahum Sarna

? What would it be like to be unable to have children? What choices do you have if you can't have children of your own?

Flawed heroes: "Our commentators find no excuses to condone Sarah's behaviour. look for no psychological explanations in extenuation of her deeds... Perhaps the Torah wished to teach us that before man undertakes a mission that will tax all his moral and spiritual powers he should ask himself first whether he can maintain these same high standards to the bitter end. Otherwise man is liable to descend from the pinnacle of altruism into much deeper depths than would ordinarily have been the case." Nehama Leibowitz This willingness to expose the central characters to criticism rather than present them as perfect, unflawed heroes is one of the marks of the vitality and contemporary relevance of the stories.

Stuck in a triangle: "Abram accepts the proposition without hesitation. Sarai's desire for a child coalesces with his own desire to attain God's promise of a mighty lineage. He eagerly takes the young Egyptian woman into his bed. Hagar conceives but Sarai's plan backfires. Young, fertile and the object of Abram's embrace, Hagar begins to take Sarai's position and authority less seriously." Dana Fewell and David Gunn

Shifted status: "In a world in which the woman was always seen as someone's property, either her father's or her husband's, the state of barrenness would include within it the real possibility of reduced status within the husband's house.. In the case of the second wife having children, there would almost inevitably be some shifting of status within the family." Noam Zion and Steve Israel.

Ch.16: 4 – 6   Abram took Hagar as a wife and Hagar became pregnant. When Hagar saw how quickly she became pregnant, she made fun of Sarai. "Look how you cannot have a child, and I got pregnant so easily. Maybe now Abram will love me more than you."

Sarai was very hurt and sad. It was unbearable for her to see Hagar pregnant. Her pain turned to anger and she accused Abram, saying, "You prayed to God to give you a child, and now you have a child. Why didn't you pray to God to give us a child? Then I too would have been blessed. Now see how Hagar makes fun of me." Abram replied, "Sarai, you decide what to do with Hagar. She is your servant." So Sarai decided: she made Hagar work very hard.

Sarai was hurt and sad and jealous. You could understand how she felt, especially after Hagar made fun of her. Those painful feelings turned to anger and Sarai made Hagar work very hard. Midrash tells that Sarai made Hagar carry heavy water buckets to the baths – work more suited to a servant than a wife of Abram, certainly not work for a pregnant woman. Some Sages say that Hagar had a miscarriage, losing the baby, perhaps because of the hard work. The Sages of Old criticize Sarai for making Hagar work so hard. By giving Hagar to Abram as a wife, Sarai had tried to do something that most women would find very difficult and, sure enough, troubles developed.

What about Abram, who told Sarai that she should decide what to do with Hagar, saying "She is your servant". Some Sages of Old criticize Abram for not looking after Hagar – Hagar was now not only Sarai's servant, she was also Abram's wife and the mother-to-be of his child. Other Sages of Old argue that Abram behaved correctly. He was reassuring Sarai by saying to her, "Hagar may be pregnant with my child, but you are still my wife whom I love and Hagar is your servant." Which of the Sages do you agree with?

Although Abram and Sarai are the patriarch and matriarch of the Jewish people, they are not seen to be perfect. Instead they are seen to be complex human beings who make mistakes, like we all do. Maybe, by seeing Abram and Sarai as real people and discussing their mistakes, we can actually learn more from them than if they were perfect. What do you think?

Ch.16: 7 – 15 Hagar ran away from Sarai into the desert. An angel found her by a spring of water and asked, "Where have you come from and where are you going?" Hagar replied, "I am running away from Sarai." "God has heard your prayer," reassured the angel, "You will have a son, and you will call him Ishmael. And from Ishmael you will have many descendants, too many to count. Now return to Sarai for she is your mistress." So Hagar returned to Sarai and Abram, and she had a son and Abram named the boy Ishmael.

The Sages of Old explain that the angel's questions – "Where have you come from and where are you going?" – remind Hagar that she had come from a special home with Abram and Sarai, and she was going into the desert, she knew not where.

The angel comforted Hagar by telling her that God has heard her prayers. Ishmael, the name of Hagar's son, means "God has heard." If we look forward into history, Hagar does have many descendants for Ishmael becomes the forefather of the Arab people.

Echoes: Ishamel the forefather of the Arab nation is the half-brother of Isaac, the forefather of the Jewish nation. The jealousy and rivalry between Sarai and Hagar seem to be echoed tragically in the conflict between Jews and Arabs in our times.

Symbol of oppression: "As a symbol of the oppressed, Hagar becomes many things to many people. Most especially, all sorts of rejected women find their stories in her. She is the faithful maid exploited, the black woman used by the male and abused by the female of the ruling class, the surrogate mother... the runaway youth... the pregnant young woman alone..." Phyllis Trible

? Ishmael becomes the forefather of the Arab people. We shall see that finally Sarai does have a son who becomes the forefather of the Jewish people. What is there in this ancient story that could explain the conflict between Jews and Arabs? What is there in this story that could also explain a closeness between Jews and Arabs?

Circumcision: continues to be a difficult mitzvah (commandment) to understand. It is a chok, a law whose reason is not given in the Torah. Nevertheless, various traditional commentators tried to understand its purpose. Saadiah Gaon argues that God created this part of man's body with a redundancy: when it is cut off, what is left is a state of perfection. Rambam holds that circumcision is a means for perfecting not man's physical but his moral being, as circumcision counteracts excessive lust. Sefer Hachinuch states that God wanted to establish a sign on the body of Jewish people, differentiating the body just as the soul is differentiated. The sign is in the reproductive organ, so that children born to that person are also touched by the covenant.

Ch.17: 1 – 11 Abram and Sarai continued to live in the land of Canaan. They lived in large tents, with the hills and the fields and the desert all around them. When Abram was ninety nine years old God came to him and said, "I am *El olam*, God the Everlasting One. Walk in my ways and be wholehearted. Now I establish my covenant between me and you, between me and all your descendants, an everlasting covenant throughout the ages to be your God. I will make you the father of many nations. And I give to you and your descendants the land of Canaan to be your land always. For your part you and your descendants shall keep my covenant. Throughout the generations every male among you shall be circumcised at the age of eight days. This shall be a covenant, a brit, between me and you: between me and you, and your children, and their children forever more." Abram did as God asked, circumcising himself, his son Ishmael, and all the other males in his house.

The covenant between God and Abram is described here. A covenant is a contract between two parties where each party must keep their side of the contract. What is God's side of the contract? God promises to be the God of Abram and his descendants forever. God also promises that Abram will be the father of many nations, and that the land of Canaan will be given to him and his descendants for always. Abram's side of the contract is that all males in Abram's household, and all males born to him and his descendants need to be circumcised.

God also asks Abram to "walk in my ways" which means to follow God's laws. God's "ways" are described in other places in the Torah as *derech tzedaka u-mishpat* – the way of justice and righteousness.

Circumcision becomes a symbol of the covenant binding parents to children, and children to their tradition and belief. The word for circumcision in Hebrew, *brit milah*, means covenant of circumcision. It is a commitment by parents to raise their sons in the tradition of the Jewish people. Still today, circumcision is central to Jewish identity. Jews continue to circumcise their sons eight days after birth and as Abram's name will be changed after his circumcision so Jewish boys are named on the day of their circumcision.

What about girls? Girls obviously do not need to have a circumcision. However, the Torah also commands that you should "circumcise your heart" (Dvarim 10:16) – that is, remove from your heart any barriers to goodness. These are barriers that both men and women need to remove.

Today a boy's circumcision is often a celebration, welcoming the child into the family. For boys – do you know about your *brit*? Where was it held? Who held you whilst the brit was being done (that person has a special name called the *sandak*). For girls – today when a girl is born some families make a *simchat bat*, a celebration welcoming the child and naming her. How was your birth celebrated?

Circumcision and birth: A number of women commentators believe that circumcision evolved as a compensation for men's exclusion from the birth experience. "Although the command to circumcise boys on the eighth day was given by God to Abraham, it was given again at Sinai in the midst of the commands of childbirth. This is not coincidental." Judith Antonelli "Childbirth is the woman's ultimate affirmation of her connection to the Creator…. Women are linked through their bodies to their mothers and their children in an endless chain of conception and birth… By performing the ritual of circumcision on their sons, men have the opportunity to bridge this gender gap and fuse with past and future generations of fathers and sons." Naomi Rosenblatt.

Historical context: "Egyptians and Canaanites practiced circumcision for reasons of health and hygiene, and as a rite of passage for males entering puberty. As is so often the case in Genesis, a local pagan ritual was adapted by the patriarchs into a monotheistic framework. By moving the date of circumcision from the beginning of adolescence to the eighth day of life, the Bible shifts its emphasis from puberty to birth, from the sexual to the spiritual. Circumcision introduces a spiritual element into the earliest stage of a child's life by acknowledging God's role in his conception and celebrating his birth as more than a merely biological event." Naomi Rosenblatt

Exposed to God: "Before Abram was circumcised he was covered over, but as soon as he was circumcised he became completely exposed to the influence of God." Zohar

What's in a name? In the ancient Near Eastern world a person's name was very significant. "The name of a man was intimately involved in the very essence of his being and inextricably intertwined with his personality." Nahum Sarna

God-given name: God gives each of the patriarchs his "destiny name". Abram changes to Abraham, and Jacob to Israel. Isaac undergoes no change of name as his name was divinely given before birth. In this way the Torah emphasizes the idea of the God-given destiny of the Patriarch.

Sarah: "More girls have been named for Sarah than for any other woman in the Torah. Her majestic name has divine origin. It was given to her when the Holy One chose her as the mother of the Jewish people." Miki Raver

? What do you know about your name? What does it mean? Why did your parents give you that name?

Ch.17: 15 Then God said to Abram: "Now your name shall be changed. You will no longer be called Abram, your name shall be Abraham, for I have made you the father of many nations. And your wife Sarai's name shall also be changed; do not call her Sarai, for Sarah is her name. I will bless her, she will be the mother of many nations and I will give to her and to you a son."

The covenant between God, and Abram and Sarai, changes their identity. God marks this new identity by changing their names. The Sages of Old explain that these new names have special meanings. In Hebrew Abraham is a shortening of *av hamon* – "father of a multitude." Sarah means "princess to all the nations."

The Sages of Old tell that the change of a person's name brings about a change of destiny. Still today sometimes when a person is very sick and at risk of dying, their name is changed with the hope of changing the course of the disease. When Abram and Sarai's names were changed to Abraham and Sarah, they too were transformed, and although they were ninety-nine and ninety years old, their faces and bodies looked young again.

Midrash tells that to commemorate Abraham and Sarah's change of name a special coin was made with their pictures on it. On one side of the coin the faces of an old man and woman were engraved, on the other side the faces of a young man and woman appeared.

And so, Abraham and Sarah always have these two sides: they are forever old and forever young. Abraham is the man who becomes a father when he is ninety-nine, but then he becomes the father of many nations. Sarah is both the woman who yearns for a child but cannot have one, and also the mother of a great nation.

On a Journey

For those who read the Torah looking for the beginning of the Jewish people, it is in the story of Abraham and Sarah that we find our first father and mother. What does the story tell us about Abraham and Sarah as our first parents?

First God called on Abraham to go on a journey. When God told Abraham *Lech lecha* – "go forth" – God didn't tell him how or where or for how long. But Abraham and Sarah listened to God's call – they were brave and adventurous, able to leave everything they knew behind. They needed to travel far away from their parents' homes, from an old way of thinking and believing to a new land, a new way of thinking and believing.

Abraham's and Sarah's travels, their *Lech lecha* in the desert, become a journey for them to change and grow. In the desert we learn more about Abraham's character, his way of being in the world, which Kabbalah calls *Chesed*. Abraham's *Chesed* means that he is open, generous and kind to others. In the desert the four flaps of his tent are always open. He loved to welcome travellers into his home, to talk with them and give them a place to eat and rest.

In the desert God came to Abraham to establish a covenant, a *brit* between God and Abraham and his children, and his children's children forever more. It is a covenant that has continued across the generations, across lands and across time till today.

As Abraham and Sarah go on their journey, their names are changed and they become the father and mother of a new people. Changing your name is very significant. Some say that when you change your name, your destiny changes. Sarai could not become pregnant but Sarah gave birth to a son. Abram did not become the father of the Jewish people, but Abraham did. By the end of the parasha Sarah is ready to give birth to a son and Abraham discovers himself ready to become the father of a people.

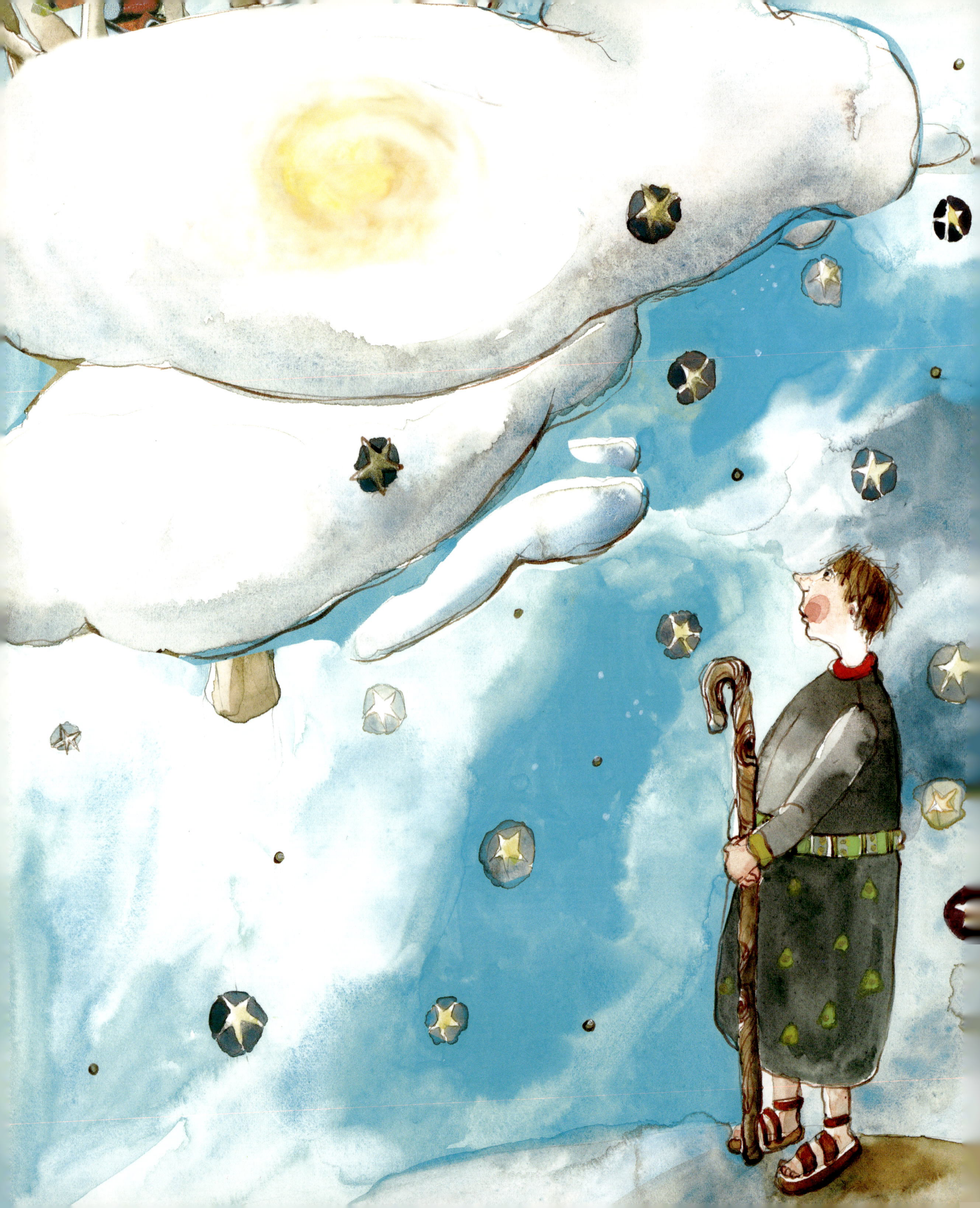

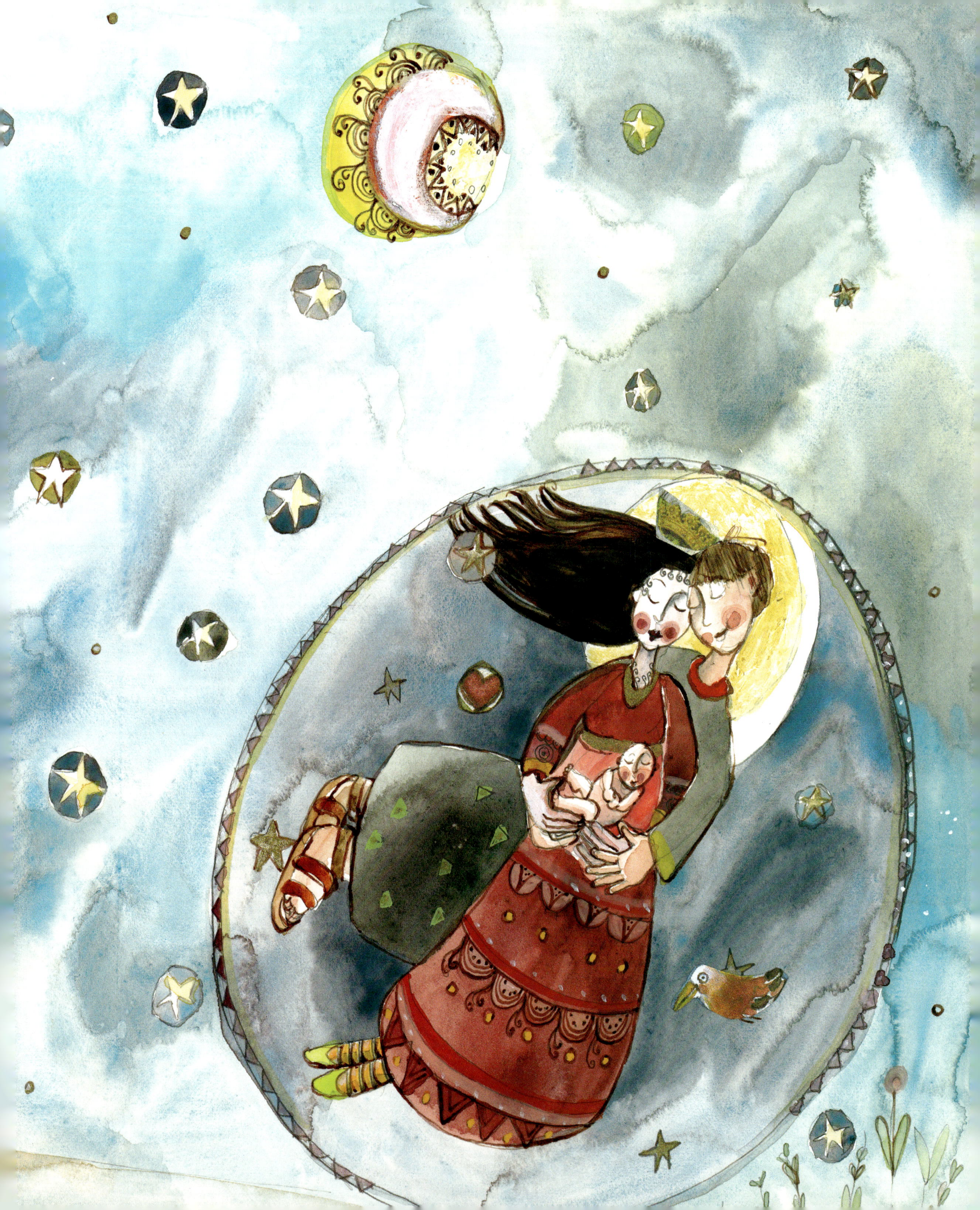

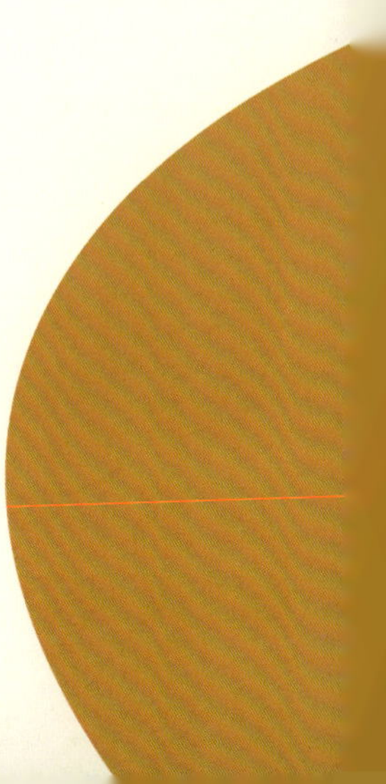

וירא

VAYEIRA

God's test and Abraham's argument

Ch.18: 1 **In the plains of Mamre on a very hot day, God came to visit Abraham as he sat at the entrance of his tent hoping to welcome travellers into his home.**

Why did God go and visit Abraham? Why is the weather mentioned? What does it matter if it was a hot day? It is believed that each and every word in the Torah is important and has a meaning. There are no extra unnecessary words. From that one sentence lots of stories have been told to fill in the gaps and help us understand the meaning behind the words.

Remember at the end of the last parasha God commanded Abraham to circumcise himself. The Sages of Old tell that the start of this parasha is three days after the circumcision and Abraham is still weak and recovering. God went to visit Abraham to cheer him up and so the Torah is teaching us how very important it is to visit a sick friend.

Kabbalah explains that God and Abraham's relationship was very special. And so here God worries about Abraham feeling sick after his circumcision, like a mother or father looking after their child when they are unwell.

And why was it so hot? God knew that Abraham's tent was always open because he loved to welcome people into his home. Midrash tells that God made the day very hot so people would not be out travelling on the hot and dusty roads. That way Abraham would not be troubled with having to look after visitors.

Lots to unpack: The richness and psychological insights of the interpretations and commentaries on the text are often so impressive. Many pages are written unpacking the levels of meaning in a seemingly bland verse, such as this one.

Without words: When God visits Abraham here there is no conversation between them. It is one of the very few cases of divine revelation without content. When one visits the sick, often words are not necessary. Sometimes there is nothing to say; it is important just to be there.

Stay seated: The word for sat yashav is spelt somewhat differently from the usual. Rashi translates yashav as "and he sat down" indicating that Abraham had tried to stand out of respect for God but God – seeing Abraham's weakness – said, "No, you sit down and rest, I will stand." There is a tenderness in God and Abraham's relationship, expressing the quality of Chesed.

? Have you gone to visit a sick friend or relative? What was the most important part of the visit? Midrash tells that visiting a sick person makes them feel one sixtieth better.

Ch.18: 2 – 6 And then Abraham saw three men coming towards him. He ran towards them saying: "Come wash your feet from the dust of the road, rest under this tree and I will prepare food for you to eat."

According to the Sages of Old, God saw Abraham was sad there were no travellers. So God brought three angels, in the shape of men, to visit him. Three angels came because there were three tasks to be done and one angel does not perform two tasks. The angel Rafael was sent to heal Abraham from his circumcision. "Rafael" comes from the Hebrew word *le-rapot,* meaning "to heal." The other two angels, Michael and Gabriel, had different tasks, as we will find out. The angels are messengers of God, and indeed all the angels' names end with the Hebrew word for God, *El*.

Legend tells that near his tent Abraham had a magical tree. This tree gave him a sign, telling him if his visitors were good people or bad people. When good people sat under the tree, the tree's branches spread over them, giving them shade. But when bad people sat under the tree, the tree's branches turned upwards, and no shade fell. When the three angels sat under the tree on the hot day, the branches and leaves of the tree spread out as far as they could, giving them lots of shade.

Angelic duties: While the angel Rafael came to heal Abraham, the angel, Michael came with the news that Sarah would soon be conceiving a son. And the angel Gabriel came regarding the destruction of Sodom and Gomorrah.

What a host! In this scene Abraham reveals his hospitality. "Nothing in the text suggests that Abraham recognizes the three strangers as the angels of the Lord they are later revealed to be. He is simply responding in character to the appearance of three strangers in his camp... Abraham reaches out to these men because he recognizes the face of God in everyone he meets."
Naomi Rosenblatt

God's marital therapy: God discusses Sarah's laughter with Abraham saying "Why did Sarah laugh, believing she is too old to bear a child – is anything beyond my power?" But God did not relay Sarah's full conversation. So as not to offend Abraham and for the sake of marital harmony God left out Sarah's comment about Abraham being too old!.

Ch.18: 9 – 12 **And so the angels stayed and they asked, "Where is Sarah, your wife?" and Abraham answered, "In the tent." And one angel said, "I will return to you at this time next year, and Sarah will have a son." Now Sarah heard the angel and she laughed at herself, saying, "How is it possible this old body will give birth to a child? And my husband too, is old."**

Midrash tells that it was the angel Michael's task to tell Sarah she would have a son. What did the angel mean by saying, "I will return to you at this time next year"? The angel drew a line on the wall of the tent and said, "When the sun crosses this point, Sarah will become pregnant, and when the sun crosses the next point she will give birth to a child." The angel was using a method of measuring time like a sundial. As the sun moves across the sky through the year, it casts shadows in different places on the dial.

And why did Sarah laugh? Sarah laughed because she thought the time had passed when she would be able to have a child, for Sarah was ninety and Abraham was ninety-nine years old. But God took Abraham and Sarah out of time and gave them a child. Midrash tells that when Sarah became pregnant, she and Abraham's faces and bodies changed and they actually looked young again.

Ch.18: 16 – 21 After the meal the angels left and walked towards Sodom. And God said, "How can I hide from Abraham – whom I love – what I am planning to do? For I have blessed Abraham to become the father of many nations. Shall I destroy the children without telling the father? And Abraham lives according to my way, doing *tzedaka* and *mishpat* – kindness and justice." So God told Abraham: "I am planning to destroy the city of Sodom and all the people who live there, because their evil is so great."

In equal measure: Originally God created the world based on justice alone, but God saw that a world based on justice alone was too harsh and could not survive. So God added an equal measure of mercy and joined it to justice.

In relationship: "Abraham is God's beloved friend, in whom He feels obliged, as it were, to confide His plan to destroy Sodom. The rhetorical question "Shall I hide from Abraham what I am about to do?" indicates the responsibilities that God has assumed toward human beings as a result of His decision to participate in a covenantal relationship with Abraham and his descendants." R. David Hartman

A Scholar of our Time suggests that when God says, "How can I hide from Abraham what I am planning to do," God is sharing with Abraham the plans about Sodom and including Abraham as God's partner on earth.

God's way is described here as "doing *tzedaka* and *mishpat*" – kindness and justice. This is at the heart of God's teachings for people's behaviour. But why is *tzedaka* – kindness first? Because justice without kindness can be cruel and cold.

Sodom was a city that had a whole system of justice without kindness – that was the evil of Sodom. Midrash tells that the land around Sodom was known to have fertile soil, the city was very wealthy and the people of Sodom were rich. Other people wanted to come and settle in Sodom too. But the Sodomites did not want to share their wealth and comfortable lives with others. So they made laws to discourage travelers from visiting Sodom. It was against the laws of Sodom to offer food or water to a traveler. If a person from Sodom did offer hospitality to a traveler they would be punished with great cruelty. Midrash tells a story about a girl who gave bread to a traveler. The Sodomites covered her with honey and tied her near a beehive for the bees to sting to death. Sodom's whole system of laws and justice was based on selfishness, protecting what it had and not sharing it with others. Sodom's principle of selfishness is the exact opposite of Abraham's principle of *Chesed* – lovingkindness and generosity.

Scholars of our Time suggest that Sodom was the first place to make anti-immigration laws. Today most wealthy countries, like the United States, Australia and Canada have immigration laws that strictly limit the number of people from other countries coming in. Perhaps as a society we need to be careful not to become too much like Sodom, developing laws that protect our own privileged lifestyles and not sharing our wealth and fortune with others.

Moral thermometer: "The treatment accorded newcomers and strangers was then and may always be considered a touchstone of the community's moral condition... Affluence without social concern is self-destructive; it hardens the conscience against repentence, it engenders cruelty and excess." Gunther Plaut

? Doing *tzedaka* (kindness) and *mishpat* (justice) is one of Judaism's main teachings for people's behaviour. Can you think of an example where kindness and justice are combined? What about an example where justice is carried out without kindness, and it is cruel?

? What sort of laws do you think wealthy countries like the United States and Australia should have in relation to allowing immigrants and refugees in?

The symphony of argument: "The dramatic confrontation between Abraham and God is told with the utmost simplicity; the cadences of repetitions vary as subtly as the repetitions of a symphonic theme. Abraham does not doubt the existence of God's justice, he only asks its extent and limitations. the important thing is that he asks altogether and that God does not reject his question out of hand." Gunther Plaut

The responsibility to question: "Not only is Abraham permitted to challenge God's actions, God invites him to do so. "Shall I hide from Abraham what I am about to do?" We learn from their exchange that one of the most solemn privileges and responsibilities of free choice is to question authority and demand justice, no matter what the personal cost." Naomi Rosenblatt

An image problem : Part of Abraham's argument with God relates to God's image in the world. Abraham says: "People will say you are not a God of justice but of destruction. First you destroy the generation of the flood and now you wish to destroy these people of Sodom." Rashi

Fully awake: "Abraham challenges God by appealing to universal moral principles. He is fully awake to his responsibilities for others and confronts God on their behalf... According to rabbinic characterizations, Abraham stands out as a socially concerned and compassionate person."
R. David Hartman

Ch.18: 23 – 32 Abraham came forward to God and said, "But what if there are fifty righteous people in the city, would you destroy the righteous along with the wicked? Shall you the Judge of all the earth not do justice?" And God said, "If I find fifty righteous people in Sodom I will spare the entire city for their sake." And then Abraham said to God, "What if the fifty righteous people lack five?" And God said, "I will not destroy it if I find forty-five righteous people." "But what if there are forty?" argued Abraham. And God said, "I will not destroy if there are forty." And Abraham continued to bargain with God and God agreed not to destroy the city if there were forty, and then thirty and then twenty righteous people. And finally Abraham said, "God, do not be angry at me, I will speak one last time. What if there are ten righteous people living there?" And God said, "I will not destroy the city if there are ten." Then God went down to Sodom to judge the people, saying, "If all are wicked, then destruction; if not, I will show mercy."

Can you imagine arguing with God like Abraham did? Questioning what God is planning to do? Perhaps God should be angry with Abraham for arguing stubbornly as he did. Maybe Jewish tradition should critisize Abraham as an argumentative old man. Instead Kabbalah and Sages of Old see Abraham as a hero, a greater man than Noah who did not argue with God to save the generation of the flood. It is quite amazing that Abraham confronts God using God's own "way": combining *tzedaka* and *mishpat* – kindness and justice.

A Scholar of our Time suggests that God was pleased Abraham was arguing, and even encouraged him. God was pleased that Abraham had his own sense of morality and was willing to argue for it. Sages of Old point out that in this story Abraham expresses the meaning of his new name – the father of many nations. He cares about the fate of all people, even the wicked people of Sodom.

Ch.19: 27 – 29 Abraham got up early the next morning and gazed down upon Sodom to see if ten righteous people were found there so the city could be saved. But God had not found ten righteous people; God had saved only Lot, Abraham's nephew and Lot's two daughters, and these had been saved for Abraham's sake. So when Abraham looked down, he saw thick smoke rising from the earth and he understood that Sodom had been destroyed.

Although it seems that God listened to Abraham's argument and weighed up the possiblity of saving Sodom, in the end God did not find even ten righteous people living there. Maybe the cruel laws of the city had influenced the ways of people living there and they had all become selfish and cruel.

Abraham's quality of *Chesed*, his lovingkindness and generosity towards others, comes through in this story of his argument with God not to destroy Sodom. Abraham becomes the example of the sort of person God hopes people will become. As the Sages of Old say, "Whoever is merciful to his fellow beings is without a doubt of the children of our father Abraham; whoever is unmerciful to his fellow beings certainly cannot be of the children of Abraham our father."

The merit of the few: "Abraham does not merely plead for the innocent but for the sinner as well, through the merit of the few righteous. The story thereby introduces the concept of merit important in biblical and especially post-biblical religion. The concept stipulates that a handful of concerned, decent and 'righteous' men could have averted Sodom's calamity by their merit." Gunther Plaut

Timeless: "When he asks 'will you sweep away the righteous along with the wicked?' Abraham poses a timeless moral question of how to mete out justice to the guilty without punishing the innocent....When we impose economic sanctions on countries run by ruthless dictators, can we justify the suffering it inevitably causes the poorest members of society? Many of Abraham's questions about the limits of justice and compassion remain unanswerable. But that does not relieve us of the obligation to persist asking them." Naomi Rosenblatt

Laughter: "Beyond all human hope, Sarah and Abraham have been blessed with a child in their old age. Sarah's initial laughter of incredulity is now transformed into the giddy laughter of joy at her long-postponed motherhood." Naomi Rosenblatt

Laughable: "The entire beginning of the Jewish people is laughable, its history, its expectations, its hopes. God waiting with the foundation of this people until its forefather had reached a 'ridiculous' high age...for a people was about to be created which was to stand with its whole existence in contrast to all historical experience." R. Samson Raphael Hirsch.

? As you continue to read the story I wonder which of Abraham's sons you think could have been called Yivkeh, God will weep?

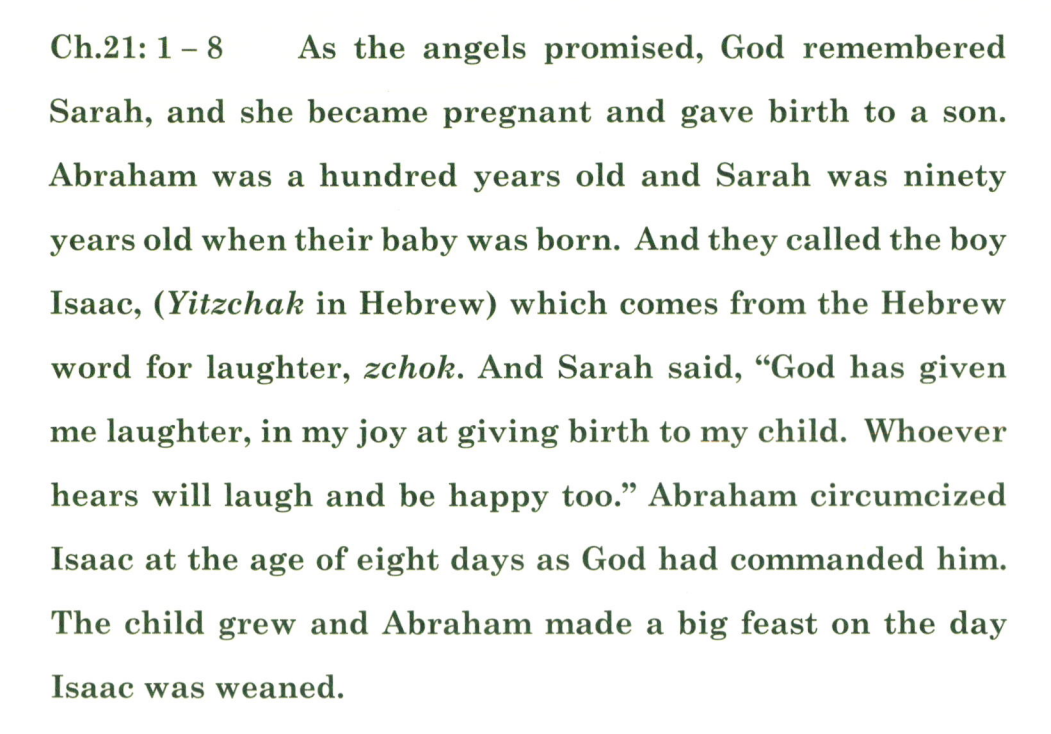

Ch.21: 1 – 8 **As the angels promised, God remembered Sarah, and she became pregnant and gave birth to a son. Abraham was a hundred years old and Sarah was ninety years old when their baby was born. And they called the boy Isaac, (*Yitzchak* in Hebrew) which comes from the Hebrew word for laughter, *zchok*. And Sarah said, "God has given me laughter, in my joy at giving birth to my child. Whoever hears will laugh and be happy too." Abraham circumcized Isaac at the age of eight days as God had commanded him. The child grew and Abraham made a big feast on the day Isaac was weaned.**

Midrash tells that on the day Isaac was born there was much happiness in the world. Other people who couldn't have children became pregnant and many sick people were cured. Even the sun and moon shone brighter that day.

Another Midrash tells that many people didn't believe an old woman like Sarah could really have a baby. They thought she must have found the child abandoned in the market and taken him home as her own. So God gave Sarah so much milk that when she breast fed Isaac she had enough milk to give other babies as well.

Yehuda Amichai, a famous Israeli poet, wrote a poem about Abraham's sons:

Abraham had three sons and not just two
Abraham had three sons, *Yishma'el* (God will hear) *Yitzchak* (He will laugh) and *Yivkeh* (He will weep).
No one ever heard of *Yivkeh*...he was the smallest and most loved.
Abraham had three sons, *Yishma, Yitzchak, Yivkeh* (He will hear, He will laugh, He will weep).
Yishma – el, Yitzchak – el, Yivkeh – el. (God will hear, God will laugh, God will weep).

Ch.22: 1 And so it happened after these words that God tested Abraham. God said "Abraham" and Abraham said "Here I am."

Why does the Torah say, "It happened after these words"? Midrash tells that these words were between God and Satan. Satan challenged God saying, "Abraham made a big feast when Isaac was weaned. He is so happy with his son Isaac that he has forgotten all about you. He did not even thank you by sacrificing one animal to you at the feast." God answered Satan saying, "Abraham has not forgotten me. Even if I said to him, sacrifice your son before me, he would do so." This Midrash suggests that one of the reasons for the Akeida, the Binding of Isaac, is a contest between God and Satan to prove Abraham's faith in God.

A Sage of Old suggests that another reason for the Akeida is to show all people how far one must go in fear and love of God. In this way the Akeida would reveal to Abraham and to others Abraham's devotion to God, a devotion that was not clear to him until it was put to the test.

Before and after: The phrase, "It happened after these words" leaves a gap in the narrative that the stories from Midrash come to fill. The Midrash provides a context for the trial of the Akeida (the Binding of Isaac) as though the Rabbis felt that God's directive to Abraham was so difficult to comprehend that they needed to provide some background or context for it.

Jewish satan: The concept of Satan exists in Judaism but it is seen as an aspect of God, rather than an independent adversary of God, as in Christian theology.

Advance knowledge: "The story begins with an uncharacteristic, explanatory sentence; 'some time afterward God put Abraham to the test'... informing the readers that this is a test gives them important information that is being withheld from Abraham... because without the explanation, the chapter will be too painful to read. By knowing in advance that what we are reading is only a test, we intuit that all will end happily." R. Joseph Telushkin

Unmatched power: "As a literary composition, this tale, known as the Akeida – is unmatched in Scripture. Austere and powerful, its every word reverberates into infinity, evoking suspense and drama, uncovering a whole mood based on before and continuing into an after, culminating in a climax which endows its characters with another dimension." Elie Wiesel

Mistranslation: "In Western literature, the episode known in Hebrew as the Akeida (the Binding of Isaac) is usually referred to as "the Sacrifice of Isaac". This mistranslation distorts the essence of the event, for at the story's end, Isaac is not sacrificed and God makes it clear that He never wants human beings to be sacrificed. I suspect that Western literature, influenced by the Chrisrian belief that God sacrificed His son for the sake of humankind, has tended to see the Akeida as a foreshadowing of that later 'sacrifice', but Jewish tradition regards it quite differently." R. Joseph Telushkin

Gently: "God says not merely 'your son' but follows it by saying 'your favored one' and then 'Isaac'. He issued the command gently, step by step, to a reluctant Abraham." Rashi

Ch.22: 2 And God said, "Take, if you would, your son, your only one, whom you love – Isaac."

Why does God repeat "your son, your only one, whom you love, Isaac"? The Sages Of Old imagine a conversation between God and Abraham but we hear only God's side of the conversation (like when we overhear someone talking on the telephone.) "Take your son," says God. Abraham says: "I have two sons." "Your only one," says God. Abraham says, "Each son is the only one to his mother" (as Sarah and Hagar each had only one son). "Whom you love", says God. "I love both", says Abraham. And only then God makes it clear, "Isaac."

Ch.22: 2 "Go forth – *Lech lecha* – to the land of Moriah and bring your son Isaac up as an offering on the mountain which I shall show you."

What is God asking Abraham to do? God is asking him to bring Isaac up as an offering. In those times people used to take one of their best sheep and kill it as an offering to God. There were even people of other religions who would kill a child as an offering to their god. Is that what God is asking Abraham to do – to kill his child, Isaac, whom he had waited so long for, as an offering? Sages of Old throughout the centuries, and Scholars of our Time today struggle to understand why God would ask this of Abraham. If Abraham sacrificed Isaac, how could he continue to teach the people around him that God is just and merciful? And according to Jewish tradition, God also has to keep all the laws given to humankind, including "Thou shalt not murder."

God has told Abraham to "go forth" – *Lech lecha* – before when God said to Abraham, "Go forth, from your land, from your birthplace and from your father's house." Then Abraham had to leave behind everything he had ever known, to give up his past. Now when God says to Abraham, "go forth," Abraham has to sacrifice his son. In doing so, he will give up his future. Abraham's life is framed between these two *Lech lechas*."

One of the Sages of Old says that God did not mean for Abraham to kill his son, rather God meant for Abraham to bring Isaac up on the mountain, like an offering, and then take him down again. Is it possible that the Akeida is based on a misunderstanding between God and Abraham?

Lech lecha x 2: The fact that the phrase Lech lecha does not occur anywhere else in the Bible emphasizes the parallels between the two Lech lecha stories. In both stories the exact ultimate destination of the journey is withheld (in the first God says only "to the land that I will show you," and in the second "on the mountain which I will show you"). Furthermore, in both the tension of the drama is heightened by the cumulative effect of the language: in the first, "Go forth from your land, your homeland, your father's house," and in the second, "Take your son, your only one, whom you love."

Misunderstanding: "Bring your son Isaac up as an offering." Rashi suggests that Abraham misunderstood God, and that the language God used allows for alternative interpretations. Rashi notes that God did not say slaughter him, because it was never His intention that Isaac should, in fact, be slaughtered, but only that he be brought up to the mountain and be prepared as a burnt offering. Therefore, once Abraham had brought him up, God told him to bring him back down."

Moral conflict: "The Akeida generally provokes an intense moral conflict in modern readers... how can moral people admire a man who is prepared to commit an act for which moral people might wish to see him executed, imprisoned for life, or consigned permanently to an asylum? In actuality the moral conflict is more apparent than real. Abraham's readiness to obey God's command shows him to be ethically deficient by later standards, but not by those of his age. God had revealed Himself to Abraham, but He had not made known to him the full ethical imlications of monotheism. Since other contemporary religious believers sacrificed sons to gods, God, in essence, was asking Abraham if he was as devoted to his God as the pagan idolaters were to theirs. Only when God makes clear He doesn't want human sacrifice does Abraham learn how evil and immoral such behaviour is." R. Joseph Telushkin

What would Sarah have done? Many women scholars have written powerfully on Sarah and her involvement/non-nvolvement in the Akeida.

Imagining Abraham's internal dialogue: "Does God really want this human sacrifice as proof of my belief and faith in Him? It is so contrary to all that I know about Him and the righteousness that has been His most consistent concern." Lippman Bodoff

Not really God's will: "But in this case it really wasn't God's will that he slaughter Isaac! Abraham's heart (discerning this) felt no love or attachment to God in this act, since it was not God's true will. That was the trial. And that is why it says 'He saw the place (Hamakon) from afar, meaning that he saw God (Hamakom) was far from him (since this commandment was not really God's will)." Sefat Emet

The Sages and Sarah: "The Sages commented that Abraham spent the entire night persuading Sarah. He could not bring himself to let her know of the plan, for he was afraid she would thwart it. On the other hand, he was afraid she would die of grief if he were to take Isaac without telling her."

Sodom and the Akeida: "The biblical and rabbinic traditions contain two contrasting themes: one that emphasizes the dignity of human responsibility, self-confidence and covenantal mutuality with God (as reflected in the story of Abraham arguing with God about Sodom) and another that demands utter silence and resignation before the inscrutable transcendant will of God." R. David Hartman

Ch.22: 3   So Abraham got up early in the morning and he saddled his donkey and he chopped the wood for the offering. He took Isaac his son and two young men and he began journeying to the place that God had told him.

Sages of Old and Scholars of our Time have wondered why the Torah points out that Abraham got up early in the morning. Was he so eager to do as God had commanded him? Or maybe he didn't want Sarah to know what he was doing so he left before she woke up. Abraham went to sacrifice Isaac without telling Sarah, but Isaac was Sarah's son too. Perhaps Abraham knew that Sarah would not let him go. What do you think? Would Sarah have sacrificed her son if God had commanded it?

And another question. Why didn't Abraham argue with God? He has argued with God before not to destroy the people of Sodom. Why doesn't he argue with God now to save his own son? A Sage of Old and a Scholar of our Time suggest that this was Abraham's test. God wanted Abraham to argue and challenge this command. Only then could God show the world that this God and God's followers would never accept the sacrifice of a child. According to this view, Abraham failed the test; he failed because he blindly obeyed God without arguing. Perhaps God was disappointed in Abraham after the Akeida. It is true that after the Akeida God and Abraham never spoke to each other again.

Ch.22: 4 **On the third day Abraham looked up and he saw the place from afar.**

The journey to the mountain, Mount Moriah, took three days. Why does the Torah tell us how long it took to get there? The Sages of Old explain that Abraham had three long days to think about what he had to do. Abraham did not obey God's command out of shock or confusion.

Midrash tells that during the three day journey Satan, disguised as an old man, came to Abraham saying, "Abraham, are you crazy, going to sacrifice the son you waited so long for?" When Satan saw that he could not change Abraham's mind he turned into a large river blocking the way. But still Abraham walked on. A Scholar of our Time suggests that the old man and the river did not really exist but were characters in Abraham's mind as he struggled to come to terms with what he was about to do.

Some say the three days of travelling to Mount Moriah felt like three thousand years. Time stood still as Abraham approached the terrible thing he was commanded to do.

Ch.22: 5 **And Abraham said to his young men, "Stay here with the donkey. I and the boy will go up and pray and then we will return to you."**

It seems that Abraham did not want his young men to witness him sacrificing Isaac. Sages of Old ask – is that because it was a private thing he was about to do, between himself and God only? Did Abraham think the young men would try to stop him? Or was Abraham ashamed of what he was going to do, and didn't want others to see?

Sages of Old and Scholars of our Time wonder why Abraham said, "We will return to you"? If Abraham went through with the sacrifice, then only he would return. Perhaps in his heart Abraham knew that Isaac would not die and both of them would return. Or maybe Abraham was testing God, saying: "You will not really make me go through with this, you are not really a God who wants me to kill my son." And so the Akeida is a double-edged test; God is testing Abraham, but Abraham is also testing God.

The old man and the river: "What is the significance of this dialogue (in the Midrash, between Abraham and the old man) which constitutes, as in many similar cases, a symbolic representation of an internal struggle? The voice of the tempter in the guise of an old man is none other than the promptings of Abraham's own heart during those three momentous days." Nehama Leibowitz

Struggling with the Akeida: The Akeida continues today to be a very confronting and disturbing story. Many different thinkers, Jewish and non-Jewish, have struggled to come to terms with it, such as Maimonides, Kant, Wiesel, Kierkegaard, Dershowitz, Bodoff.

A double-edged test: "God subjected Abraham to it, yet at the same time Abraham forced it on God. As though Abraham had said; I defy You, Lord. I shall submit to Your will, but let us see whether You shall go to the end, whether You shall remain passive and remain silent when the life of my son – who is also Your son – is at stake." Elie Wiesel

Proceed as commanded: Abraham passed the test of the Akeida when he showed God that he was prepared to proceed as God commanded with faith that the God of justice and righteousness in whom he believed would never, and could never, let that sacrifice come to pass." Lippman Bodoff

Isaac and the crucifix: There is a visual similarity between the image in Judaism of Isaac himself carrying the wood for his sacrifice and the image in Christianity of Jesus carrying the cross. The visual similarity underscores the contrast between the two sacrificial situations. In Christianity Jesus is sacrificed to atone for man's sins; in Judaism Isaac is not allowed to be sacrificed.

Moriah and Golgotha: Elie Wiesel writes that in Christianity the threat hanging over Isaac is seen as a prefiguration of the crucifixion, "except that on Mount Moriah the act was not consummated; the father did not abandon his son. Such is the distance between Moriah and Golgotha. In Jewish tradition man cannot use death as a means of glorifying God. Had he killed his son, Abraham would have become the forefather of a people – but not the Jewish people."

Ch.22: 6 – 8   Abraham took the firewood for the offering and placed it on his son, Isaac. He took the fire and the knife in his hand and the two of them went together. Then Isaac spoke to his father saying, "My father," and Abraham answered, "Here I am, my son." And Isaac said, "Here is the wood and the fire, but where is the lamb for the offering?" "God will provide the lamb for the offering, my son," answered Abraham. And the two of them went together.

The language in the story of the Akeida is very strong and poetic. Scholars of our Time look at the language in this most central sentence: "God will provide the lamb for the offering, my son." The sentence starts with "God" and ends with "son" – the two most important relationships in Abraham's life, now in conflict with each other. What does Abraham mean when he says, "God will provide the lamb for the offering, my son"? Is he telling Isaac that he will be the offering? Or does he have a deep intuition, a glimpse into the future that God will, in the end, provide a lamb?

"My son," "my father" – the words emphasize the closeness of Abraham's and Isaac's relationship even as the sacrifice is about to begin.

"And the two of them went together." Scholars of our Time explain that the first time the Torah writes this phrase, Isaac did not understand that he himself would be the sacrifice. The second time the same words are written, Isaac understands, and still "the two of them went together;" the one to bind, the other to be bound, the one to sacrifice, the other to be sacrificed. "They went together, still close to one another though everything already separated them."

Ch.22: 9 – 10 **They arrived at the place. Abraham built an altar and arranged the wood. He bound his son, Isaac, and placed him on the altar on top of the wood. Abraham stretched out his hand and took the knife to slaughter his son.**

Legend tells that Isaac told his father to bind him, tying him hand to foot. For Isaac said to his father, "I am a strong boy and you are old. I'm worried that when I see the knife in your hand I may tremble and push against you for the desire for life is strong. So bind me tightly for I am afraid, afraid of being afraid." And Isaac also said, "When you tell my mother, make sure she is not standing near the well or on the roof lest she fall and hurt herself." As we shall see in the next parasha, Isaac is right to be worried about his mother when she hears of what happened

Tears were streaming from Abraham's eyes as he looked down on his beloved son. Isaac looked up at his father crying. He gazed at the sky and saw the heavens open. The angels stood in rows upon rows, crying and weeping, and their tears fell into Isaac's eyes. We shall see that those angel tears changed Isaac's eyesight forever. Isaac had become the centre of the universe; time had stopped.

Beating heart: "As a chld I read and reread this tale, my heart beating wildly; I felt dark apprehension come over me and carry me away. There was no understanding the three characters. Why would God, the merciful father, demand that Abraham become inhuman, and why would Abraham accept? And Isaac, why did he submit so meekly?" Elie Wiesel

Heart wrenching: Abraham's mind must constantly be focusing on the sacrifice itself. Isaac is his most beloved son. What will the boy think when he sees his father tie him to the altar, and raise a knife over his throat? That Isacc's last memory of life will be of being killed by his father must wrench Abraham's heart most of all." R. Joseph Telushkin

Joint offering: Elie Wiesel writes that the Akeida was Abraham and Isaac's joint offering. They were equals in the Akeida in spite of their opposing roles. A Kabbalistic interpretation suggests that in the Akeida Abraham and Isaac had to swap their roles. Usually Abraham represents Chesed (lovingkindness) and Isaac represents Gevura (strength based on restraint). Abraham had to overcome his Chesed to go through with the Akeida and Isaac had to overcome his Gevura to give himself up to sacrifice.

Ch.22: 11 – 13 And then an angel of God called out from heaven saying, "Abraham, Abraham!" He answered, "Here I am." And the angel said: "Do not raise your hand against the boy, do not do a thing to him, for now I know that you are a God-fearing man, you did not withhold your beloved son from me." Abraham looked up and saw a ram caught by its horns in the thicket. He went and freed the ram and offered it up as a sacrifice instead of his son.

The angel stops Abraham from hurting his son, and Isaac is not sacrificed. In the end we see that God does not really want Isaac to be sacrificed, God never wants the sacrifice of a child.

A Scholar of our Time explains that this parasha gives us two very different models of people's relationship with God. The story of Abraham and the Akeida suggests a relationship where people have to obey all of God's commands without questioning. Even when a command seems awful, or against our beliefs, or beyond our ability to understand. So Abraham had to obey God's command to sacrifice his son.

The other model of people's relationship with God, suggested in the story of Sodom, is quite different. In that story Abraham does not accept what God says and he argues with God about destroying the people of Sodom. In fact God seems to encourage Abraham's arguing for what he believes is right. What do you think about these two models of people's relationship with God?

There is a Midrash, sounding very much like a fairy tale, about the ram that Abraham sacrificed. After it was sacrificed the ram's soul returned to heaven. But the ram longed to do something more in the world of people and so God sent it back to earth. Now it was no ordinary ram for God had given it horns so long they reached all the way to heaven. In this way the ram could be in both worlds at once, with its feet on the earth and its horns in heaven.

Ram's horn: "Why do we sound the horn of a ram? Because the Holy One, blessed be He, said; 'Blow me a ram's horn that I may remember unto you the binding of Isaac the son of Abraham, and I shall account it unto you for a binding of yourselves before Me.'" Talmud

Stayed: "The sacrifice, though commanded, was not exacted. Abraham's hand was stayed before the fatal act was completed. This showed, once and for all, clearly and unmistakenly, that in contrast to what was imagined of the heathen deities worshipped by Israel's neighbours, the God of Israel did not demand human sacrifice of his worshippers." Samuel Driver

Two different models: "…the interaction of these two traditional Judaic themes: the theme of human adequacy and dignity in participation with God and the theme of human terror and submission when faced with the all-demanding might of God." R. David Hartman

Model of Submission: "What was the most precious possession of Abraham: with what was he concerned the most? Isaac. Because the son meant so much to him, God instructed him to retreat, to give the son away… Precisely because of the supremacy of the intellect in human life, the Torah requires, at times, the suspension of the authority logos… Whatever is most significant, whatever attracts man the most, must be given up." R. Joseph Soloveitchik

? Do you think Abraham passed the test or not? What was the test?

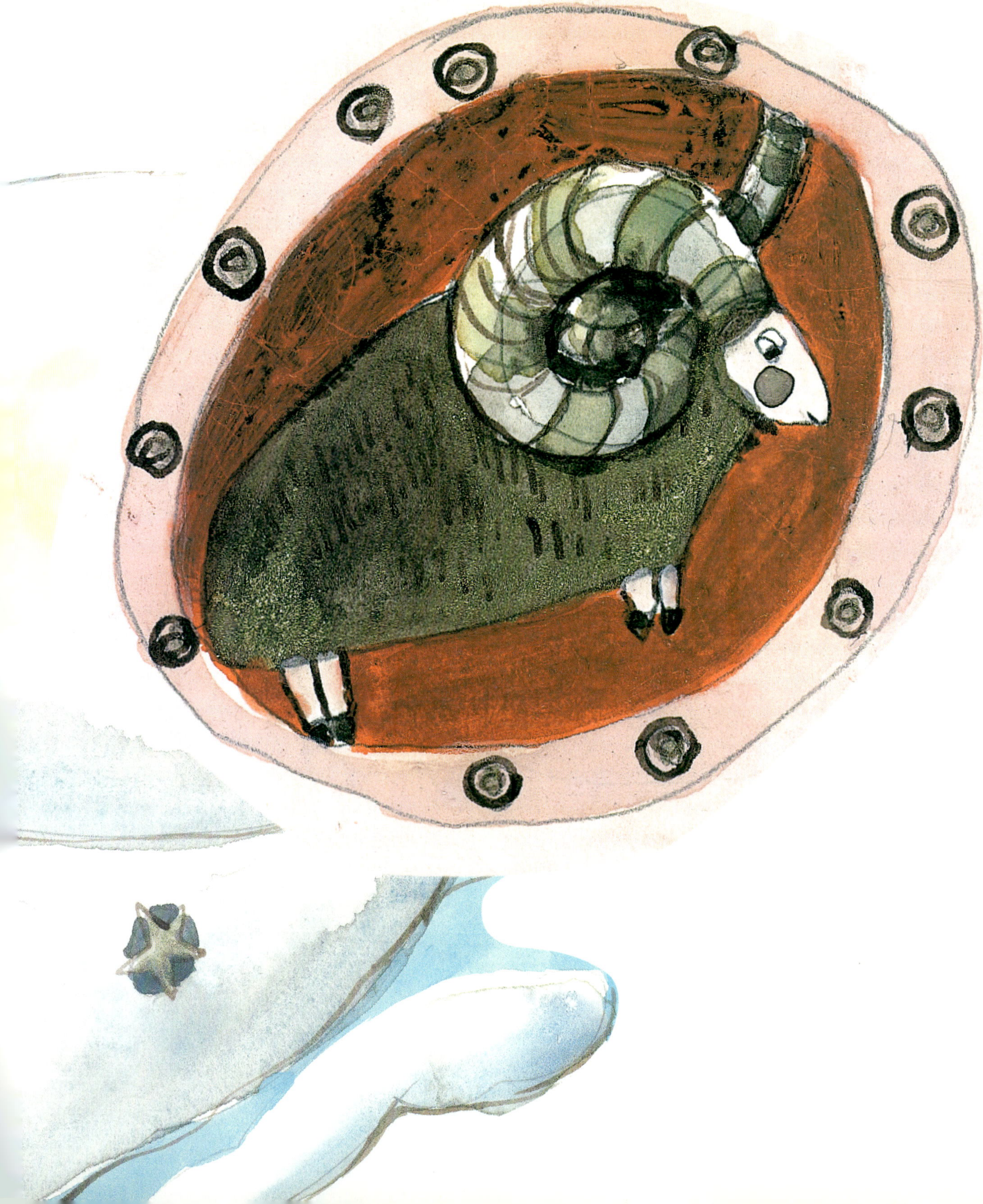

Ch.22: 15 – 17 The angel of God called to Abraham a second time from heaven, "Because you have not withheld your beloved son I will truly bless you. Your children's children will be as many as the stars of the sky, and the sand on the seashore. And all the nations of the earth shall bless themselves through you."

A story from Midrash imagines a conversation between Abraham and God. When Abraham heard the angel's voice he did not cry out with joy or relief. Instead he began to argue with God. "Well, then, my God," said Abraham unabashedly, "I could have pointed out to You before that Your command to sacrifice my son contradicted Your promise that I would be the father of a people. I could have spoken up, but I didn't, I held my tongue. In return, I want You to make me the following promise: In the future when my children and my children's children throughout the generations act against Your law and against Your will, You will also say nothing and forgive." "So be it", God agreed, "Let them but retell this tale and they will be forgiven." So every Rosh Hashana when God is judging our deeds, we remind God of the Akeida in our prayers. "Remember when Abraham our father bound Isaac his son upon the altar. Abraham overcame his *Chesed*, his lovingkindness, to do Your will. So may your lovingkindness overcome your anger towards us."

Struggling with Sodom and the Akeida

The parasha of Vayeira traces Abraham and Sarah's journey, their struggle and finally their joy on having a child. We see Abraham's quality of *Chesed*, his lovingkindness, reflected in his tent that is always open to travellers, in his hospitality and feeding people as they rest from their journey.

The parasha seems to describe two different models of people's relationship with God. In the story of Sodom Abraham argues with God, and God seems pleased that Abraham has his own sense of morality. In Jewish tradition Abraham is seen as a greater man than Noah because he did argue with God to try to save people. Abraham's way of showing kindness with justice becomes the example of how God wants people to lead their lives.

But then at the end of the parasha, there is a different model of people's relationship with God. God asks Abraham to sacrifice the son he has waited so long for and Abraham does not argue. Many people over many centuries have struggled with the story of God's command to Abraham to sacrifice his son. It remains, still today, a difficult and disturbing story. The opinions about the story seem to fall into two groups.

One group argues that God did ask Abraham to sacrifice his son as the ultimate test of his faith in God. Abraham's willingness to sacrifice Isaac would prove without a doubt that he held nothing back from God – not his son, not his reputation (Abraham would lose all his followers after such an act), not his future (Abraham's future of becoming a great nation cannot be fulfilled if Isaac is killed). This group argues that people need to obey God's commands without questioning, even when a command seems awful, for we cannot understand God's ways.

People in the other group are very uncomfortable with the whole idea that God would ask Abraham to sacrifice his son to prove his faith.

Rashi, the famous Sage of Old, argues that God did not mean for Abraham to kill his son, rather God meant for Abraham to bring Isaac up on the mountain, like an offering, and then take him down again.

Others argue that Abraham's test was that God wanted him to protest and challenge the command to sacrifice his son. God wanted Abraham to argue, just as he had argued to save the people of Sodom. God wanted to teach Abraham never to kill in God's name or even at God's command. God was testing Abraham to see if he would remain loyal to God's law (given to Noah after the flood), not to kill. Abraham would pass the test only if he stood up to God and said, "I can't do it; its contrary to Your Law."

Some say that just as God was testing Abraham, so Abraham was testing God, as if to say "You will not really make me sacrifice my son." If God had failed the test and let Abraham kill his son, then Abraham would have broken the covenant with God. "If the God I have found demands the same kind of immorality that I saw in my father's idol worship, I must be mistaken and I must look further for my God".

A Scholar of our Time Elie Wiesel, writer and Nobel Peace prizewinner argues that both Abraham and God failed the test. No God should ever ask a father to kill his child, and no father should ever agree to do so.

What do you think of the story of the Akeida? Which group, if any, do you agree with?

Whichever opinion you agree with, the Torah tells us that something as terrible, as powerful as the Akeida, cannot easily be contained and ended. Abraham and Isaac cannot go down from the mountain and return to their normal lives as though nothing had happened.

The story tells that after the Akeida there were dramatic changes in people and relationships. We shall read in the next parasha of what happened to Sarah after the Akeida. And it seems that Isaac, looking up at the heavens and awaiting his death, was a changed person. What about Abraham and Isaac's relationship? They were so close as they walked up the mountain together. The Torah does not tell us of their walking together like that again. Even Abraham and God's relationship seemed to change. From the beginning of parashat Lech Lecha, till the end of parashat Vayeira, God and Abraham have a close relationship and the Torah records many conversations between them. But after the Akeida, God and Abraham never speak again.

For centuries many writers and thinkers have struggled with the story of the Akeida, and we too continue to struggle with it. And like Abraham we also struggle to find a model for relating to God that feels right.

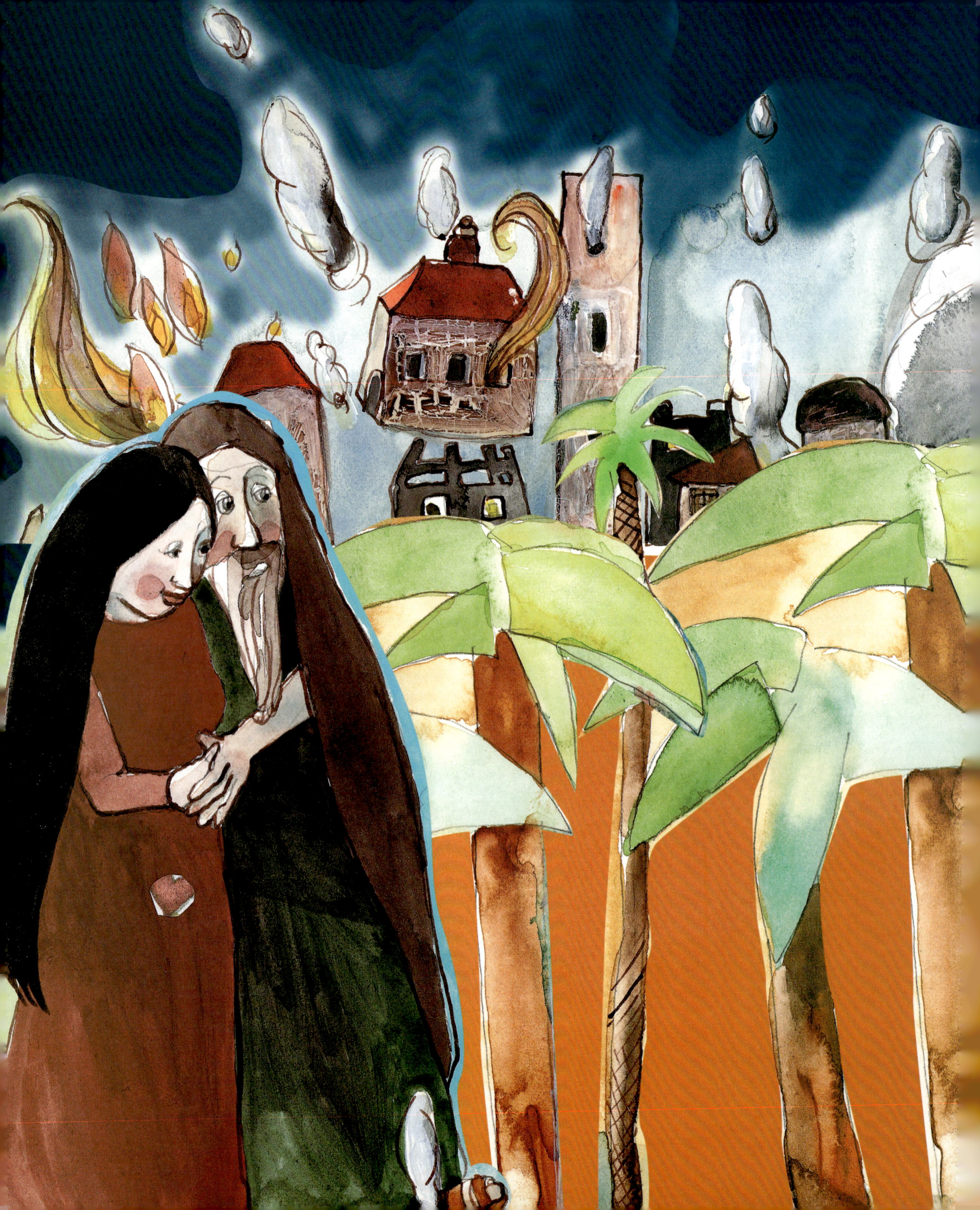

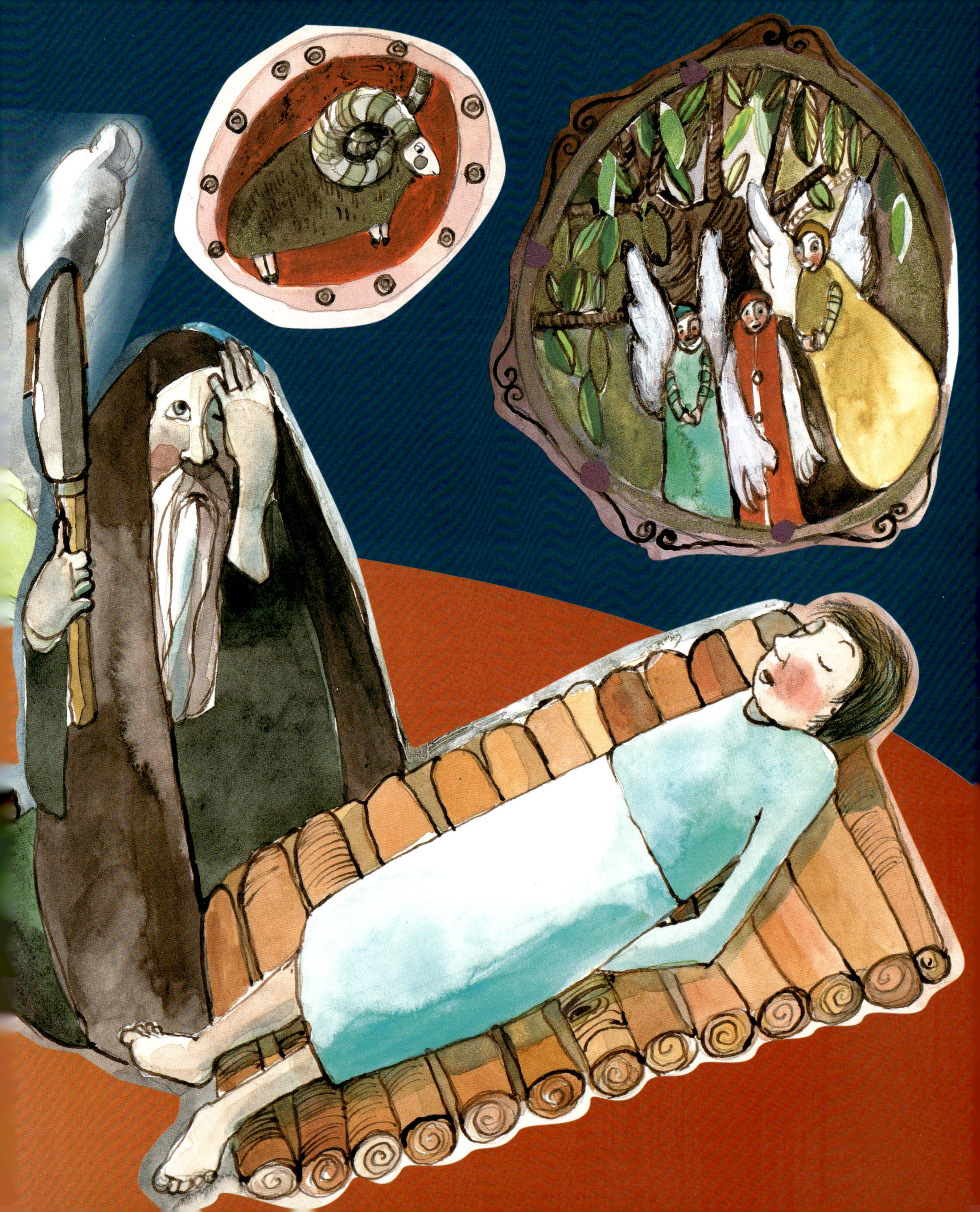

חיי שרה

CHAYEI SARAH

The life of Sarah

Inexplicable cost: "The death of Sarah is narrated directly after the Akeida, because as a result of the tidings of the Akeida – that her son had been fated for slaughter, and had been all but slaughtered – she gave up the ghost (her soul flew away) and died". So Rashi summarizes a number of Midrashim whose central thesis is that "Sarah is the true victim of the Akeida, her death is its unexplicated, inexplicable cost. What happened at the Akeida cannot be neutralized, though the sacrifice is not literally consummated." Avivah Zornberg

All or part of me: A compelling insight into Sarah's death comes from a book called "Sacred Fire" written by R. Shapira in the Warsaw ghetto in the years 1939 – 1942. Shapira writes 'Sarah died in order to show God that a Jew should not be expected to suffer unlimited levels of anguish. Even though a person with the mercy of God, survives and escapes death, nevertheless elements of his capability, his mind and his spirit are forever broken and as a result of his ordeal, lost to him. In the final analysis, what difference does it make, whether all of me or part of me is killed." Shapira's insights into Sarah's suffering and death are powerful and poignant given the suffering and death he saw around him each day in the ghetto. His words take on a myriad of meanings when seen through his context.

Transforming: "The shofar blasts on the New Year are to transform Sarah's death into atonement, because the Teru'ah – the broken shofar tone – is groaning and wailing."

? What do you think Sarah would have done if God had told her to bring her son up on the mountain as a sacrifice?

Ch.23: 1 – 2 Sarah died in Kiryat Arba in the land of Canaan. Her lifetime came to one hundred and twenty seven years.

This parasha is called The Life of Sarah. It seems like a strange name given the parasha starts with her death. But then maybe not so strange. Perhaps a lot of what happens in the parasha unfolds as a result of Sarah's death and comes to fill in the gap left by her death. Let's see what you think.

Sarah died just as Abraham was coming down from Mt. Moriah where he had nearly sacrificed Isaac in the last parasha. Is it just a coincidence that Sarah's death is the first thing to happen after Isaac's near sacrifice? Or is there a connection between the two events? Midrash fills in the gap between the end of the last story and the beginning of this one.

One Midrash tells that Satan was so angry he lost the contest with God that he took his revenge out on Sarah. Satan went to Sarah saying, "Your husband Abraham took Isaac, your only son, and sacrificed him to God." On hearing this Sarah was so shocked that cries of grief poured out of her heart and she died.

Another Midrash tells the story a bit differently. In this version Isaac himself told Sarah that his father had almost sacrificed him. "Were it not for the angels I would be dead," exclaimed Isaac. On hearing this Sarah died, not because her son had actually died but because her beliefs in life and her love for her husband were completely destroyed. How could her husband do such a thing? How could their God ask him to do it?

What would have happened had God told Sarah, not Abraham, to sacrifice her son? Scholars of our Time imagine such a conversation between Sarah and God where Sarah pleads with God, "Take me for your sacrifice, not my son." In this version of the story Sarah died to replace her son.

These stories are all slightly different but they have one thing in common – Sarah could be the real victim of the Akeida. She, not Isaac, is the one who dies. Within these stories even the possibility, the idea of the sacrifice of a child, has terrible consequences.

Jewish tradition has made sure we remember Sarah's cries every New Year, at Rosh Hoshana as we blow the shofar. For the *Teru'ah*, the broken shofar notes, sound like her crying.

CHAYEI SARAH

Ch.23: 2 Abraham came to mourn Sarah and cry over her death.

Midrash tells of a great sense of loss in the world when Sarah died. Abraham wept for the loss of his life-long companion. Many other people in the land mourned her death also.

A legend about Sarah's tent tells of what a special person she was. The doors of Sarah's tent were always open and a cloud of holiness always floated above the entrance. Sarah's dough for making challah was magically blessed. After eating her challah, guests went away feeling full and did not feel hungry again for many hours. And Sarah's Shabbat candles glowed all week, their light lasting with the spirit of Shabbat from one week to the next. But when Sarah died her tent was left in darkness and all the magic of her tent disappeared.

At home in a tent: Rabbi Soloveitchik writes that the special qualities of Sarah's tent embody the ideals to which a Jewish home should aspire. Her wide open tent doors reflect generosity and hospitality. "Your home should be wide open and the poor should be as members of your household" (Avos 1.15) The blessing built into Sarah's dough consists of satisfaction – a contentment with one's material goods. The Shabbat candles glowing all week suggest that the spirit of Shabbat, an atmosphere of rest and sanctity prevail in the household.

Back to the real world: Various traditional commentators are bothered by the fact that the Torah records in lengthy detail the dealing and bargaining over the burial plot. They suggest that in moving from the spiritual heights of the Akeida to the business world the story indicates that one cannot live on such spiritual heights alone.

Practical details: Perhaps Abraham's buying of the burial plot is a way for Abraham to gain some control and comfort at her death by attending to the practical details of her burial. "Fussy attention to detail, whether the rituals of burial and mourning or the negotiations with the cemetery, is the hallmark of a mourner struggling to feel some control." R. Burton Visotsky

Love and burial: "With the Cave of Machpela, Abraham discovered them all: the intensity of his love for Sarah, the depths of his roots in the earth, and his own need to remain rooted – connected and caring and belonging... Along with the cave of Machpela, Abraham discovered himself, and so came at last to inherit the land of Israel, a land as uniquely and specifically his as Sarah was uniquely and specifically his." R. Matis Weinberg

A bargain? The parasha provides a glimpse into ancient Middle Eastern bargaining. At first Ephron, the owner of the land, offers it to Abraham as a gift. But it seems this is just polite bargaining etiquette for when Abraham repeats his desire to pay full price for the land so that no – one could ever challenge his ownership, Ephron quotes what seems to be a highly inflated price, four hundred shekels. Abraham chooses not to haggle over the price but accepts it and pays immediately.

Ch.23: 3 – 20

After crying over Sarah's body, Abraham got up and said to the people of the town, "Let me buy a place to bury my beloved wife. Speak to Ephron that I may buy the Cave of Machpelah which is in his field." And Abraham bought the Cave of Machpelah and the field and trees, paying Ephron the full price of four hundred silver shekels. And so Abraham buried Sarah in the cave.

After Sarah's death, Abraham wanted to bury her in a piece of the land of Israel that he owned himself. Although God has promised the land to him, Abraham did not actually own any land and so he had to ask permission to buy a small burial plot. Scholars of our Time explain that only after Sarah died did Abraham realise how connected he was to her, and to the land. So the first land Abraham owns in Israel is a place that stands for the love between a husband and a wife.

Abraham had chosen a very special place to bury Sarah – the Cave of Machpela. Legend tells that this was the place where Adam and Eve were buried. Until the time of Abraham, angels guarded the cave, burning a fire near it to keep people away.

What do you think of the contrast between God's promise of the land to Abraham and the fact that here Abraham has to ask the townspeople permission to buy a small burial plot?

Ch.24: 1 – 4 Now Abraham was old and God blessed him *bakol*- with everything. And Abraham said to his senior servant Eliezer, "Swear to me that you will not take a wife for my son Isaac from the daughters of the Canaanites. Rather go to the land of my birth, to my relatives, and find a wife for him there."

Abraham was old, one hundred and thirty seven years old, and he was blessed with everything; a long life, children, honour and wealth. Scholars of our Time explain that the parasha gives us an approach to ageing that is very different from our modern times where youth is valued so much. Old age was seen as a time of blessing when one has a sense of contentment and completion in one's life.

There was only one thing missing in Abraham's life and left for him to do, and that was to find a good wife for his son, Isaac. Abraham wanted to find a wife for Isaac who would learn the ways of his family and his God. Abraham was worried that if Isaac took a wife from the daughters of the Canaanites, he would be influenced by their beliefs and worship idols and not live according to God's way.

Obedience and marriage: Why did Abraham command Eliezer that Isaac not take a wife from the daughters of the Canaanites? Why didn't Abraham command Isaac directly? Intriguingly Halacha states that a son is not required to obey a parental order not to marry the woman of his choice.

Ageing: Old age in the Torah is seen as a process of construction not of deconstruction. "All the days of a person's life are laid out above: one by one they come soaring into this world. If the person leaving the world merits, he comes into those days of his life, they become a luminous garment." So R. Matis Weinberg quotes form the Zohar and expands "Old age allows us to 'wear the days of our life' as a single garment – a totality, integrated and complete. Ageing is the opposite of the deconstruction of the self. It is a process of internalization, integration, consolidation and reconciliation."

Elder: The word zaken, "elder" in Hebrew is seen in the Talmud as a contracting of ze kana – "this one has it."

Choosing a bride: "Wary of the dangers of mixed marriages and assimilation, Abraham feels more secure going back to 'the old country' to select a bride for his son. By bringing the bride from so far away, he hopes that she will be absorbed psychologically, spiritually, and socially into her new family in Canaan." Naomi Rosenblatt

? How do you think old age is seen in our society today?

Isaac the middle patriarch: Many commentators see the fact that Isaac plays no part in the choice of his wife as consistent with his relative passivity or his Gevura – withholding quality. In comparison with the other patriarchs, Isaac doesn't have the vision and charisma of Abraham or the drama and conflicts of Jacob. The Akeida is the event with which he is most identified, the experience of which is understood by many to contribute to his passivity (as a survivor of trauma). Apart from the Akeida, Isaac encountered few life challenges. He inherited great wealth from his father and so did not have to struggle financially. And, unlike Jacob, he never had to struggle with the hardships of living outside the land of Israel, and juggling four wives and thirteen children.

Arranged but not compelled: The Torah writes that if the chosen woman does not wish to follow Eliezer then his promise to return with a wife becomes null and void. So Abraham is careful to ensure that Isaac's wife is not coerced into marriage.

? Imagine being on a debate about the advantages and disadvantages of marriage arranged by the parents. What arguments could be put forward for each side?

Ch.24: 5 – 8 "But what if the woman refuses to come with me?" asked Eliezer. "Should I take your son back there?" "No, you must not take him back there! God, who took me from the land of my birth and promised this new land to my children, this God will send an angel before you and you will find a wife there for my son. But if the woman does not agree to follow you, you are released from this promise." And Eliezer swore to Abraham to do as he asked.

These words "God, who took me from the land of my birth and promised this new land to my children, this God will send an angel before you," are the very last words spoken by Abraham in the Torah. Sages of Old explain that they express Abraham's belief in God and his confidence that everything will turn out as promised.

Abraham who has just bought his first piece of land in Israel and buried his wife there feels very connected to the land. It is very important to him that Isaac not leave the land of Israel. Of the three forefathers Abraham, Isaac and Jacob, Isaac is indeed the only one who never left the land.

Isaac does not choose his own wife. Rather, Abraham sends Eliezer off to find a wife for him. Today we would call this an arranged marriage. Most of us can't imagine our parents choosing a husband or wife for us. We expect to fall in love and marry a partner of our own choosing. But perhaps there are some advantages in parents being involved in choosing a partner for their son or daughter. What do you think?

Ch.24: 10 – 14 So Eliezer set out with ten camels laden with precious gifts and travelled to the town of Nahor. He arrived at the town in the evening when girls were coming out to draw water from the well. Eliezer made his camels kneel down by the well and prayed, "God, be gracious to my master Abraham. When the girls of the town come to draw water, give me a sign. When I say, 'Please lower your jar so I may drink' let the one who answers, 'Drink and I will water your camels as well' be the one whom You have chosen for Isaac."

Eliezer prays directly to God asking for a sign to tell him which girl is to be the wife for Isaac. What is the sign? The Sages of Old point out that the only important sign for Isaac's future wife is her kindness and generosity – on seeing a traveller tired from his journey on the dusty roads, she must give him water to drink and water his camels too. She must be generous to strangers and kind to animals.

Scholars of our Time point out that the character test of kindness and generosity was not an easy one. Do you know how much water one camel needs to drink to regain its fluids after a long journey? One camel needs twenty-five gallons of water and it takes a camel about ten minutes to drink this amount of water. Can you work out how many gallons of water the bride needed to draw from the well and for how long would the camels be drinking? Anyone would be exhausted after that job!

? What are the qualities you would look for in a partner – a husband or wife?

Healing energy: Avivah Zornberg sees in Rebecca's energy a healing that is needed for both Abraham and Isaac after the Akeida. "In an obvious sense, as she runs back and forth at the well, eagerly providing for the needs of the servant and the camels, she resembles Abraham welcoming his angel guests – impatient, energetic, overflowing with love (Chesed). For an Isaac, withdrawn, haunted by the shadows in his mother's tent, she will re-evoke the hopeful involvement of an Abraham, connecting, integrating, generating life."

Ch.24: 15 – 21 Eliezer had barely finished speaking when Rebecca, who was very beautiful, appeared with a jug on her shoulder. She went down to the well and filled her jug. Eliezer ran toward her asking for water. "Drink, my lord," she said, and quickly lowered her jug. When he had drunk enough she said, "I will also draw water for your camels until they drink their fill." So she hurried and emptied her jug into the trough and kept running to the well to draw water for all his camels. Eliezer stood gazing at her, astonished and speechless. It seemed God had made his journey successful. Now Eliezer wondered whether Rebecca would agree to follow him back to be Isaac's wife.

Scholars of our Time explain the importance of the well as a meeting place in biblical times. People did not have running water in their homes and so girls went to the well on the outskirts of the village to draw water. They lowered their buckets into the well by a rope and carried the water home or emptied it into a trough for the animals to drink. At the well the girls also told each other the latest news from their village.

Rebecca came from Abraham's family in Haran. She was Abraham's brother's granddaughter. The Sages of Old tell that the women of that family and that area were known to have strong characters. Rebecca certainly passed the character test of showing kindness and generosity.

As Rebecca runs energetically back and forth to the well, she reminds us of Abraham welcoming his angel guests and preparing a feast for them. Indeed according to Kabbalah, Rebecca overflows with the same energy of *Chesed*, kindness and generosity, as Abraham. There is a moment of suspense as Eliezer watches, he is fascinated by Rebecca's energy and it reminds him too of his master Abraham.

Ch.24: 22 – 27   As the camels finished drinking, Eliezer gave Rebecca two heavy gold bracelets and asked, "Whose daughter are you?   Is there room at your father's house for us to spend the night?" She answered "I am Rebecca, Bethuel's daughter, the granddaughter of Milca and Nahor. We have room for you and plenty of straw for your camels." Eliezer bowed and thanked God, saying: "Blessed be God who has guided me on the way to the house of Abraham and Sarah's relatives."

Midrash tells that Rebecca put the two bracelets on her arm and they fit perfectly. So Eliezer knew she was the right wife for Isaac. For Abraham had given him the bracelets, saying "If the girl passes all the other signs this will be the final sign."

Well done: "In biblical times a town's well was a social grazing ground... every response and movement by Rebecca in this scene reveals an important facet of her personality... The psychosocial test that the servant puts Rebecca through is critical to the future of the story. Circumstances will change. Her marriage will have its ups and downs, its shifting dynamics. But Rebecca's assertiveness and self-confidence will remain constant. The character traits illuminated by this episode in Rebecca's youth will stand her in good stead throughout her life and throughout her marriage to Isaac." Naomi Rosenblatt

? In biblical times the well was a meeting place for young people. Where is "the well" today where young people go to meet?

Ch.24: 28 – 54 Rebecca ran ahead to tell her family all that had happened. The family welcomed Eliezer to their home, bringing him food to eat and straw for the camels. But Eliezer would not eat until he had told them the whole story, of how in their old age Abraham and Sarah had a son, and how God had guided him on this journey to choose Rebecca as a wife for this son, Isaac. Rebecca's father, Bethuel, and brother Laban, answered, "As the matter comes from God, we cannot refuse you. Take Rebecca to be a wife for Isaac." Eliezer thanked God and gave gifts of gold and silver to Rebecca and delicious fruits for all. And they ate and they drank and slept the night there.

Why does Eliezer repeat the long story of how Isaac was born to Abraham and Sarah when they were old and the signs that helped him choose Rebecca? Sages of Old explain that in his story Eliezer wanted to impress on the family how God had guided him to find Rebecca. He also told the family of Abraham and Sarah's wealth and mentioned that Isaac was their only son. So the family would realize that Isaac was a "good catch" for Rebecca.

Retelling: Eliezer's retelling of the story is different in a number of aspects from the way the story is originally told, and various commentators have sought to explain the reasons for the differences. Abarbanel explained that the changes were intended to gain the confidence of Rebecca's family and to persuade them of the importance of binding themselves to Abraham through the marriage of Rebecca to Isaac. R. Samson Raphael Hirsch explained that Eliezer made a point of not arousing suspicion and expressed the retelling in a manner to make the situation acceptable to Rebecca's family.

Greedy hospitality? Some commentators suggest that Laban was attracted by Rebecca's new gold jewellery and the obvious wealth of the servant coming with camels laden with gifts. In future stories Laban emerges as a deceiving person (he deceives Jacob into marrying Leah instead of Rachel) so his behaviour here has been interpreted as disingenuous, greedy and scheming. Unlike Rebecca, Laban only invited Eliezer into his home after he took note of the jewellery and wealth.

? Can you think of a time when you repeated a story in a particular way to make a point or emphasize an aspect?

Ch.24: 54 – 61 The next morning, Eliezer said, "Let me return home now," but Rebecca's mother and brother insisted, "Let her stay with us awhile and then she will go." They agreed to ask Rebecca herself, saying, "Will you go with this man?" And she answered, "I will go." So they blessed Rebecca and she and her maidens mounted their camels and followed Eliezer on the long journey back to Isaac.

Rebecca's cloth: "Why is this woman-child so eager to go forth into the unknown? Apparently she's cut from the same risk-taking pioneering cloth as her relatives Abraham and Sarah. Like them, she is prepared to trade in her comfortable city life for the rigours of a desert existence...Perhaps she has heard stories about Abraham and Sarah, about how they tired of the materialistic life – which her brother Laban exemplifies – and sets off in search of a more meaningful existence." Naomi Rosenblatt

Scholars of our Time explain that the whole story of Eliezer choosing Rebecca as a wife for Isaac reveals a lot about her personality. At the well Rebecca's kindness and generosity shone. We also saw she had lots of energy and worked hard. Here Eliezer asks Rebecca to leave her family, travel with him to a faraway place and marry a complete stranger. And she says yes! What sort of qualities would Rebecca need to agree to go? Confidence, a sense of adventure and bravery would surely help! Rebecca has reminded us of Abraham before – here she reminds us of him again. When God asked Abraham to leave behind his birthplace and his father's house he immediately agreed. And so when Rebecca was asked to leave behind her birthplace and her home she answered "I will go." Perhaps Rebecca had heard of Abraham and Sarah, their new way of life, their covenant with God. Maybe she was excited to be part of this new people with different beliefs.

Rebecca's mother and brother ask her if she agrees to go with Eliezer and become Isaac's wife. From this the Sages of Old learn that a woman can be given in marriage only when she herself agrees.

? This story tells of how Rebecca leaves her home and family. Have you ever left your home, for a short time, or a long time? Who did you leave behind? What was it like?

Future shock: "What Rebecca sees in Isaac is the vital anguish at the heart of his prayers, a remoteness from the sunlit world of Chesed that she inhabits. Too abruptly, perhaps, she receives the shock of his world. Nothing mediates, nothing explains him to her. 'Who is that man?' she asks, fascinated, alienated. What dialogue is possible between two who have met in such a way?" Avivah Zornberg

Prayer times: According to tradition Abraham instituted the morning prayer, Shacharit; Isaac the afternoon prayer, Minchah; and Jacob the evening prayer, Ma'ariv.

Ch.24: 63 – 65   Towards evening Isaac went out into the fields to pray. He looked up and saw the camels coming. Rebecca also looked up and seeing him, asked: "Who is that man in the field walking towards us?" "That is Isaac," answered Eliezer. Rebecca slipped down from her camel, reached for her veil and covered herself.

Isaac went out to pray in the evening when the heat of the day had cooled. He liked to get away from the noise of the camp and walk alone in the fields. According to Midrash, Isaac's prayer as the day cooled became *Mincha*, the late afternoon prayer. A Scholar of our Time describes how Isaac felt, walking in the field, waiting for his new wife to be brought to him. Ever since his mother died Isaac had felt sad, sensing something missing in his life. Now he wondered what his new wife would be like, and hoped they would be happy together.

Why did Rebecca slip down from her camel when she saw Isaac? Sages of Old explain that she did not want to meet Isaac riding high on the camel whilst he was walking towards her on foot. Other Sages of Old say that Rebecca fell from the camel. Why did she suddenly fall? Because she got a shock when she saw Isaac, so different from herself.

Midrash asks, "How did she see him?" "What did she see in him?" And then answers: "She saw him majestic and was dumbfounded in his presence." Rebecca saw Isaac as awesome, praying to his invisible God, so different from the idols of her family. And perhaps she also saw him as so different from herself – serious, silent, troubled after his experiences of the Akeida and his mother's death. Here he was, her husband-to-be, so different from her and her sunlit outgoing ways.

And then Rebecca reached for her veil and covered herself. Scholars of our Time explain that Rebecca veiled herself because she was suddenly aware of their difference, as if to protect herself from his suffering. As we shall see in the next story, there does seem to be a veil between Rebecca and Isaac throughout their marriage. She never confronts him directly when they differ. Instead, as we shall see, she uses other means to guide the events in her home.

Can you think of a time today when Jewish women put on a veil? Rebecca's act of veiling herself before she met Isaac is remembered today in a ceremony before a Jewish wedding called *Badeken*. Before the *chuppah* the groom is led to the bride and lowers a veil over her face.

Ch.24: 66 – 67 Eliezer told Isaac all that had happened. Isaac took Rebecca into his mother Sarah's tent and she became his wife. He loved her and so was comforted after his mother's death.

Midrash tells that although Sarah had died years before Isaac still missed her. Every time he went into her tent and saw it in darkness he was saddened. But now things began to change.

Remember the special, almost magical qualities of Sarah's tent? When Isaac took Rebecca into her tent they reappeared. And so the doors of the tent were wide open again and the cloud of holiness returned. The Shabbat candles glowed and the dough of the challah was blessed. Rebecca brought love and energy to Isaac, and so Isaac was comforted and found new hope for the future.

Loss and comfort: "Isaac was comforted after his mother's death" – poignant words that have been the focus for many interpretations. According to R. Samson Raphael Hirsch these are among the most lofty words in all the history of mankind. "A forty year old man cannot be consoled for the death of his mother until he finds the right wife. Such is the importance of the woman, mother and wife in Israel".

Mothers and sons: According to Rashi "It is human nature that as long as a man's mother is still alive, he is involved with her." It seems that only when Isaac finds a life partner in Rebecca is he able to finally separate from Sarah and her death.

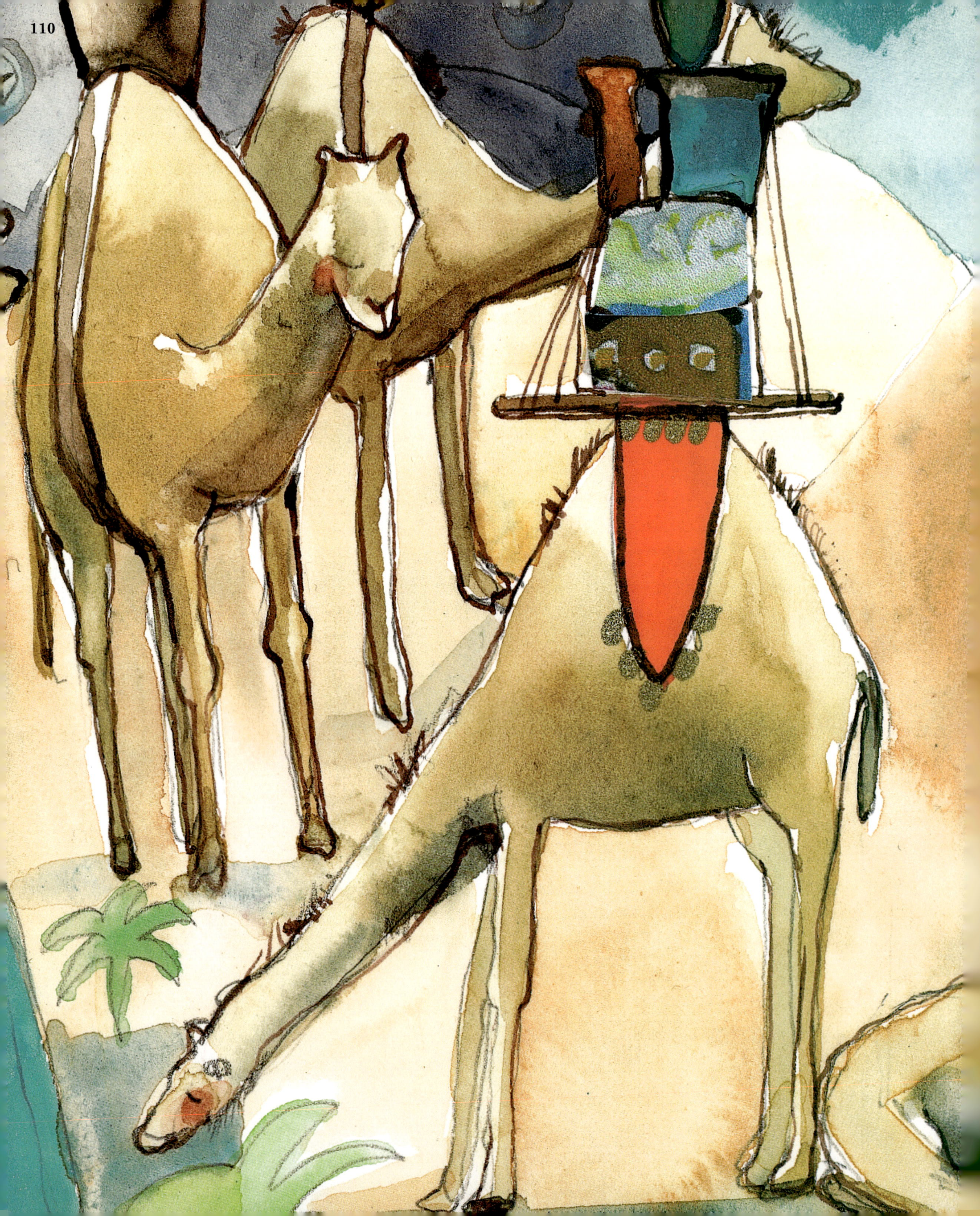

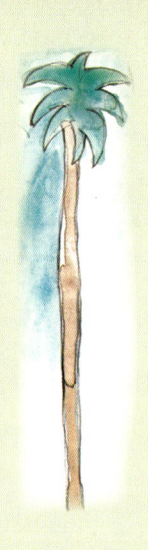

Looking back on Sarah's life,

and then, moving on.

Now we can understand why this parasha is called The life of Sarah. Even though the parasha begins with Sarah's death, the story throughout is bound up with her life and the gap left by her death.

It is only after Sarah's death that Abraham buys his first piece of land in Israel. Only after her death does Abraham realize how deep are his connections to her and to the land. And so he grasps the importance of buying a burial place for the whole family in the land of Israel.

Isaac, too, misses his mother. After her death he visits her empty tent shadowed in darkness and feels again the large hole in his life. And so the choice of a wife, a partner for Isaac, is so central. Eliezer chooses Rebecca on seeing her kindness and generosity, her energy and strength. There is something in Rebecca that reminds him of Abraham. Eliezer senses that this woman will be right for Isaac and right for the family. She will heal some of the pain still lingering from Sarah's death. And so Eliezer leads Rebecca swaying on her camel on the long journey back to Isaac.

The meeting between Rebecca and Isaac is mysterious. Something strange happens as she slips, or falls off her camel, and veils herself. And then Isaac and Rebecca go together into Sarah's tent. He learns to love her and she helps him move on from missing his mother. The tent opens up and becomes full of light and blessing again as before.

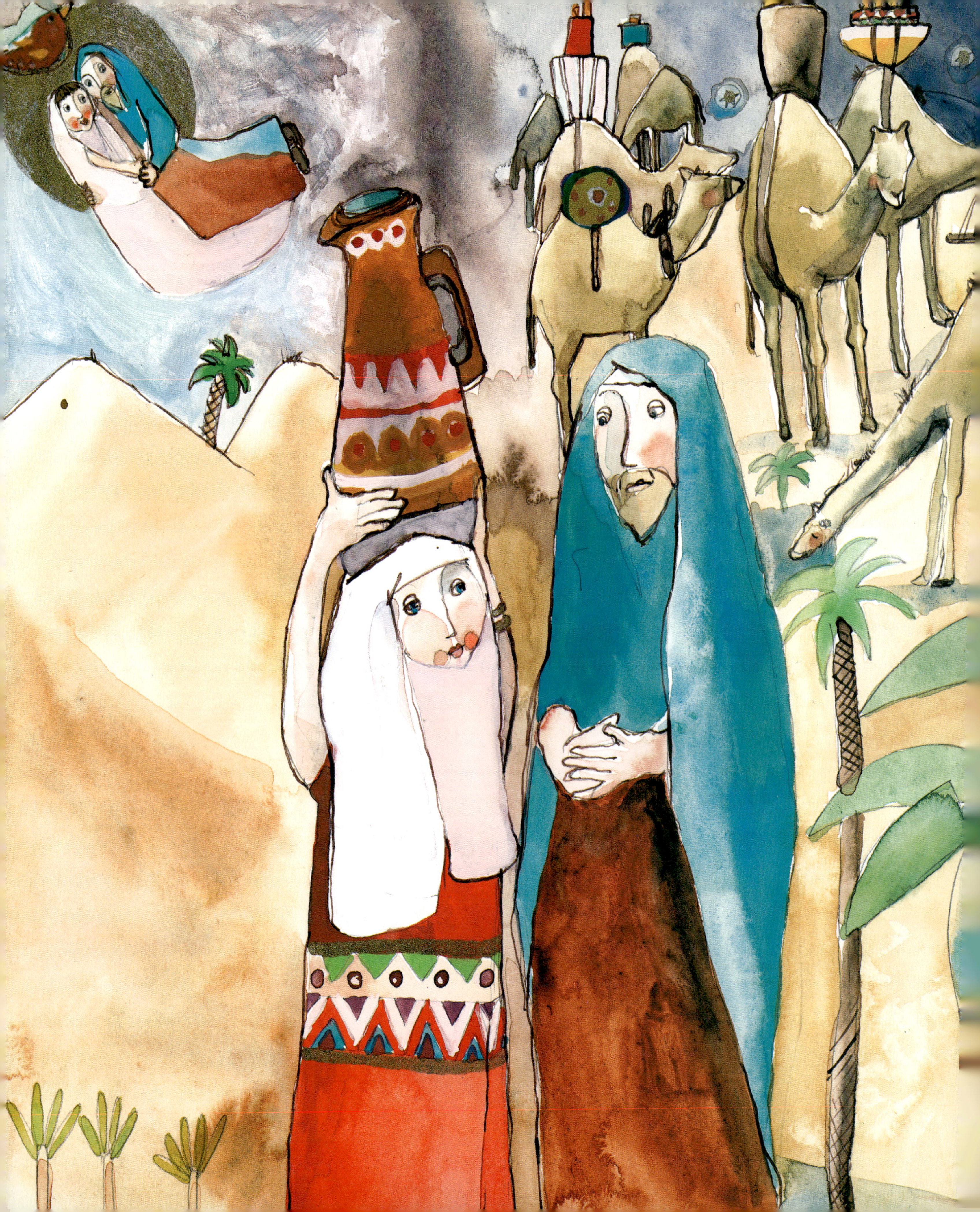

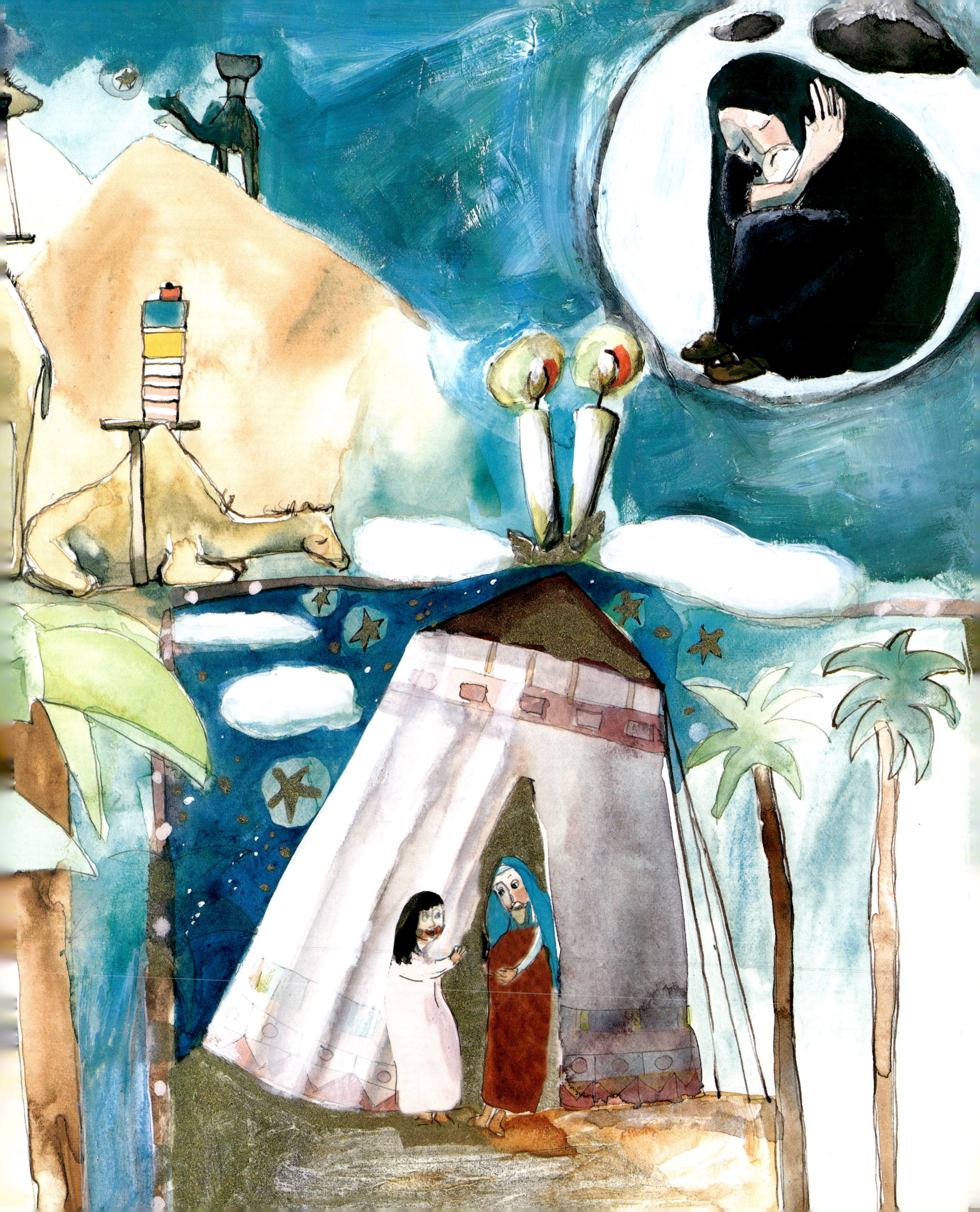

תולדות

TOLDOT

The story of Esav and Jacob

Extreme loving: Kabbalistically Abraham brought a quality of Chesed – expansiveness and lovingkindness into the world. But Kabbalah teaches that any one quality on its own, even a positive quality like Chesed, becomes extreme. And so expansiveness without boundaries is seen as problematic, diffuse, unfocused, misguided, even dangerous.

Harmony and balance: Kabbalah teaches a need for balance between the different qualities, a need for Chesed – expansiveness to be channelled with boundaries. The quality of Gevura – strength provides boundaries; it directs physical, intellectual or spiritual energy into a defined shape so it can achieve a goal. "It (Gevura) harnesses and shapes dispersed energy into sharp relief." R. Laibl Wolf

? Like father, like son. Like mother, like daughter: In what ways are you like your father or mother? In what ways are you different?

Ch.25: 19 These are the children of Isaac, son of Abraham. Abraham became the father of Isaac.

Why does the Torah repeat itself and tell us twice what we already know, that Abraham is the father of Isaac? Midrash tells that Isaac's way of life and good deeds were like his father's. When Abraham and Isaac passed by, people would exclaim, "You are fortunate Abraham to have such a son, and you Isaac are fortunate to have Abraham for a father." "He is his father's son" is a saying in many languages. Although Abraham was the father to other sons, they did not follow in his ways.

The Sages of Old tell that Abraham and Isaac looked very alike. Some people gossiped that an old man like Abraham could not have a child so God made their faces so similar no-one could doubt who was Isaac's father.

Kabbalah suggests that the Torah is telling us something deeper about the relationship between Abraham and Isaac. According to Kabbalah, Abraham represents *Chesed* - lovingkindness and openness. He is the man whose tent flaps are wide open in all directions to welcome travellers on the road. This Abraham gave birth to Isaac, a very different sort of personality. According to Kabbalah, Isaac does not represent *Chesed* but rather its opposite, *Gevura*. *Gevura* is strength – the sort of strength that comes from concentration and discipline, like when you lift up a heavy weight and your muscles tighten and your mind focuses. *Chesed* involves openness but *Gevura* involves closing up and being focused. While Abraham's tent flaps were wide open Isaac closed the flaps of his tent. We shall see that Isaac is a man who lives a quieter life – he is not called by God to go on a journey, rather he stays still and focused near his tent. Even though they are so different, Abraham's *Chesed* – lovingkindness gave birth to Isaac's *Gevura* – focused strength.

Ch.25: 20 – 21 Isaac was forty years old when he married Rebecca. After many years Rebecca had still not been able to become pregnant and have a child so Isaac prayed to God on her behalf. God listened to his prayer and Rebecca became pregnant.

Like Sarah, Rebecca also had difficulty becoming pregnant and having a child. Other mothers of important people in the Torah had difficulty becoming pregnant too. The children of these women are seen as special. If you wait a long time to have a baby then that child feels very special to you.

Why did Isaac pray on Rebecca's behalf? The Sages of Old explain that God had promised Isaac he would have children but Isaac wanted to be sure he would have children only with Rebecca (and not another woman, as Abraham had his first son with Hagar.) So Isaac prayed to God, "Let the children you give me be born only by Rebecca my beloved wife."

Sages of Old also tell that Rebecca prayed for a child alongside Isaac. Rebecca and Isaac travelled together to Mt Moriah and pitched a tent on top of the mountain. Isaac prayed in one corner of the tent, Rebecca prayed in the opposite corner and God's spirit hovered between them.

The Torah uses an unusual word for "prayed". Instead of the usual *vayitpalel* it writes *vayeater*. Midrash connects the word *vayeater* to the word *atar* which means a pitchfork. What does a pitchfork have to do with prayer? Just as a pitchfork turns hay from one place to another, so prayers can turn your destiny from one place to another.

Monogamy: Isaac was the only one of the patriarchs who was monogamous throughout his life. Unlike Abraham and Jacob he never took another wife or concubine. Like many couples struggling with infertility, Abraham and Sarah experienced a lot of tension around their prolonged childlessness (with Abraham taking Hagar as a wife, Sarah's hurt when Hagar became pregnant etc). In contrast the traditional commentators emphasize the unity and harmony between Isaac and Rebecca as they struggle to have a child.

Whose prayer? Did God listen to Isaac's or Rebecca's prayer? The Sages compare the efficacy of Isaac's prayer (the prayer of a righteous person who is the child of a righteous person) to Rebecca's prayer (the prayer of a righteous person who is the child of a wicked person). A famous saying states "In the place where penitents stand even the wholly righteous cannot stand." However in this case the text suggests that God listened to Isaac's prayers.

Barrenness: "The issue of barrenness is extremely serious in the world of the Bible in general and Genesis in particular. Apart from the meta-theme of the need to pass over the covenant agreement with God... the problems of infertile women in the biblical world would be very complicated and serious." Noam Zion and Steve Israel

? Do you know of a woman who had to wait a long time before she could have a child? What was it like for her?

The children clashed inside her: Avivah Zornberg explains that the verb for "clashed" – va-yitrotzetzu comes from the word rootz meaning "to run". And so the boys ran into each other in conflict and they also ran in opposite directions. Some traditional commentators argued that each twin was drawn to a different world, the physical as compared to the spiritual. But other commentators argued that both twins wanted the wholeness of existence, and therein lay the conflict. The struggle between the twins has been understood by traditional commentators to represent a conflict between two different nations/ideologies/spiritualities.

Male empathy: The traditional commentators, although all men, were effective in imagining Rebecca's thoughts and feelings during her difficult pregnancy. One example is Sforno's suggestion of Rebecca's unspoken words "If my pregnancy is so unusually difficult that I am facing imminent death in childbirth, why did my husband pray that I should be the one to bear his children?" In biblical times death during childbirth was not uncommon.

? Today pregnant women can have an ultrasound to show a picture of their baby in the womb. What do you think an ultrasound of Rebecca's twins would look like?

Ch.25: 22 It turned out Rebecca was carrying twins. But the children struggled so much inside her that Rebecca cried out, "Why is this happening to me?" and she went to ask God.

Midrash tells that Rebecca went from tent to tent asking all the women around her if they too had experienced so much pain in their pregnancies. The pain was so strong she worried that the babies might die inside her and that she might die too. It turned out this was no normal pregnancy; something extraordinary was happening inside her.

The Sages of Old tell that Rebecca was carrying twin boys who were destined to be enemies. Already in the womb they were clashing – arguing that the space was not big enough for the two of them and fighting about who would be born first. "They kicked and wrestled in the watery darkness, two bodies feeding off one placenta." How could Rebecca's womb contain them when we shall see that the whole world would not be big enough for them to live in peace? Imagine how Rebecca felt as the mother of two sons who were fighting each other even before they were born.

Midrash tells that the twins ran into each other in conflict but they also ran in opposite directions. Whenever Rebecca passed a non-Jewish temple one baby struggled to be born and whenever she passed a Jewish temple the other baby struggled to be born. The Midrash is already hinting that each of the boys will represent different ways of being in the world and different religions.

Ch.25: 23   And God answered her, "Two nations are in your womb, two different peoples will separate from inside you. Power shall pass from one nation to the other and in the end the older shall serve the younger."

From the very beginning of the story there is rivalry between the twins. God tells Rebecca that each of the twin boys she is carrying will be the forefather of a nation. But the two nations will never be powerful at the same time, rather when one rules the other will be defeated. In the end the nation of the one who is the first born will serve the nation of the second twin.

The Sages of Old and the Midrash suggest who these two nations are. The nation descending from the older twin is Edom, which later is identified with Rome, and the nation from the younger twin is Israel. At no time in history were Rome and Israel powerful at the same time.

God tells Rebecca this important information about the future of her children. Scholars of our Time suggest that by telling Rebecca, God gives her the responsibility to see that the covenant of Abraham goes to the right son. Strangely Rebecca never shares this information about the boys with her husband Isaac. He is "left in the dark". Some Scholars of our Time suggest that it was not God speaking to Rebecca, but her motherly intuition telling her what would be.

In context: In Midrashic and Talmudic sources Esav is identified with Rome and Christianity. The traditional commentators characterized Esav in very negative terms and in identifying Esav with Christianity, they also characterized Christianity negatively. Such views may seem very uncomfortable and even dangerous for some readers today. It is important to understand the historical context within which these traditional commentaries were written, a period when Jewish people were persecuted under Roman and Christian rule, and the writing of such commentaries expressed Jewish frustration and anger at Christian oppression, Crusades etc. In those times Christianity also espoused very negative views about Judaism. Today in an age of greater objectivity and tolerance, and interfaith dialogue, the views of both Judaism and Christianity towards one another have changed.

Comforting: "Indeed there must have been something comforting in thinking of the Romans as the present-day equivalent of biblical Esav, for just as God helped Jacob triumph over his physically larger and stronger brother, so He might help the Jews to throw off the Roman yoke." James Kugel

The fight to be first: According to a Midrash describing the conflict between the twins as to who would be born first, Esav said to Jacob "If you do not let me be first I will emerge through the stomach wall and kill our mother." This Midrash is representative of those Midrashim described earlier which depict a very negative character for Esav.

Dichotomy: The Torah text clearly sets up a contrast between Esav and Jacob, but the characterization of that dichotomy is drawn in different terms by different commentators. Many traditional commentaries and Midrashim depicted the dichotomy in extreme terms of evil and righteousness, accentuating the differences between Esav and Jacob, and providing various stories which depict Esav in very negative terms, and others which depict Jacob only positively. Contemporary scholars depict the differences between the twins in more psychological, less value laden terms. In teaching this story to our children we need to be clear about the stories and values we want to pass on.

Antihero: Contemporary scholars recognize the negative attitudes of the traditional commentators towards Esav and understand their views in their historical context. "If Jacob was made out to be altogether virtuous and studious, then Esav's image was likewise modified by early interpreters — if anything, in even more radical fashion. He became utterly wicked, a crafty, bloodthirsty embodiment of evil." James Kugel "Esav is a paradigmatic antihero of midrashic literature." Michael Rosenak

? A Scholar of our Time imagines making a movie about the twins. Which actors would you cast to play Esav and Jacob?

Ch.25: 24 – 26   When Rebecca gave birth the first twin came out covered all over with red hair, so they named him Esav. Next his brother emerged holding onto Esav's heel so they called him Jacob.

Midrash describes a competition between the twins as to who would be born first. Esav, the stronger twin, fought his way out of the womb winning the race to be the firstborn son. Then Jacob came, following close behind, grasping Esav's heel as though to pull him back inside.

Esav and Jacob are very different twin brothers, and they look completely different from one another when they are born. Sages of Old tell that when Esav was born he was so hairy he already looked grown-up. The name Esav comes from the Hebrew word *esev* meaning "grass", because Esav's head was covered with hair as a field is covered with grass. The name "Jacob" comes from the Hebrew word *ekev*, meaning "heel", because he was holding onto his brother's heel.

Ch25: 27   Esav became a skilled hunter, a man of the fields. Jacob was a simple man who stayed in the tents.

The differences between the boys became clearer as they grew up. As a skilled hunter, a man of the fields, Esav loved to be outdoors, in nature. He was a man of action who used his physical ability and strength. As a hunter he was good at trapping animals and killing them.

On the other hand "Jacob was a simple man who stayed in the tents." In contrast to his brother, Jacob wasn't "field-wise", or as we would say today "street-wise." He wasn't big and strong, instead he stayed close to home. According to the Sages of Old, Jacob stayed in the tents to study Torah. He stayed in the tents of Abraham and Isaac and learnt from them. Whilst Esav used his strength to hunt, Jacob used his mind to study.

The Torah story is setting up a contrast between the two boys, a contrast that will soon turn into a competition. But when people are different you can describe their differences in a number of ways. Sages of Old and Scholars of our Time have different ways of describing the contrast between the boys.

Many Sages of Old and Midrash described Esav as wicked – they presented him as cunning and violent, a hunter who liked to shed blood and kill animals. There are many stories about Esav's wickedness. One Midrash tells that in the fight about who would be born first Esav said to Jacob, "If you do not let me be born first I will come out through our mother's stomach and she will be die." On the other hand the Sages of Old and Midrash described Jacob as only good and righteous.

Why did these Sages of Old present Esav so negatively and Jacob so positively? If you read the Torah story itself it describes good and bad qualities for both Esav and Jacob. It is important to take into account the times in history when these Sages of Old lived. They lived in the Middle Ages when the Jewish people lived under Roman and Christian rule and many of these governments made life very difficult for the Jews, oppressing them and discriminating against them. Also in those times Christianity itself expressed negative views about Judaism. The Sages of Old saw Esav as representing the ruling non-Jewish nations and Jacob as representing the Jewish people. They expressed their sense of injustice and anger by presenting Esav as evil, and hoping that one day Jacob the righteous would be victorious over Esav.

Also as we shall see in the story Jacob, not Esav, is the son chosen to carry on Abraham's covenant. Perhaps the Sages of Old focused on Jacob's good qualities and Esav's negative qualities to help us understand why Jacob and not Esav was chosen.

Scholars of our Time suggest another way of understanding the differences between the twins. Each twin represents a different side within each of us, a different side of personality. Esav is the physical and active person hunting in the field while Jacob is the gentle and thinking person who stays at home studying. There are many twins in ancient stories and fairy tales, where each twin represents one side of a complete personality but lacks the qualities the other has. They are like two sides of a puzzle that need to come together to make a whole. This parasha follows the story of the two twins and we shall see whether either can learn to develop the qualities of the other and so become a more complete person.

Modern insights: Contemporary scholars recognize the negative attitudes of the traditional commentators towards Esav: "While the Bible shows Esav as a flawed but far from terrible person, the Esav depicted in many rabbinic sources is unequivocally evil" Rabbi Joseph Telushkin. In his book "The Bible As It Was" James Kugel gives a detailed description of how the traditional commentators "make Jacob into a model of virtue and Esav into the opposite." "The literature of Midrash, dealing with Esav against the backdrop of Roman oppression and duplicity, considers Esav an evil man, the wicked father of an idolatrous and oppressive nation." Michael Rosenak

Psychological differences: Contemporary scholars present the differences between Esav and Jacob in a different, more psychological, less value laden light: "Esav is most clearly visible using his limbs... while Jacob is one who 'sits in tents' essentially limbless, all mind... If Esav has chosen to be a hunter...then Jacob must assume the opposite role, the passive, limbless scholar, absorbed in the worlds of his father and grandfather." Avivah Zornberg

? If you were teaching this story at a school what ideas would you want to pass on about Esav and Jacob? What would be your challenges in teaching this story?

Ch.25: 27   The boys grew up.

Sages of Old and Scholars of our Time explain that underlying the words "The boys grew up" is a description of Esav's and Jacob's upbringing by their parents. As we have seen, Esav and Jacob were very different personalities. But their parents tried to educate them in the same way.

A Scholar of our Time criticizes Isaac and Rebecca for having the same approach and expectations for two such different boys. If Esav loved being outdoors, using his body, and Jacob was happy indoors reading, how could you treat them the same and teach them the same way? A Hebrew proverb says "Raise a child in accordance with his way." This means that you have to take into account the child's personality to raise him or her in the best way. Today we know that children have different personalities, and do not all learn the same way. So the Hebrew proverb fits well with modern approaches to education.

What would have happened if Isaac and Rebecca had understood Esav's personality better and been able to direct his physical strength and skills in more positive ways? Maybe there would have been less competition between the twins and Esav and Jacob would have remained brothers in spirit as well as in flesh.

Courting disaster: "To try to bring up a Jacob and an Esav in the same college, make them have the same habits and hobbies, to want to teach and educate them in the same way for some studious, sedate, meditative life is the surest way to court disaster." R. Samson Raphael Hirsch. "Hirsch's criticism is that Isaac and Rivka thought that only a tent dweller could be a noble Jewish character. Consequently, they educated Esav as though he ought to have Jacob's tent – dwelling nature. They forgot that the Torah is given to an entire people and hence must be suited to every temperament." Michael Rosenak

Progressive proverb: The Hebrew proverb "Raise a child in accordance with his way" echoes a progressive approach to education. Contemporary psychological and educational theories understand that children are born with different inherent and biologically based temperaments and learning styles.

Simple yet diverse: "The great task of the Jew is simple and straightforward as regards its basic content, but the modes of its fulfilment are as varied and complex as the differences in individuality and the diversity of life that result from these differences." R. Samson Raphael Hirsch

Nature or nurture: Michael Rosenak looks at the story of Esav and Jacob as a case study for thinking about the influence of nature or nurture on character. "Was Esav born incorrigible, a 'bad lot' irredeemable by education? Or is he a classic example of those who, due to miseducation or parental neglect, go wrong?"

? Do you think parents should treat all their children the same?

Ch.25: 28   Isaac loved Esav, for he liked eating the meat from Esav's hunt, but Rebecca loved Jacob.

It is unusual for parents to love one child so obviously more than the other. The fact that the two brothers were rivals and that each parent loved one more than the other is an ominous start to the story – it feels like something bad is going to come out of this.

Why did Isaac love Esav? The simple explanation is that Isaac loved the meat Esav brought him to eat and in this way Esav was a good son to his father.

Scholars of our Time have another explanation. They suggest that Isaac was attracted to qualities in Esav that he himself did not have – a case of opposites attract. Isaac was a quiet man – in the whole of the Torah he says only a few words (remember he was nearly sacrificed in the Akeida, imagine the effect that might have had on him). He didn't travel around much and preferred to stay near the tents. Kabbalah suggests that Isaac, with his quality of gevurah, was a closed and quiet person. Perhaps this quiet Isaac was attracted to Esav's outdoor energy and strength – he loved his adventurous son for being what he had never been.

And Rebecca loved Jacob. Jacob stayed at home close to his mother and he learnt to cook with her (we hear about his cooking next). Also Rebecca knew of God's prophecy, that the covenant of Abraham would pass on to Jacob, not Esav.

Marital tension and male bonding: "Many families that harbour underlying tensions between the mother and father have a tendency to split into two camps... their competition reflects the opposing forces at war within their family, and specifically, within their parent's marriage... As old age descends upon him, Isaac retreats from the demands of his marriage and his leadership position into a simpler relationship with Esav that revolves around traditional male bonding and food." Naomi Rosenblatt

Damaged duo: The love between Isaac and Esav could be based not on being opposites but on being alike. Many see Isaac after the Akeida as a survivor of trauma, suffering from "Post Traumatic Stress Disorder". Isaac, damaged by his experience, saw in Esav also a person damaged, flawed, and he reached out to help him.

Opposites attract: "That Isaac's sympathies were more inclined towards Esau, Rebecca's to Jacob can moreover easily be explained by the attraction of opposites...that Esau's lusty active nature appealed to him (Isaac)... saw in him a force which he had lost... Rebecca, on the other hand saw in Jacob's whole being a picture of a life unfolding (as she had never seen) in her father's house." R. Samson Raphael Hirsch

? Do you think opposites attract? Or are people drawn to others who are similar to them?

Weary of life: Rabbi Soloveitchik explains that Esav is exhausted not just because of the exertion of the hunt but because he lacks direction to give meaning to his life. He is wearied by what he experiences as the meaninglessness of life and the inevitability of death.

Justifying Jacob: In a bid to present Jacob as blameless, a traditional commentator justifies his behaviour as follows: "Learn from this that a righteous person is permitted to use artifice to obtain a sefer Torah or a sacred object in the possession of a wicked person."

The power of translation: Literary scholar Robert Alter translates Esau's words even more graphically and vulgarly: "Let me cram my maw with this red-red (ha-adom ha-adom haze)." According to Alter, Esau is "too inarticulate to recall in his hunger or his sheer boorishness the ordinary Hebrew word nazid, "stew."

? How would you describe Esav and Jacob's characters in this story?

Ch.25: 29 – 34 **One day when Jacob was cooking a lentil stew, Esav came in from the field exhausted. "Give me some of that red stuff to gulp down. I'm starving," said Esav. "First swear to me and sell me your birthright," answered Jacob. "Well, I am going to die anyway, so what use is my birthright?" So Esav swore to him and sold Jacob his birthright. Jacob gave Esav bread and lentil stew and Esav ate and drank and got up and went away. That was how Esav gave up his birthright.**

What is the birthright? Scholars of our Time explain that in biblical times the birthright was a very special honour given to the first born son. The birthright son had special privileges: after his father's death he would take his place as head of the household and he would receive a double portion of land.

The story about the lentil stew tells us more about the characters of the two brothers. What does the story tell us about Esav? Esav came in from the field asking for "red stuff" to gulp down. He was so hungry and impatient he couldn't even think of the name of the food. "And he ate and he drank and he got up and he went away." Sages of Old point out the many verbs used quickly one after the other. Esav was in a hurry, he didn't think much about what he was doing and he showed no regret. Ruled by his needs and feelings of the moment, Esav lived only in the present and did not think about the future. So he didn't value the birthright and was happy to sell it for a bowl of lentils.

And what about Jacob? Whilst the Sages of Old and Scholars of our Time see this story as showing Esav's shortcomings they also see some negative qualities on Jacob's part. Jacob obviously wanted the birthright – he thought about the future and wanted to be a link in the chain going from Abraham through Isaac onwards. But to get what he wanted Jacob took advantage of Esav, getting the best deal for himself. The trade of birthright for bread and lentils was far from even.

Ch.27: 1 – 4   When Isaac was old and his eyes were dimmed from seeing he called his older son Esav saying, "I am old now – who knows how soon I may die? So take your bows and arrows and go hunt me some game out in the field. Prepare me a tasty dish to eat and then I will give you my blessing before I die."

Scholars of our Time explain that it was the custom in biblical times for a father to bless his children before he died. In those days the blessing was as important as a legal will today.

Why does the Torah say Isaac's eyes "were dimmed from seeing" when the simple meaning is Isaac had become blind in his old age? A story from Midrash tells how Isaac lost his eyesight from seeing too much. When Isaac was bound on the altar ready to be sacrificed he looked up into the skies. At that moment the clouds parted and the angels looked down at Isaac and cried. Angel tears fell into Isaac's eyes, and his eyesight was changed forever.

The Sages of Old suggest that Isaac's blindness was not just a physical blindness. Isaac was blind to Esav's faults – he was too influenced by the good food Esav brought him to eat. So Isaac could not see the personalities of his two sons clearly, to be able to choose which one of them was more suited to carry on Abraham's tradition.

How does blindness change an older person's life? Older people who become blind lose their confidence to find their way around, to get out and do things. Instead they feel safer staying at home. This is how it was with Isaac who preferred to stay at home in his tent.

Darkness imprinted : "What Yizchak experienced in his youth, helplessly shackled, his eyes alone free to pierce the heavens, is 'imprinted' forever on those eyes. The Akeida leaves him an after-image, a kind of inverted residue, which only in old age assumes its original blinding quality... Survivor of unbearable trauma, he lives an apparently successful life... but after a lifetime of achievement the deep imprint of the Akeida develops, and the whole world falls into darkness."
Avivah Zornberg

Preparing for death: In preparing for death some people choose to compose an ethical will expressing their values, hopes and loves. The deathbed blessing of people in biblical times expressed some of these ideas.

Ch.27: 5 – 10 Rebecca had been listening at the tent flap and now she called Jacob. "I overheard your father tell your brother: 'Hunt some game and prepare me a tasty dish so I may bless you before I die.' Now, my son, listen to my words and do as I say. Bring me two good goat kids from the flock and I will cook them just the way your father likes. Then you take the dish to your father so that he will bless you before he dies."

Vacuum: "As Isaac recedes into the passivity of old age, he leaves a leadership vacuum in the family, which Rebecca must fill. As with many couples where a husband becomes incapacitated by illness, the wife, Rebecca, evolves into the dominant member of the marriage, forced to make independent decisions on behalf of the family's future. But she has to work covertly from 'within the tent.' She does not have the option of replacing her infirm husband and conferring the blessing on Jacob herself." Naomi Rosenblatt

Needing therapy: "A reader senses that Isaac and Rebecca's marriage was far from perfect, they certainly did not communicate well... Unquestionably, the tensions between the twins parallel at least some of the tensions between the parents." R. Joseph Telushkin Family therapists would have a field day with these family dynamics – the poor communication between the marital couple (why didn't Rebecca tell Isaac about the prophecy? why didn't Isaac tell her his intention to bless Esav?), the family split into two dyads, (Isaac and Esav, Rebecca and Jacob), the competition between the sons.

? This story shows what happens to people who have no power in a society. Like Rebecca, they may have to resort to indirect ways to gain power and influence in their world such as trickery and violence. Can you think of different times and places in history where people have not had power and how it has affected their behaviour?

A sense of drama is building up. Only Rebecca knows which of the sons is the one chosen to carry on the covenant. But she did not tell Isaac and Isaac is about to bless the wrong son. Knowing Esav and Jacob's personalities Rebecca saw that Jacob was more suited to receive the special blessing, and she felt she had to organize things so that would happen.

But what sort of mother would trick her old, blind husband into blessing one son instead of the other? Sages of Old and Scholars of our Time critisize Rebecca for her trickery. And we shall see later in the story, Rebecca ends up paying for it. Her favourite son Jacob leaves home for twenty years and Rebecca never sees him again.

Scholars of our Time have another way of understanding Rebecca's behaviour. Isaac had become old and blind and no longer acted as a leader of the family. Rebecca was a strong and clever woman, and knew what should happen with her sons. But Rebecca lived in a time and place in history where men made all the decisions and women had little power. Perhaps Rebecca resorted to trickery because she had no other way of doing what she knew was right and what God had told her.

Ch27: 11 – 17 Jacob wasn't sure about his mother's plan. "But my brother Esav is hairy and my skin is smooth. What if my father touches me and realizes I am tricking him, then he will curse me, not bless me." But Rebecca said, "The curse will be on me my son, just do as I say." So Jacob brought the goats and Rebecca cooked the tasty dish. Then she dressed Jacob in Esav's clothes and covered his arms and neck with the hairy skins of the goats. She gave Jacob the tasty dish she had cooked and he took it to his father.

Rebecca worked busily to disguise Jacob with Esav's clothes and the goat-skins so he would feel hairy like Esav. But did Rebecca really think she could trick Isaac with a few hairy goat skins? It was obvious Isaac would realize he had been tricked when Esav came back from the hunt ready to be blessed himself. What was Rebecca doing?

A Scholar of our Time has a fascinating explanation for Rebecca's behaviour: her plan was that Isaac should realize he had been tricked. Rebecca believed that Isaac could not see his two sons clearly and had been tricked into believing Esav should carry on Abraham's covenant and so receive the blessing. Once Isaac saw how easily he had been tricked with the disguise of the goat-skins and the tasty food he would realize he had been tricked before, tricked into thinking that Esav not Jacob deserved to carry on the tradition and receive the blessing.

And what do you think of Jacob's behaviour? He wasn't worried about tricking his father and cheating his brother. He was only worried about being found out and getting cursed. Many Sages of Old and Scholars of our Time critisize Jacob. Others argue that he didn't do anything wrong. He was a good son who respected his mother and obeyed what she told him to do. What do you think?

Stuck: "Jacob's untenable position, pinioned between a strong-willed mother and an emotionally inaccessible father, comes to a head in the blessing scene when he must either defy his mother or deceive his father." Naomi Rosenblatt

The moral issue: Nahum Sarna explains what he sees as the Bible's moral position on Jacob's deception. "The Bible is not here condoning what has been obtained by trickery. On the contrary, the way the narrative is handled makes clear that Jacob has a claim on the birthright wholly and solely by virtue of God's pre-determination... Jacob is portrayed as having acquired the birthright, first, by heartless exploitation of his own brother, and then, by the crafty deception practiced upon his blind old father. Scripture... wishes to disengage the fact of Jacob's election from the improper means the young man employed in his impatience to formalize his predestined, independent right to the heirship."

Proactive pragmatist: "And while it is easy for us to fault Rebekah for using deception to achieve her goal, she emerges as a proactive pragmatist who is willing and able to make tough decisions when the circumstances demand... God speaks to Rebekah, not Isaac, about the future leadership of the family, and she does not shrink from the responsiblity that receiving His prophecy confers on her." Naomi Rosenblatt

Face to face: "Jacob was finally facing his father, poised to ask for the blessing and the love he had always craved. But this moment of truth, for which he had waited a lifetime, was doomed to deception. "Come close and kiss me, my son." Jacob stiffened. Did he dare kiss his father and risk detection? He moved closer to the old man, and they embraced. Jacob buried his head in his father's neck and kissed him, searching in vain for memories of this fatherly embrace. Perhaps they dwelt only in his dreams. He choked back a sob, clenching his teeth against the tears exploding in his eyes."

Naomi Rosenblatt

Transformation: Avivah Zornberg suggests that Jacob's impersonation of Esav indicates the beginning of a deep psychological transformation in Jacob. "It evokes the disappearance of the old self-constructed Jacob and the birth of a new hybrid being... Jacob lays claim to the perceived energies of his twin brother... what Jacob has gained in his impersonation of Esav is a sense of power in his limbs."

? Do you think Jacob was right or wrong to trick Isaac and get the blessing? We shall see that while the Torah does not make an obvious moral jugdment, the story itself, and what ends up happening to Jacob, and to Rebecca, speak for themselves

Ch.27: 18 – 29 Jacob went to his father and Isaac asked, "Which of my sons are you?" "I am Esav your first born," answered Jacob, "Please sit up and eat and then bless me." And Issac said, "Come closer so I can touch you to see if you are really my son Esav or not." And when Isaac touched him he said, "The voice is the voice of Jacob but the hands are the hands of Esav. Come closer and kiss me, my son." As Jacob kissed him Isaac smelled him and said, "The smell of my son is like a summer field blessed by God." And Isaac blessed him, "May God give you the dew of heaven, the richness of the earth and plenty of corn and wine. Let peoples serve you and nations bow to you. God will give you and your children the blessing of Abraham, that you will inherit the land God promised to your grandfather Abraham."

Jacob disguised himself and pretended to be Esav. What happens when you pretend to be someone else? Scholars of our Time suggest that Jacob does not simply pretend to be Esav but actually takes on some of Esav's qualities as his own. "The voice is the voice of Jacob and the hands are the hands of Esav." Before there had been a split between the twin sons – Jacob was the one who sat in tents, learning, discussing, using his voice. And Esav was the one who hunted in the fields, active, using his hands. But now Jacob is taking on the hands of Esav, growing a part of himself that is more physical and active, taking opportunities to succeed in the world.

We shall see in the next parasha that Jacob leaves his quiet life in the tents near his parents and lives a more active physical life. He becomes a shepherd, tending sheep in the fields, and he marries and has many children. Jacob must take on some of Esav's qualities to become a forefather of the Jewish people.

Sages of Old and Scholars of our Time agree that the Torah seems to criticize Jacob's trickery. Jacob's whole life's journey from the time of the trickery till his death is marked by hardship. For the story tells how Jacob is tricked himself a number of times: first by his father-in-law and then by his own sons. And whilst Jacob's father, Isaac, and his grandfather, Abraham, both lived to a ripe old age, Jacob describes the years of his life as "few and hard."

Consequences: "Sin and deceit, however justified, bring in their train ultimate punishment." Nehama Leibowitz, although not a critic of Jacob, draws this conclusion.

Legally blessed: "Instead of insisting on his unconsciousness at the time of the blessing, instead of withdrawing words of blessing extorted from him under false pretenses, Isaac tells his beloved deprived son, Esau, "indeed, he is blessed."...After the deception, Isaac himself unexpectedly ratifies the transaction. A dramatic event – the use of certain words called a "blessing" – has transpired. Regardless of moral judgments in the narrative itself or by generations of readers, that dramatic event is here ratified."
Avivah Zornberg

Terror: "Why is Isaac afraid? He said, 'Perhaps I have sinned in blessing the younger before the older, I have changed the order of the relationship.'"
Rashi A Midrash describes Isaac's terror: "He saw gehinnom, the abyss, open beneath him." Isaac realized that he had inverted the correct order of things by blessing Jacob instead of Esav. He felt the expected structure of things fall away and this created in him a sense of terror.

Unconscious insight: "Without question, Isaac preferred Esav... Isaac's favoritism was so strong he couldn't hide it. Yet at a less conscious level, Isaac realized that the great mission God had entrusted to his father, Abraham, and to him – to make God known to the world – could be carried on only through Jacob. He himself lacked the strength of character to deny the blessing to Esau, but when Jacob appeared, disguised as his brother, he went along with the deception, knowing that Jacob was worthier of the blessing."
R. Joseph Telushkin

Ch.27: 30 – 33 As soon as Jacob had gone, Esav returned from the hunt. He had cooked the tasty dish and brought it to his father, ready to receive the blessing. "Who are you?" asked Isaac, confused. "I am your firstborn son, Esav." Isaac began to tremble with a great sense of terror. "What... who was it, then, who brought me a tasty dish before you did? Because I blessed him and he must remain blessed."

In a flash Isaac realized he had been tricked. He had given the blessing to Jacob instead of Esav, and so had reversed the correct order of things by which he must bless the firstborn first.

But at the same time Issac also realized, with shock, that he had been wrong all along. Suddenly he saw that Jacob, not Esav is the right son to carry on the covenant. Only now when Isaac saw how easily he had been tricked did he realize that he had been mistaken all along about his sons.

"He must remain blessed." A Scholar of our Time explains that, in biblical times, once a blessing was given it could not be taken back.

Ch.27: 34 – 40   When Esav heard this he wept wildly and bitterly and begged, "Bless me too father'. But Isaac answered, "Your brother came with trickery and took away your blessing." Esav cried, "Have you but one blessing? Bless me too." So Isaac blessed him, "May God give you the richness of the earth and the dew of heaven above. Yet you shall live by your sword and you shall serve your brother. But when you grow restless you will throw off his yoke from your neck."

Reading this story we feel Esav's sorrow. Esav the strong and tough hunter breaks down crying, so upset was he to be tricked and miss out on the blessing. Esav clearly valued this blessing and begged his father to find a blessing for him too. The Sages of Old, who usually focused on Esav's wickedness, here understand his tears and pain.

Scholars of our Time note that even now when Esav was so upset he did not accuse his father in anger. He could have said, "You only have two sons, how could you get us mixed up?" Instead all he said was, "Bless me too father".

Esau's pain: "Biblical commentators have long struggled with this chapter. (Anti-semites also have a field day with it, seeing in Jacob the prototypical, wily, and scheming Jewish businessman.) Most commentators, Christian and Jewish, speak of Jacob in respectful terms; still, one would have to have a heart of stone to remain unmoved by Esau's pain, and to have no qualms about Jacob's lies." R. Joseph Telushkin

Tragic: "Esav is surely one of the most tragic figures of the Bible." R. Bradley Artson

Sympathy: "Esau bursts into wild and bitter sobbing. Unquestionably, this time the Bible's description of Esau's anguish is intended to evoke the reader's sympathy. On the previous occasion, Esau exaggerated his hunger, demanded food like a barbarian, and showed no understanding of his birthright's significance. But this time Esau's behaviour has been appropriate." R. Joseph Telushkin

Right or wrong: "Suppose a father has the power to bestow a life – transforming family mission on only one son, but for some perverse reason plans to bestow it on his least worthy child... Rebecca knew – God had told her – which son was more worthy. Knowing what she did, should Rebecca (and Jacob) have gone along with Isaac's plan to bestow the blessing and the power that went with it on Esau? To do so would have constituted a betrayal of both their mission and their descendants... One can certainly make a powerful case for the rightness of Jacob's behaviour. Yet, a literary analysis of later episodes in Genesis strongly suggests a powerful undercurrent of biblical disapproval."
R. Joseph Telushkin

Ch.27: 41 – 45 Esav hated Jacob because of the blessing and he decided, "When my father dies I will kill my brother Jacob." Rebecca told Jacob that Esav was planning to kill him and she sent him away to her brother Laban's house in Haran. "Stay with Laban until your brother's anger cools. When he forgets what you have done, I'll send for you to come back." So Jacob went away to Laban's house. No-one could have guessed how long he would be away, for it was a very long time.

Rebecca sent Jacob away to protect him from Esav's anger. But in sending him away Rebecca also paid a price for her part in deceiving Isaac. Rebecca loved Jacob but Jacob was to stay away for twenty years, marrying and having twelve sons and a daughter. Rebecca would never see Jacob again, and she would never see his children.

Competing Visions

The parasha of Toldot is a challenging one, telling the story of twins Esav and Jacob who are very different from one another. But only one of these boys will be chosen to carry on God's covenant with Abraham and become the third forefather of the Jewish people.

The story sets up a contrast between the twins and the competition between them is fierce. But there is a big difference between the way the Sages of Old and Midrash describe the characters of Esav and Jacob and the way the Scholars of our Time describe them.

The Sages of Old lived in the Middle Ages under Roman and Christian rule, when Jews were oppressed. They saw Esav as the ancestor and the symbol of their oppressors and so imagined Esav as dishonest, violent and evil.

But Scholars of our Time, no longer living under oppressive Roman or Christian rule, see Esav and Jacob quite differently. Instead of seeing Esav as evil and Jacob as righteous they see their different personalities, each with positive and negative qualities.

So the place and time in history when you live can affect the way you understand stories and people. The seventy faces of the Torah, the different ways of understanding the Torah stories, are influenced not only by who you are, but also by when you live, and where and how. We need to be aware of how we want to understand and remember the story today.

Both Jacob and Esav represent an extreme way of being. Jacob is always indoors studying, Esav is always outdoors hunting; neither is ideal. Like the twins in fairy tales, each needs the other's qualities to be whole.

When it comes to the importance of carrying on the covenant, keeping the traditions of Abraham and Isaac, Esav doesn't seem to care much. Living in the present, not thinking about the future, he is not worried about carrying on the covenant. And so he sells his birthright for a bowl of lentils. But perhaps Jacob cares too much. He takes advantage of Esav to get the birthright and he tricks his father to get the blessing. So the story of Toldot can make us feel uncomfortable. Jacob the deceiver gets the blessing and he goes on to become the third forefather of the Jewish people. But it is the process of feeling uncomfortabe and discussing and struggling with the story that is important. As a philosopher wrote "The essence of morality is a questioning about morality." In the difficult choice between the twins, both of whom are not ideal, the story tells – it is better to care too much than to care too little.

And Jacob does improve over time. While pretending to be Esav, Jacob starts to develop some of Esav's positive qualities. He develops the "hands of Esav" to go with "the voice of Jacob." We shall see in the next stories that he leaves his parents' home and goes out into the world. He lives in nature and becomes a shepherd, marries and has many children. So he becomes a more whole person, comfortable indoors and outdoors, using his mind and body, living his life in the present and the future.

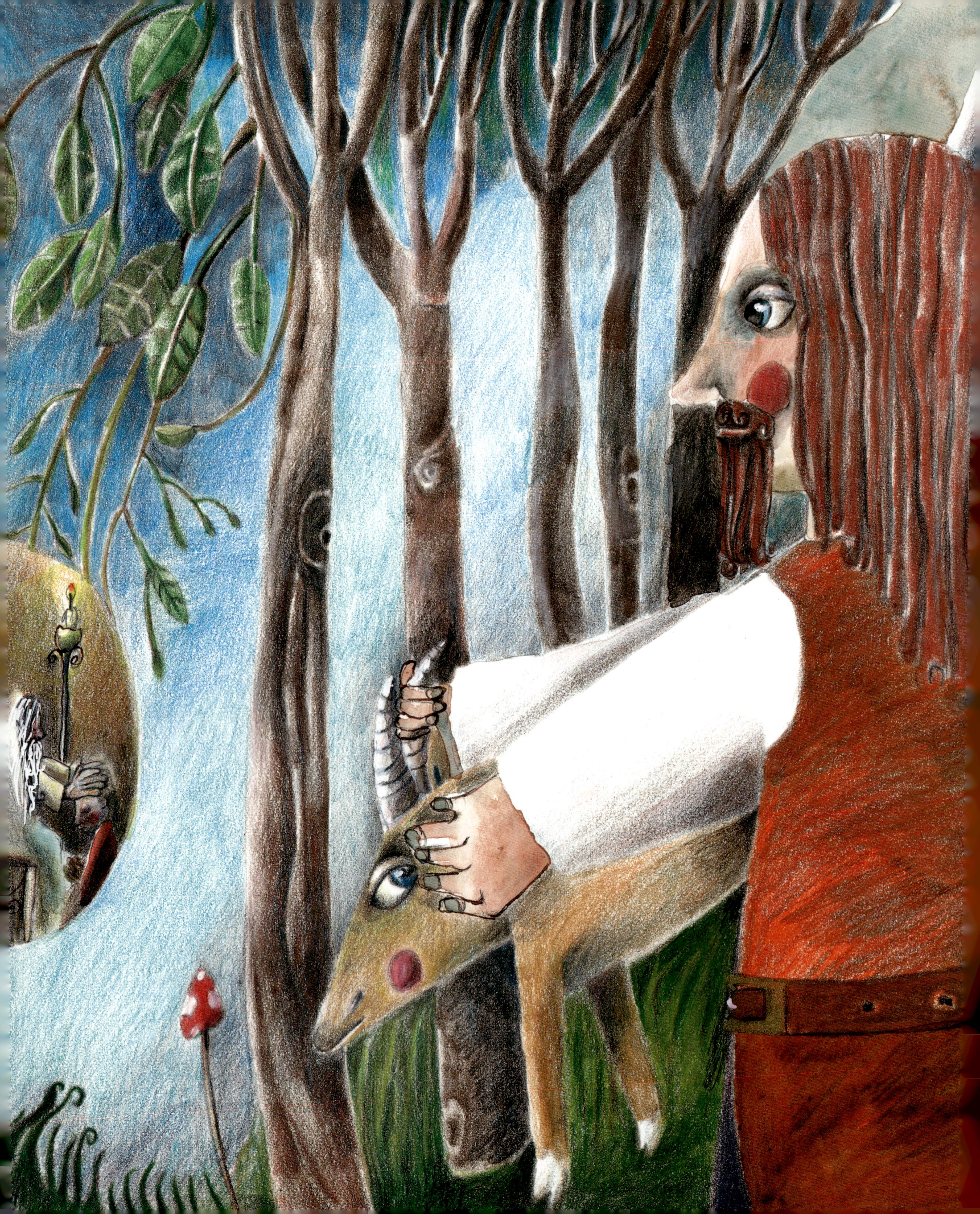

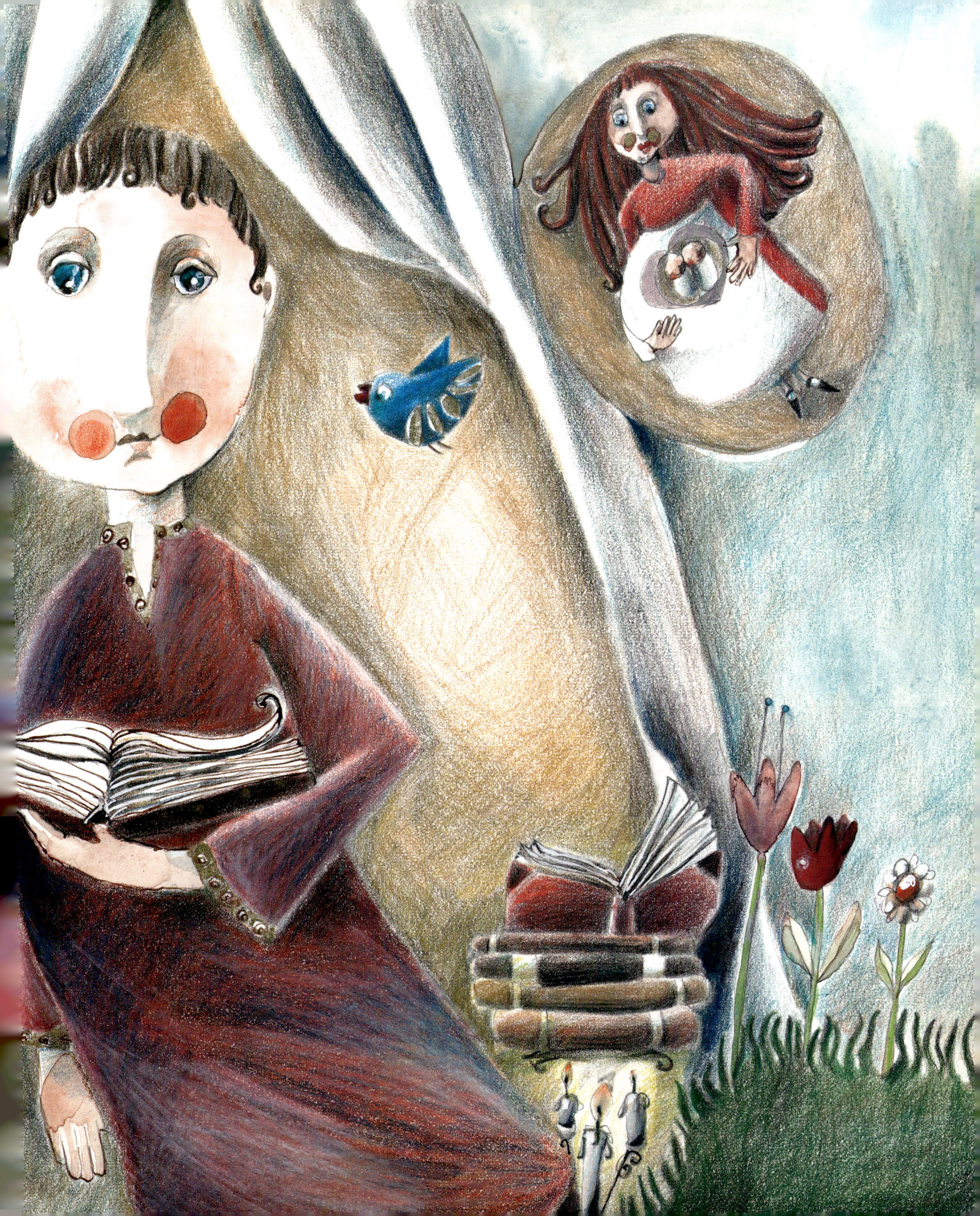

וֵיצֵא

VAYETZE

And Jacob went out on his journey

Setting out alone: "Jacob had not yet grasped the magnitude of his exile... all he knew was that he was terribly alone – banished from his homeland, despised by his brother, shamed before his dying father... like many mythic heroes, Jacob must seek out his destiny and forge his adult identity away from his clan." Naomi Rosenblatt

In exile: Jacob's journey away from his parents' home is compared to an exile. He is the only patriarch who suffers the harshness of living outside the promised land, in exile, and so his journey is seen as a metaphor for the experience of the Jewish people in exile.

? Imagine you are Jacob leaving your parents' home and walking alone across the stony land. What are your thoughts and feelings?

Ch.28: 10 Jacob set out from his parents' home and journeyed towards Haran.

In the last parasha Jacob got the blessing from his father but it cost him a lot. His brother Esav was full of anger at him, and so Jacob had to flee his parents' home, never to see his mother again. Jacob also had to leave the land promised to his grandfather and father, and cross into a different land where he would stay for twenty years.

Scholars of our Time compare Jacob's journey away from his parents' home with Abraham's. Abraham left his birthplace and his parents' home when God called him. He left with a wife and a band of followers and he began his journey toward the land that God promised him. But Jacob leaves alone, and God has not spoken to him. And rather than moving towards the promised land Jacob moves away from it.

Kabbalah compares Jacob's travelling away from his parents' home to a person climbing down a deep and dangerous well. When climbing down a deep well you need to tie yourself to the top with a strong rope lest you fall down and are lost forever. There is a sense of danger as Jacob moves away – perhaps in Haran he will forget about his parents' ways and the covenant with God. We shall see that before Jacob goes down to Haran he ties himself to the ways of his parents with a promise.

Ch.28: 11 **He came to the place *Hamakom* and stayed there overnight because the sun had set. Jacob took some stones, put them under his head as a pillow and lay down to sleep.**

It seems Jacob's sleeping in that place was no accident – in fact God organized things so Jacob would have to sleep there. Sages of Old tell that God made the sun set early so Jacob would have to stop. He had wanted to keep going but the darkness was so deep "he found the world like a solid wall before him." A Scholar of our Time writes that Jacob did not just arrive at the place, he actually crashed into it. For God had changed the laws of physics and geography and had moved the place forward to meet Jacob.

And what or where is "the place" – *Hamakom*? Sages of Old explain that "the place" is Mt Moriah. In the past this was the place of the Akeida, where Jacob's father was bound in sacrifice. In the future this will be the place of the *Bet Hamikdash*, the Temple, where Jews will pray to God. "The place" – *Hamakom* is also one of the names of God. The scene is set for something mysterious to happen – it is dark, Jacob is alone and he has crashed into a strange place.

Crash: The Hebrew word for "he came" *vayifga* is a very unusual word to express arriving at a place. In keeping with the idea that God brought the place forward to meet Jacob, Avivah Zornberg explains that "vayifga suggests a dynamic encounter with an object travelling toward oneself. The force of the meeting is palpable but mysterious."

Dark night of the soul: As Jacob begins his journey and leaves the promised land the sun sets. Twenty years later when Jacob makes the return journey to his parents' home the story tells of a sunrise. Rashi suggests that Jacob's twenty years outside the Promised land (living at the home of his deceiving uncle Laban), is a time of spiritual darkness.

? If you were making a movie of this scene where Jacob came to the place *Hamakom*, how would it look? What sounds or music would there be?

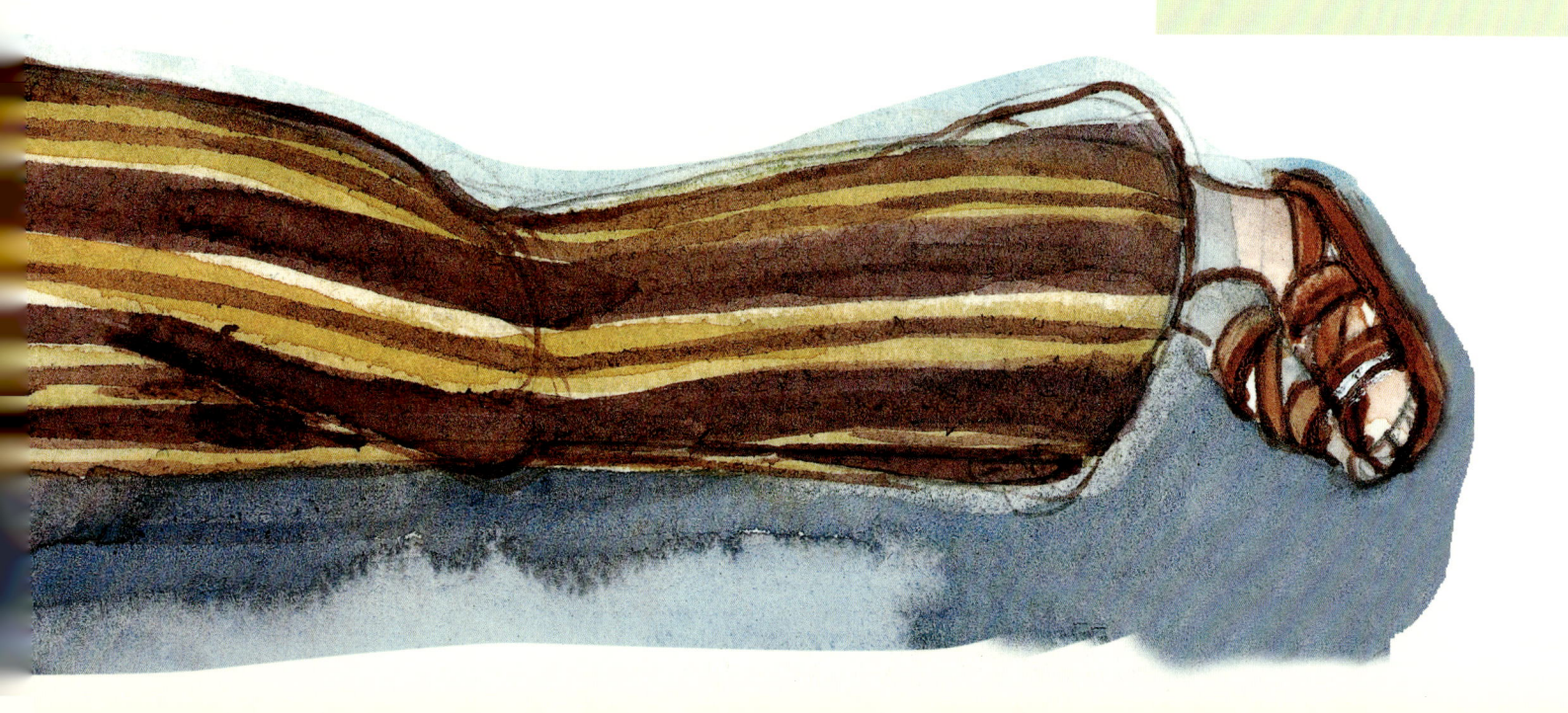

A ladder upwards: "The ladder expresses his desire for upward transcendance, for deliverance from his earthly conflicts." Naomi Rosenblatt

A ladder to God? "The image of the ladder reaching the sky recalls the image of the Babylonian temple tower (as in the Tower of Babel). The Babylonians believed the tower served as a meeting place between God and man (with man ascending and God descending the tower). But in Jacob's dream only angels go up and down. The divine and humans do not meet – the gap between them is unbridgeable by physical means." Nahum Sarna

The ladder as history: Midrash suggests another meaning for the dream. Accordingly, the angels in the dream are kings of nations climbing up and down the ladder of history. The king of Babylon goes up and down, the king of Greece goes up and down, and the king of Rome goes up and down. The dream shows Jacob that many nations will rise and fall in the history of the world, and so Jacob should not be afraid that his people will always live under the rule of another nation.

A ladder in Poland: Elie Wiesel suggests a harrowing meaning of the dream formed by his own experiences in the Holocaust. "In his dream Jacob saw a ladder whose top reached into heaven. It still exists. There are those who have seen it, somewhere in Poland, at the side of an out – of – the – way railroad station. And an entire people was climbing, climbing towards the clouds on fire. Such was the nature of the dread our ancestor Jacob must have felt."

? What do you think Jacob's dream of the ladder and the angels could mean?

Ch.28: 12 As Jacob slept he dreamt: And behold there was a ladder rising up from the earth with its top reaching the heavens, and angels of God were going up and down on it.

Jacob's dream of the ladder is the first dream recorded in the Torah. Sages of Old, Midrash and Scholars of our Time have all discussed the meaning of this dream.

What could a dream of a ladder and angels going up and down it mean? A Scholar of our Time explains that the ladder is Jacob's own wish to climb up out of his difficulties and find better times. The angels are Jacob's messengers to God asking for help and comfort on his journey.

Sages of Old suggest the ladder represents the ups and downs of life. "The affairs of men are comparable to a ladder... for a single day can carry one person up the ladder of life and another down." Perhaps Jacob caught a glimpse of the ups and downs of his own future.

But why do the angels go up the ladder first and then come down? You would think angels live in heaven and need to climb down the ladder to earth before they climb up. Sages of Old explain that Jacob dreamt this dream just as he was about to leave the borders of the land promised to Abraham. The angels that accompanied Jacob in the promised land do not cross its border and so they climb up to heaven. Other angels come down the ladder to accompany Jacob on the continuation of his journey.

Ch.28: 13 – 15 And in the dream God stood beside Jacob and said, "I am God, the God of Abraham and Isaac. I give to you and your children the land on which you are sleeping. Your descendants shall be as many as the grains of dust on the earth, and they shall spread out to the west and the east, the north and south. Remember that I am with you to protect you wherever you go. I will bring you back to this land and will not leave you until I have fulfilled this promise."

This is the first time God speaks to Jacob and what a speech! God renews the promise made to Abraham and Isaac, promising Jacob the land and many descendants. Scholars of our Time point out that there is a new element in God's promise to Jacob – God promises to be with Jacob and protect him wherever he goes. Perhaps Jacob felt so lonely and afraid, with his brother's anger behind and an uncertain future ahead, that he needed God's promise of protection.

God promises to give Jacob and his descendants "the land on which you are sleeping". But that wouldn't be much land! Sages of Old tell that God folded up the whole of the land of Israel beneath the sleeping Jacob. Like a parent who hides a present under the pillow of their sleeping child!

"I am with you": God tells Jacob "I am with you." What does it mean to experience God as with you? Does it mean you are protected from suffering and evil? Michael Rosenak explains: "A religious approach that we find in Torah... is that although there is much evil in the world, God may be petitioned to give the individual strength to cope with it, to put it into perspective... To be "near" God does not mean to be protected from history or inevitable suffering and death, but to "see" in the midst of these that "I am continually with You, You hold my right hand."

Vertical and horizontal: "The vertical image of the ladder on which the angels ascend and descend (but where are the essential wings...are angels not made to fly) is contrasted with the horizontal image of Jacob's sleeping body and the spreading out of his descendants to the west, east north and south." Avivah Zornberg

Sulam and Sinai: The Hebrew word for ladder (sulam) and the word Sinai both have the same numerical value. So Midrash tells that in his dream God showed Jacob the giving of the Torah at Mt Sinai and said: "If your descendants observe this Torah, they will ascend like these angels; if not, they will descend like them." Genesis Rabbah

? Have you ever had a dream that you knew was important? How did you know? What did you feel when you woke up?

Ch.28: 16 – 22 **When Jacob woke up from his sleep he felt shaken. "Surely God is in this place and I did not know. How awesome this place is, none other than the house of God and the gate of heaven." And Jacob took the stone he had used as a pillow and set it up as a memorial stone and he called the place Bet – El, House of God. And Jacob made a promise to God: "If you remain with me, protect me and give me bread to eat and clothing to wear, then you shall be my God."**

Upward ladders: "Like Jacob we all face difficult passages through life – troubling nights when we are consumed by fears… and like Jacob we are always standing before the 'gateways to heaven.' Ladders are constantly being lowered into our lives… sometimes they take the form of a teacher or friend… other times they appear as personal or professional opportunities. But it falls to us to take the first steps, one rung at a time, beginning at the bottom of whatever ladder we face." Naomi Rosenblatt

I did not know: "When can man experience God's nearness? Only when he is suffused by 'I don't know', when he himself knows that he does not know and does not pretend to have wisdom and insight." Panim Yafot

Holy place: "Any place where God lets down the ladder. And how are you to know where that will be? Or how are you to determine where it may be, but by being ready for it always?" John Ruskin

Dreaming: "There is a profound intimation here about the dynamics of sleep, about loss of consciousness and the possible gifts of unconsciousness, about knowing and dreaming." Avivah Zornberg

? Jacob said "God is in this place" and he felt the place was holy. What do you think makes a certain place holy? Where is the place where you feel most spiritual or holy?

Jacob felt shaken when he woke up. He didn't say to himself, "It was just a dream, I'll forget about it" – rather he realized the importance of the dream : God was speaking to him. The dream is a turning point for Jacob – from now on he has a new confidence in the direction of his life. And he is no longer on his own – he has the feeling that God is with him.

What does Jacob mean when he says, "Surely God is in this place and I did not know?" According to Sages of Old he means "If I had known God was in this place, I would not have fallen asleep." Jacob feels it is not proper to sleep in a place of God (sort of like falling asleep in the middle of synagogue)! But if Jacob had not slept, he would not have dreamt of ladders and angels, and he would not have received his first message from God. Sometimes our dreams tell us things we don't know when we are awake.

Remember when Jacob first lay down to sleep he used a few stones as a pillow. But now the Torah writes that "Jacob took the stone he had used as a pillow and set it up as a memorial stone." How did the few stones turn into one? Midrash tells that Jacob took twelve stones representing his twelve sons who would become the twelve tribes of Israel. The twelve stones became one stone, telling Jacob that his twelve sons would become one people in the land. Jacob remembered the problems he and his brother Esav had in growing up together so he knew how difficult it could be for twelve brothers to get along well together. He would be pleased to know that his twelve sons would one day come together as one people.

Ch.29: 1 – 11 Jacob lifted up his legs and arrived at Haran. He saw a well in a field, some shepherds and three flocks of sheep waiting to drink from the well. A huge stone covered the mouth of the well, so only when all the flocks gathered could all the shepherds together roll the stone off to water their sheep. Jacob asked the shepherds if they knew Laban, Rebecca's brother. "Yes" they answered "and there is his daughter Rachel, coming with her sheep". When Jacob saw Rachel he rolled the stone off the well and watered her sheep. And he kissed Rachel and cried.

What does "Jacob lifted up his legs" mean? A Scholar of our Time explains that after his dream Jacob woke up with a new confidence and strength. Knowing that God was with him his heart lifted up his legs and he strode with a sense of lightness and freedom, almost like flying.

Why was the stone covering the well so heavy that you needed many people to roll it off? Sages of Old tell that the people in Haran did not trust each other to take only a fair amount of water. They chose a stone that needed their combined strength to roll it off and so they could only water their sheep when they were all together.

How did Jacob manage to roll that huge stone off on his own? Sages of Old tell that when Jacob saw Rachel it was love at first sight. Jacob knew that he wanted to marry her and share his life with her. That rush of love gave Jacob the superhuman strength to roll the huge stone off the well – impressive for a first date! (Scientists confirm that in extreme situations a chemical called adrenalin is secreted into the bloodstream giving a rush of strength.) Jacob, who in our last parasha was a "man of tents", now becomes a man of action. He has taken on some of his brother Esav's strength and has managed to combine the "hands of Esav" with the "voice of Jacob".

And why does Jacob kiss Rachel and then cry? These are the first tears in the Torah. Sages of Old tell that when Jacob falls in love with Rachel he cries because he realizes what he has missed his whole life – a partner and soulmate. Midrash tells that Jacob also cries because he has a glimpse into the future and sees that Rachel will not always be with him.

Flying: "Jacob responds to his fate with a long-legged leap, inspired with the knowledge that in his 'walking' God is with him... Light and wide-striding, Jacob is, in effect, almost flying." Avivah Zornberg

The well of meetings: A generation before, Abraham's servant Eliezer had met Rebecca beside a well near Haran. But the differences between the two scenes are significant. "The servant had an impressive entourage of camels and gifts for the bride's family. Jacob arrives on foot as a ragged fugitive, with nothing to offer his future father-in-law but the labour of his body." Naomi Rosenblatt

Love at first sight: "The first moment that Yaacov set eyes on gorgeous Rachel, he kissed her and he wept. He was enchanted by her. The smooth-skinned, expressive man held nothing back. Theirs was love at first sight, a marriage made in heaven." Miki Raver

? Do you believe in love at first sight? What does it mean to you?

? Have you ever experienced a burst of adrenalin like Jacob, giving you extra strength?

Bride price: Jacob offered Laban seven years of work as a bride price for Rachel. Nahum Sarna explains that it was customary for a man to pay the father of the bride for his daughter. Some brides were more costly than others, depending on her family status, looks etc. As Jacob had no property he offered his years of labour. Was seven years of labour a high or low bride price? We don't know.

? Like Jacob we can experience time as moving by fast or slow. Have you ever felt time fly by (like when the summer holidays seem to finish so fast) or drag slowly?

Ch.29: 13 – 20 Rachel took Jacob to meet her father Laban. And Jacob said to Laban: "I will stay with you and work seven years to marry Rachel, your younger daughter," for Jacob loved Rachel. Laban had two daughters. The older one, Leah, had tender eyes and Rachel, the younger one, was beautiful all over. So Jacob worked seven years for Rachel but they seemed like only a few days to him because of his love for her.

Rachel was considered more beautiful than Leah. Midrash tells that Leah had "tender eyes" because they were red and puffy from crying. Leah had overheard a plan that Rebecca's two son's Esav and Jacob were to marry Laban's two daughters, the older to the older and the younger to the younger. At the thought of marrying Esav, Leah cried and cried until her eyelashes fell out.

Sages of Old explain that Jacob's love for Rachel was so strong that it transformed time, making seven years seem like only a few days.

Ch. 29: 21 – 31 After the seven years, Jacob reminded Laban of their agreement. That night, Laban made a wedding feast and then in the darkness he took Leah as a wife to Jacob. When morning came Jacob saw it was Leah and not Rachel who had been married to him. He said to Laban, "Why have you deceived me? I worked seven years for Rachel. Why have you done this to me?" And Laban answered him, "It is not our custom here to marry off the younger before the older. Work for me another seven years and I will give you Rachel also as a wife." Jacob agreed and married Rachel too, and he loved Rachel more than Leah.

Laban deceived Jacob, swapping Rachel for Leah on the wedding night. This reminds us of Jacob's deception when he pretended to be Esav and tricked Isaac into giving him the blessing. When Jacob complains, Laban says that unlike what Jacob did in deceiving Isaac, the younger cannot take the place of the first born. Jacob doesn't argue with Laban – perhaps he feels guilty about tricking his own father and so he accepts Laban's deception as his punishment.

It is not clear just how Laban managed to swap Leah for Rachel. The Torah story is short and leaves a lot to the imagination. This is where the Sages of Old and the Midrash wove stories to fill in the gaps.

Sages of Old tell that Laban made a big wedding feast so that Jacob would get drunk and be confused. Perhaps Leah was wearing a veil and Jacob could not see her properly. And where was Rachel? Maybe Laban locked her up on the wedding night so she could not warn Jacob.

Some tell that Jacob and Rachel had made a code of secret signs – touching the right big toe, thumb and earlobe – for the wedding night. But when Rachel saw that Laban swapped her for Leah she did not want Leah to be humiliated. And so she taught her the secret signs.

Kabbalistically: Leah and Rachel represent different worlds. Leah represents the concealed world, the veiled world whilst Rachel represents the revealed world. Leah's marriage to Jacob was hidden, accomplished by a veil, whilst Rachel was met openly at the well and married openly.

Deceiving: "All that night she (Leah) acted the part of Rachel. As soon as he rose in the morning 'behold it was Leah,' he said to her: 'Daughter of the deceiver! Wherefore hast thou tricked me?' Said she to him 'And thou, why did thou deceive thy father when he said to thee: Art thou my son Esau?'" Midrash Tanhuma

? Why do you think Laban tricked Jacob into marrying Leah? Was it because an older daughter had to be married before her younger sister? Couldn't Laban have told Jacob about this custom before he first agreed to work for Rachel? Or couldn't Laban have found a husband for Leah in seven years? In the Torah story Laban is described as a dishonest man.

? Can you imagine a conversation between Rachel and Leah after the wedding of Jacob to Leah?

Two kinds of love: *Rachel represents "a romantic love that draws its sustenance from longing, from separation and distance, from premature death – a love full of expectations, dreams, and memories. On the other hand, we have the love of a faithful woman, (Leah), the woman who remains beside her husband, works, and struggles in the daily round with him, bears him most of his children, and whose love is constant, stable and real. Leah's relationship with Jacob was without the drama, the elation, and the dejection that characterized his love for Rachel." Adin Steinsalz*

What's in a name? *The names Leah calls her sons signify her changing relationship to her husband and herself. Each of her first three sons "embodies yet another desperate attempt to win her husband's love. 'Reuben' – means the Lord has seen my affliction, now my husband will love me, 'Shimeon' – because the Lord heard that I was unloved and gave me this one also, 'Levi' – my husband will become attached to me for I have borne him three sons. With the birth of her fourth son Judah, Leah finally achieves the inner strength to stop craving her husband's approval. Judah is a source of pure joy, in and for himself. 'This time I shall praise the Lord." R. Bradley Artson*

To be a woman: *Rachel and Leah can be seen to struggle with the same dichotomies of female identity as women today. "One is beautiful, one is homely. One is fertile, the other barren. One is the archetypal mother, the other is the perennial love… neither feels whole." Naomi Rosenblatt*

? If you were Rachel writing a diary about longing to have a baby while your sister Leah gives birth to many, what would you write?

Ch.29: 31 – 35, Ch.30: 1 – 13 **When God saw that Leah was unloved, God gave her many children. Leah had six sons, Reuben, Simeon, Levi, Judah, Issachar and Zebulun, and one daughter, Dinah. When Rachel saw that she did not become pregnant she felt jealous of her sister and said to Jacob, "Give me children or I will die." Rachel gave her handmaid to Jacob and Jacob had two sons with her, Dan and Naftali. And Leah gave Jacob her handmaid too, and Jacob had two more sons with her, Gad and Asher. God heard Rachel's prayers and she became pregnant and gave birth to a son. She named him Yosef, meaning "May God give me another son."**

At this point Jacob has four wives, ten sons and a daughter. That's a lot of family! We shall soon see that Jacob has two more sons and these twelve sons become the twelve tribes of Israel. But all was not peaceful in this large family. Rather a storm of mixed emotions swirled. Leah loved Jacob but Jacob did not love her. Jacob loved Rachel but Rachel was sad she didn't have children and she was jealous of Leah. Both Rachel and Leah gave their handmaids to Jacob in a race to have more children. Everybody seems to want what they haven't got. Rachel had love but wanted children. Leah had children but wanted love.

Midrash tells that once when she was pregnant, Leah prayed for her sister Rachel to have a son. Rachel did have a son and the baby Leah was carrying turned out to be a daughter instead, Jacob's only daughter, whom she called Dinah.

The Sages of Old and Scholars of our Time tell stories helping us imagine how Leah and Rachel felt as the two wives of Jacob. The situation was difficult for both of them, as two sisters married to the same man. Each suffered a sense of sadness in her life and was jealous of the other. In many ways Leah was the most unhappy of the Matriarchs. Jacob saw her as the wife he was tricked into marrying and at first did not really love her. God saw that Leah was unloved and gave her many children. And Leah names her children hoping that through them Jacob will come to love her. As time passes Jacob becomes more aware of Leah's inner beauty. He sees what a strong mother she is and realizes that the people of Israel will be descended more from Leah's sons than from Rachel's. And so with time Jacob grows to love Leah.

"Give me children or I will die," Rachel's voice bursts out with pain and frustration. Why does she say "I will die"? Rachel feels that her life without children does not have joy and meaning. There is a hint of tragedy in Rachel's words – Rachel does have children but, as we shall see, she will die giving birth to her second son.

Rachel's peom: The much loved Hebrew poet Rachel, who died in 1931, a childless woman, wrote of her longing for a son, and compared herself to the biblical Rachel.

If only I had a son, a little child,
bright, with black curls,
To hold his hand and to walk slowly
Down the paths of the garden,
A child. A little one.
I would call him Uri, my Uri.

The short name is soft and pure,
A fragment of brightness,
I'll call out to my dark little boy, Uri.

I will yet become as bitter as the mother Rachel.
I will still pray like Hannah at Shilo.
I will yet long for him.

Give me children or I will die: "Whether she means by this that she would prefer death to barrenness, or that she feels that she is living a state of "death-in-life"...her desperation is clear." Noam Zion and Steve Israel

Rachel's voice: "My dear sister, Leah, how often we fought and how jealous we were of each other. You lusted after a love that was not for you, and I lusted after sons I could not have... My sister, the two of us have been barren, you from love and I from children." Penina Adelman

Textual life span: Ilana Pardes writes of the different possibilities for character development between men and women in the Bible. Jacob's character changes and develops significantly through the stories. In contrast female characters such as Leah and Rachel do not develop as much. "Female characters, however, are not so fraught with development. Their textual life-span is limited… The biblical woman appears on stage only when she is marriageable, and her stay there is determined, generally speaking, by the impact of her maternal position on the status of her favourite son. Rachel actually dies in childbirth, but other biblical mothers simply vanish from the scene once their offspring are on their own."

Echoes of rivalry: The rivalry between Leah and Rachel echoes historically. "The Leah – Rachel relationship has an enduring influence on the structure of Jewish nationhood, first revealed in the antagonism between the sons of Leah and Rachel's son Joseph. Later it becomes one of the factors in the great historical rivalry between Leah's tribes, led by Judah, and Rachel's tribes, led by Joseph's son Ephraim. It was represented in all the conflicts and clashes between the kingdom of Judah and the kingdom of Israel – Samaria." Adin Steinsalz

Ch.30: 22 – 43, Ch.31: 1 – 16 Jacob worked for fourteen years for Laban. He then worked another six years as a shepherd for himself, and his flocks of sheep and goats became many. Jacob became a wealthy man with a large family, four wives, eleven sons and a daughter. Laban and his sons became jealous of Jacob's success, and said that all Jacob's wealth should belong to them. Jacob saw that Laban's attitude to him had changed. Then God said to Jacob: "Return to the land of your fathers and I will be with you." Jacob spoke to Leah and Rachel and they agreed to leave their father's house. "Whatever God has said to you, do," they said to Jacob. So Jacob lifted his children and wives onto the camels. He led his flocks of sheep and goats, and the camels loaded with his belongings, and he began the long journey back to the land of his father. As Jacob approached the promised land, angels met him. When Jacob saw them he said "This is a Godly place," and named it Machanayim, meaning "two camps."

It was time for Jacob to separate from Laban, to look after his own family and future, and to return home to the land of his father.

Why did Jacob call the place Machanayim, meaning "two camps"? Some Sages of Old explain that there were two camps of angels, the angels who looked after Jacob outside the borders of the promised land, and the angels who now came to meet Jacob to accompany him into the land of his father.

Others Sages of Old say the two camps are the camp of angels on one hand and Jacob's own camp on the other. Jacob's camp was looking for God's protection. The angels' camp was looking for people who would follow God's ways. When these two camps met, Jacob called the place Machanayim.

From Jacob – a man of the tents,
to Jacob – a man of the world.

At the beginning of this story Jacob left his parents' home and the promised land, fleeing from his brother's anger. The sun set and night fell, it was dark and Jacob was all alone. In the next story the Torah tells of a sunrise as Jacob prepares to cross the border back into the promised land, returning to his parents' home. Sages of Old suggest that all of Jacob's time living at Laban's house, twenty years, was like one long night. In a different land, amongst different people, Jacob had to manage alone.

But then Jacob was not completely alone. As he set out on his journey Jacob saw the angels climbing up and down the ladder, like a changing of the guards, as new angels took over to accompany him. God too promised Jacob, "I will be with you." And then the angels appear again at the end of this story as Jacob is about to cross back into the promised land.

Perhaps the angels and God did watch over Jacob during the twenty years. For Jacob came to Laban's house, alone, with nothing except his body ready to work. Twenty years later he left, a husband with four wives, a father with eleven sons and a daughter, a wealthy man with flocks of sheep and goats and camels. We read about how Rachel and Leah struggled as the two wives of Jacob and how they become the third and fourth matriarchs of the Jewish people.

During the journey away from his parents' home, as he becomes a husband and a father, we see Jacob change. He is no longer a "simple man of tents", he is now a strong and self-made man, head of a large family. Jacob still has the "voice of Jacob", the knowledge of one who has studied and has his own relationship with God, but now he also has "the hands of Esav". After twenty years of looking after the sheep in the hot sun and the cold nights Jacob has become strong. He has changed but he will change yet some more before he finally becomes the third patriarch of the Jewish people.

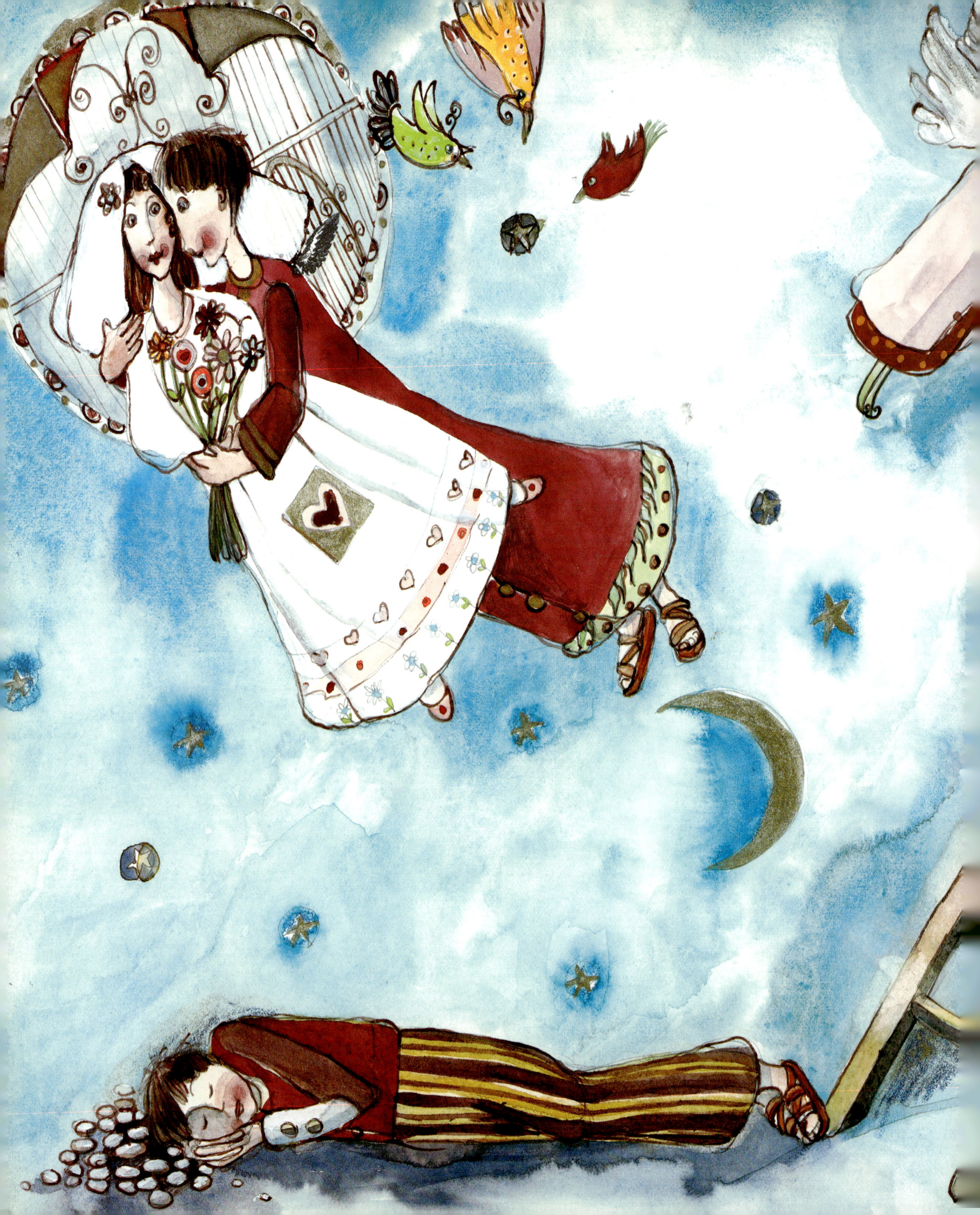

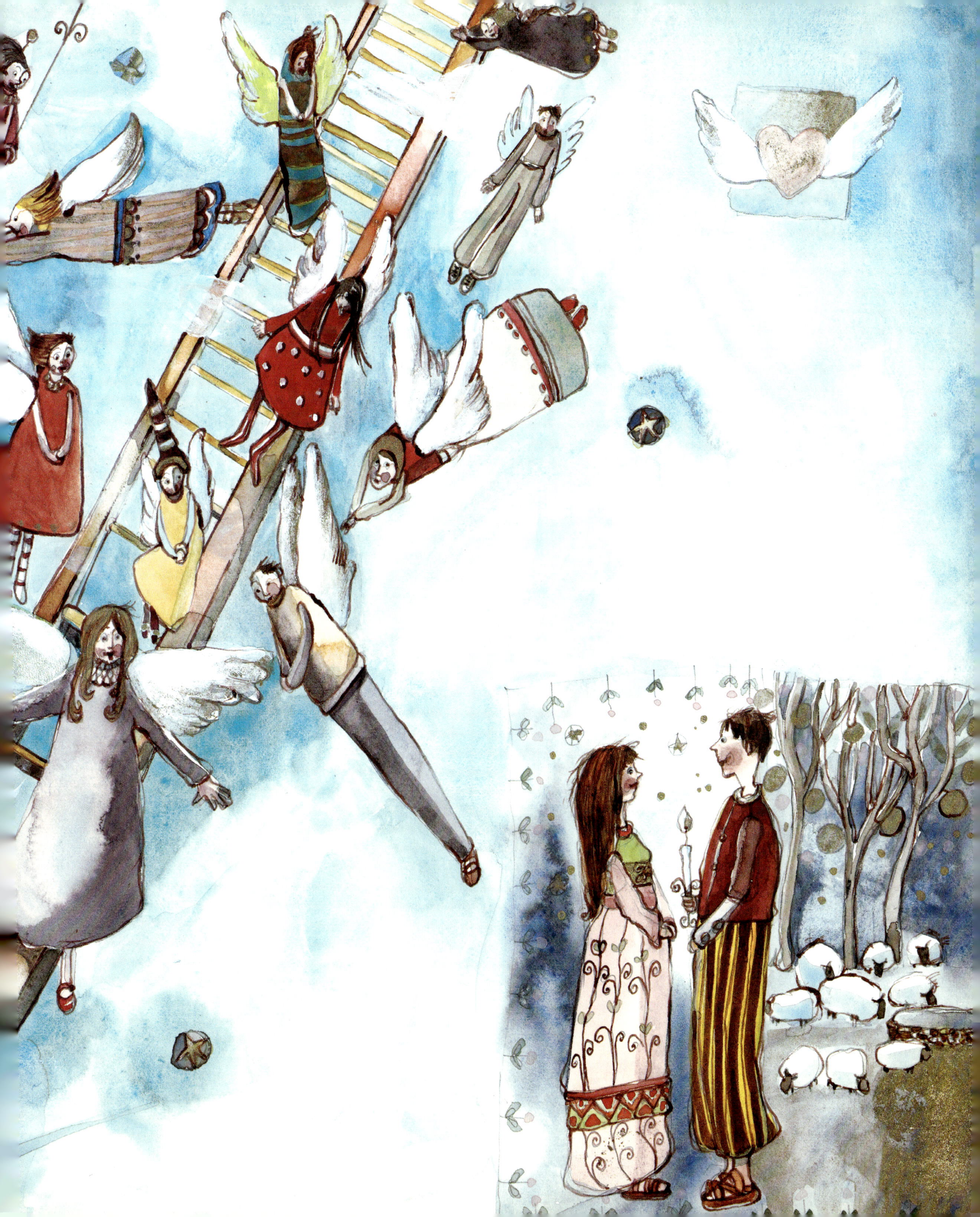

וישלח

VAYISHLACH

The journey home

A stranger: Jacob placates Esav by insisting that one of the main issues of Isaac's blessing has not, in fact, been realized in him – he has no power, he is marginal to all societies. "I have not become powerful or important but have simply been a stranger (ger). It is not worth your while to hate me for father's blessings, since he blessed me, 'Be master over your brother' and you see that has not been fulfilled in me." Avivah Zornberg

Ch.32: 4 – 6 Jacob sent the angels ahead to meet his brother Esav in the land of Edom. He told the angels to say "My lord Esav, I have lived with Laban until now and worked hard for many years. Now I come to make peace with you."

Twenty years have passed since Jacob left his parents' home, fleeing Esav's anger. Jacob did not know if his brother's feelings towards him had changed. Did Esav still want to kill him? Or would he be pleased to see his long lost brother? The story tells how each of the brothers behave as they prepare to meet each other after such a long time.

Why did Jacob call his brother "My lord"? (Can you imagine ever calling your brother 'My lord'?) Some Sages of Old explain that Jacob called Esav "My lord" to show he respects him as his older brother and wants to make peace with him. Other Sages say that Jacob was wrong to try and flatter Esav. What do you think?

Sages of Old focus on the Hebrew word the Torah uses for "lived" – *garti* when Jacob says "I have lived with Laban". According to Gematria, (which explains a word's meaning in terms of the numerical value of its letters), the word *garti* adds up to six hundred and thirteen, which is the number of commandments given in the Torah. When Jacob says *garti* with Laban, the hidden meaning is "I lived with Laban in a strange land but even there I kept God's way, keeping all six hundred and thirteen commandments."

Ch.32: 7 – 9 The angels returned to Jacob saying, "We went to Esav and he is already on his way to meet you, with four hundred men." Jacob became very frightened and divided his people into two camps, thinking "If Esav attacks one camp, maybe the other camp will escape."

Why was Jacob so scared? He thought that if Esav was coming to meet him with four hundred men he must be planning to attack with his army and take revenge on him. Although it was twenty years ago since Jacob tricked Esav and took the blessing, in Jacob's mind it felt like yesterday.

Scholars of our Time explain that when you have a fight with someone and then you don't see them for a long time, facing them again can be scary. Sometimes you worry and worry about what happened and the worry and fear build up in your imagination and get bigger over time.

Jacob divided his people into two camps, putting his wives and children behind and his servants in front. He hoped that if Esav and his four hundred men attacked, his family could run away and be saved.

Frozen in time: "One of the realities of a broken relationship is that if there's no move to healing, if what you do is run away from it, then the moment gets frozen in time and perhaps even amplified. Jacob has had twenty years to replay Esav's hatred." Roberta Hestenes

Fright and anxiety: Rashi says that Jacob suffered both fright and anxiety: fright – that he might be killed by Esav, and anxiety – that he might end up killing Esav.

? Have you ever had a fight with someone and then not seen them for awhile? How did you feel when you met them again next time?

Courage: The Sages say that Jacob's courage was built out of many kinds of readiness – readiness for war, for peace, for prayer. Some say that Jacob's behaviour in the face of threat is a guide to the Jewish people in similar situations, that Israel in exile must always be willing to recognize the varying and sometimes conflicting elements in any situation.

Out to impress: The Torah text tells that Jacob sent the livestock to Esav drove by drove, keeping a distance between droves. "Why did he not send Esav all the flocks mixed together? In order to astonish him at the immensity and range of the gift… Subtly Jacob plans the presumed effect of his gift. For maximum impact, he allows the suspense of a space between flocks, playing with Esav's constant surprise, as he assumes that the procession of animals has ended – only to find it begin again." Avivah Zornberg

Tomorrow: "Jacob was worried. Understandably so. Tomorrow he might die. His brother, whom he hadn't seen in twenty years, would not come to the appointment alone; he would be accompanied by at least four hundred armed men… Jacob was afraid. He had been fortunate all his life; it could not go on indefinitely, not beyond this night. Tomorrow it would all be over." Elie Wiesel

Ch.32: 10 – 22   Then Jacob prayed to God to protect him and his wives and his children. And he sent a gift to Esav, a gift of many sheep and donkeys, goats, cows and camels.

Sages of Old explain that Jacob prepared to meet Esav in three different ways. He prayed to God. He prepared to make peace, by sending gifts to Esav. And he prepared for war, by dividing his camp into two.

What did Jacob pray? Many years ago, when Jacob dreamt of the ladder and the angels, God made a promise to him, "Remember that I am with you to protect you wherever you go." Now, in his prayer Jacob reminded God of that promise, and asked God to protect his wives and children as well.

Jacob sent the many animals to Esav as a gift and a peace offering. Remember that in biblical times sheep, goats, donkeys, cows and camels were expensive possessions (like expensive cars today), so Jacob's gift was very generous. Maybe that was Jacob's way of asking Esav to forgive him for what happened in the past.

What image would Esav have of Jacob before they even met? Scholars of our Time suggest that Esav would think Jacob had become rich and powerful, someone to be respected. Maybe Jacob wanted to impress his brother Esav.

Ch.32: 23 – 25 During the night Jacob got up and took his wives and his children and all his possessions and crossed the Jabbok river. And then he crossed back over the river and so he was alone on the other side.

Scholars of our Time tell that in many legends and myths the crossing of a river symbolizes crossing an important boundary in one's life. Crossing the Jabbok river was important for Jacob. He was crossing the border back into his father's land and coming face to face with his brother after so many years. He was also crossing the boundary from his youth to his adulthood and going to meet those he loved and feared.

"And so he was alone." The noise of the children, the camels, sheep and donkeys over the other side of the river quietened as they all settled back to sleep. Jacob had chosen to cross back over the river to be alone in the quiet of the night. He had a lot to think about as he looked back over his life and thought about the future ahead. Jacob knew that his life was about to change. His meeting with his brother was unpredictable, there might be a battle, one of them might even die. He also thought of the covenant his grandfather and father had made with God – was he, Jacob, ready to become the next patriarch and leader of his tribe? So much to think about. That's why Jacob had chosen to leave the others and be alone.

Solitude: "There is a connection between divine and human solitude: man must be alone to listen, to feel, and even to fight God, for God engages only those who, paradoxically, are both threatened and protected by solitude. God, traditionally, elects to speak to His chosen in their sleep because that is when they are truly alone..." Elie Wiesel

Crossing the Jabbok : "Since ancient days, crossing a river has been the symbol of overcoming hazard and going forward to new experience. In this sense, Jacob passing over the Jabbok to meet Esau crosses the watershed of his life. Everything that has happened to him since he obtained both birthright and parental blessing by doubtful means has been tainted with his own guilt and his brother's enmity. Jacob can fully face his own past only as he seeks reconciliation with Esau, and this he can only do as he becomes a different man." Gunther Plaut

? When have you, like Jacob, chosen to be alone to think things through? Is there a special place you like to go to think?

Surreal: "It was a silent struggle, silent and absurd. What did the stranger want? Nobody knew, not even Jacob. They wrestled until dawn, neither uttering a word…" Elie Wiesel

Existential struggle: Martin Buber saw Jacob's wrestling with the angel as a metaphor for each individual's struggling with life's existential questions. And so the image of this wrestling, the two entwined together, has become a powerful symbol for our struggle with others and our struggle with ourselves.

The struggle in me: "I often don't know whether I'm struggling with God or with myself. And if I'm struggling with myself, I'm struggling with both the demonic and divine in me." Bill Moyers

A dream: Some traditional and contemporary commentators see the struggle as having taken place in a dream. "There are things which become so fixed in one's mind that they have a physical effect." Abarbanel

? Who do you think the angel-man was? Maybe your idea about his identity is different from those suggested by the Sages of Old and Scholars of our Time?

Ch.32: 26 – 27   Suddenly a man appeared and began to wrestle with Jacob. They struggled in the dust, entwined together, wrestling until the break of dawn.

Who was this man who suddenly appeared and started wrestling with Jacob? His identity is mysterious and unclear. Over the centuries Sages of Old and Scholars of our Time have wondered who he was, and suggest different identities for him.

Is he Esav's guardian angel come to do battle with Jacob on the night before he meets Esav? (Remember Esav and Jacob have wrestled with each other before, when they fought in their mother's womb about who would be born first)

Maybe the wrestler is the angel of death? For Jacob feared the possibility of his own death in a battle the next day with Esav.

Or is he the good angel, Michael, come to wrestle with Jacob and give him some practice and encouragement before he meets Esav? So Jacob's success in wrestling the angel would give him confidence that he could face his brother without fear. As the angel will say at the end of the fight: "You have wrestled with the divine and human and won."

Then again, maybe it was all an inner struggle. Jacob was wrestling with himself, with his conscience, with his sense of guilt about how he had tricked his brother to get the blessing. So many possibilities for who that wrestler could be, and still the mystery remains.

Sages of Old explain that the Hebrew word *va-ye'avek*, which means "he wrestled," describes how Jacob and the angel-man fought. They were entwined together and knotted around each other, struggling as they tried to push each other down to the ground.

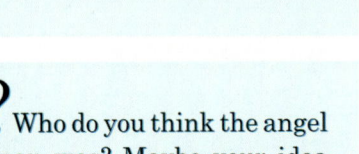

Ch.32: 26 – 27 When the angel-man saw that he could not defeat Jacob he struck his hip, injuring it. "Let me go" he said, "for the dawn is breaking".

The angel-man injured Jacob's hip but Jacob did not surrender even though he was in great pain. Then as the dawn arrived and the early light of morning began to creep across the Eastern sky the angel-man himself wanted to get away and escape.

Kabbalah explains that the angel-man had power in the dark of night but became powerless in the daylight. Legends and myths tell of creatures who have powers and magic in the night but lose their power with the break of day. What do you think will happen when the angel-man loses his power?

Confusing: "A confused and confusing episode in which the protagonists bear more than one name; in which words have more than one meaning and every question brings forth another... Theirs was an awesome fight, yet in the end they had to give up, neither being able to claim victory. Both were wounded: Jacob at the hip, the angel in his vanity." Elie Wiesel's commentary on Jacob wrestling with the angel is poetic and intriguing, tracing the mysteriousness of the encounter.

Echoes: Jacob's wrestling with the angel has been echoed in English literature in tales of warriors being visited by dreams or angels before a great battle.

He did not know: "While he struggled Jacob did not know the nature of his opponent. Perhaps this is the way it had to be, for when a man struggles with a force beyond himself, he can, at the moment, not be sure whether it is God or Satan who is his adversary... Both will engage him almost beyond endurance. The great agony of the soul is precisely that during the struggle we are in doubt and "the man" may get away before we know his name. The mystery may never be completely unravelled: this is part of the ambiguity of man's meeting with God." Gunter Plaut

? Can you think of any creatures in legends and myths that have power in the night and become powerless in the day?

Struggling with God: "The people of Israel... is a history of a struggle with God, of opposition to God, of being wounded by God in the struggle, and yet of being blessed by God, too."
John Barth

Inner victory: "Blessedness could only be claimed as his birthright when he had prevailed over his doubts and fears, when he had wrestled against his darkest demons."
Naomi Rosenblatt

The struggle for blessing: "It will no longer be said that the blessings came to be yours through manipulation and deception Ya'akov, but rather openly, and through struggle Yisrael." Rashi

Meaning in suffering: "I will not let you go unless you bless me." What did Jacob mean by this? He meant "I will not part from this experience unless I find a meaning to my suffering". Suffering of itself does not heal. Only suffering that has a meaning, and is accepted willingly, has the power to heal, to transform an individual into a whole person: that is, someone who is undivided, who can come to terms with himself, and even with his enemies, as Jacob did with Esav and Laban." Esther Spitzer

? Do you like the name *Yisrael* "Those who wrestle with God" as a name for the Jewish people? Why, or why not?

Ch.32: 27 – 31 "I will not let you go," said Jacob "unless you bless me." "What is your name" asked the angel-man. "I am Jacob." "Your name shall no longer be Jacob," said the angel-man. "It shall be *Yisrael* – Israel, which means 'God wrestler,' because you have wrestled with divine and human and won." "Please, what is your name?" inquired Jacob. "Why do you wish to know?" asked the angel-man, and he blessed Jacob. Jacob named the place Peniel, which means "face of God." "For I have seen God face to face," said Jacob, "and I have survived."

What is the blessing Jacob asks for from the angel-man? Sages of Old and Scholars of our Time explain that Jacob asked him to agree to his right to the blessing given by Isaac. So Esav would accept that the blessing belonged to him and not hate him anymore.

Why does the angel-man change Jacob's name to Israel? Remember Jacob's name comes from the Hebrew word *ekev*, "heel," because Jacob came out of his mother's womb holding onto Esav's heel. The name Jacob had the meaning of one who comes second, always trying to catch up. But now Jacob's name is changed to *Yisrael,* - Israel, "God wrestler," and with this change of name the angel-man gives Jacob a powerful message. If Jacob can win in a wrestle against a divine being (or against his own inner fears and doubts) he has no reason to fear his own brother.

Midrash tells "There are three names by which a person is called:
One which his father and mother call him, And one which people call him,
And one which he earns for himself.
The best of all is the one that he earns for himself."

The name Israel became the name for all the Jewish people, who are called the Children of Israel. It seems such a strange name for a people – Those who wrestle with God. Strange but maybe also very appropriate, for Jews throughout history have wrestled with God – arguing, challenging, accusing and pleading as we struggle to understand God's ways.

Ch.32: 32 – 33 The sun rose for Jacob as he passed Peniel, limping on his hip. Therefore the Children of Israel must not eat the sinew around the hip bone of animals because the angel-man injured Jacob on the hip.

Finally the sun rose, morning light filled the air, and the angel-man disappeared as suddenly as he had appeared. Jacob had won the wrestling match but he was injured. Some say he continued to limp all his life, reminding him of that mysterious struggle in the night.

A Sage of Old explains that the commandment not to eat the hip bone is meant to remind us of Jacob's fight. Just as Jacob fought the angel-man through a difficult night and eventually made it back to his homeland, so too the Jewish people will fight through difficult circumstances and return to their homeland.

Limping : "This encounter with God has meant pain for Jacob and pain for the people of Israel as well – the pain of struggling with God, of experiencing God as the Adversary… There's a long biblical tradition in the Book of Job and other places of God taking an adversarial position."
John Barth

Alone: "Each of us alone with God: Behind the mask of face and deed Each wrestles with an angel."
Jesse Sampter

Different encounter: "By the morning I was lame. Yet I did not let go until with the coming of the new day I had wrestled the blessing of reassurance from my creator… And as the sun rose again upon me I went limping down the ford thinking how unlike my youthful encounter with the God of my fathers on that journey out to Haran was this one." Irving Fineman

Reconciliation: "Esav's readiness to make peace with his brother comes as a surprising climax to the carefully prepared encounter. Esav's retainer of four hundred men allows us to suppose that he did not originally come with peaceful intentions, especially since his scouts must have informed him that Jacob was unarmed. Esav expected to meet the old Jacob, the hated sibling who had overtaken him with cleverness and guile. He was prepared for violence. But in the brothers' fateful meeting all is suddenly changed. The reconciliation occurs because it is Israel, not Jacob, whom Esav meets, and Jacob is a new man who asks forgiveness, if not in words then in manner, who limps towards him with repentant air and not deceitful arrogance... The essentially simple and uncomplicated Esav, who himself has matured, senses this at once and runs to kiss his newly found brother."
Gunther Plaut

Jacob and Israel: "When Abram becomes Abraham, he's no longer Abram. But Jacob always remains Jacob. He's referred to as Jacob more times than he's referred to as Israel. He has two names from now on and that's what makes him so fascinating. His identity is complex. He's constantly in a struggle between the two sides of his identity. Its not a transformation but an evolution."
Avivah Zornberg

? Have you made peace with someone you were fighting with? What did you do? How did you feel?

Ch.33: 1 – 4 The next day had arrived. Jacob looked up and saw Esav coming towards him with four hundred men. Suddenly Esav ran out to meet Jacob and embraced him. He threw his arms around Jacob's neck and kissed him, and they wept.

Jacob had lived in fear of Esav for twenty years. What a surprise when Esav hugged him and kissed him. Esav seems to have forgiven Jacob for what happened in the past and is happy to see his long-lost brother.

Some Sages of Old believe Esav came in peace to Jacob, others think he was still angry and wanted to hurt Jacob. They base their different views on the way the Hebrew word for kiss *neshika* is written with a series of unusual dots above it. Those who say Esav was coming in peace suggest that he kissed Jacob with all his heart, and the dots above the word *neshika* emphasize this. Those who say that Esav wanted to hurt Jacob remind us that the word *neshika* is very similar to the word *neshicha* which means bite. Esav actually wanted to bite Jacob, but then Jacob's neck turned hard as marble, and that's why Esav cried, from pain!

A Scholar of our Time suggests that originally Esav did not come in peace, for he brought four hundred men with him. But Esav saw that Jacob had changed. He was no longer the old Jacob who had tricked him out of the blessing. He was now a new Jacob, an Israel, who had worked hard for many years and now limped towards him, asking to be forgiven, wanting to make peace.

Ch.33: 5 – 11 Esav looked up and saw all the women and children and he asked "Who are all these?" Jacob answered, "These are the children God has given me." And Esav asked, "Why did you send me all those gifts?" "To make peace with you," answered Jacob. "I have enough, my brother," said Esav. "Let what you have remain yours." But Jacob said, "No, please accept my gifts, for God has been gracious to me and I have plenty." So Esav accepted the gifts and he travelled back to his home in Seir. And Jacob travelled to Sukkot, on the way back to his parents' home.

At last the time for peace has come. After years competing with each other as children: after Esav threatening to kill Jacob: after twenty more years when they didn't see each other, finally the brothers make peace. What is it that allows them to make peace with each other? We shall see in the words they use.

What does Esav say when Jacob explains that he has sent him gifts to make peace? "I have enough, my brother. Let what you have remain yours." Perhaps Esav is speaking about more than sheep and camels and donkeys. Perhaps he also means "I have enough, let the blessing remain yours, I don't need it anymore." And what does Jacob answer? "Please accept my gifts... I have plenty." And so the brothers make peace with each other when they no longer need to compete or judge themselves by what the other has, when each is happy with what he has. Perhaps we can only make true peace with others when we are happy with who we are and what we have.

Both Esav and Jacob have changed. In the earlier parasha, Toldot, they were competing with each other – for the birthright, for the blessing, for their parents' love, for their chances of success in the future. Now they have grown up and matured. Both are husbands and fathers with many possessions. Now each can say, "I have enough, my brother", "I have plenty". Sages of Old have a saying: "Who is the man who is happy? He who is satisfied with his lot, with what he has."

At the end of this scene Esav goes home to Seir and Jacob travels on to Sukkot. The brothers do not go and live near each other, side by side. Scholars of our Time explain that Jacob knew that even though he and Esav had made peace with each other, they were still very different and needed to live apart.

Confirmed: "The blessings were tenuously held in Jacob's hand. When were they confirmed? Here Esav said "My brother, let what is yours remain yours." Bereshit Rabbah

Separate ways: The Torah text is much more detailed about the process of Esav and Jacob going their separate ways. In the text Esav offered to escort Jacob back to his home in Seir. But Jacob declined saying he would follow at a slower pace with his children and cattle. However Jacob does not follow Esav to Seir, he turns off to Sukkot instead. Thomas Mann in his novel "The Tales of Jacob" describes the scene: "It was a polite refusal, and Esav, rather gloweringly, understood it as such... Jacob thanked him and said there was no need, if only he found grace in the sight of his lord – so that the emptiness of his words stood revealed. Esav shrugged his shaggy shoulders, turned his back on the fine and false one, and went hence into his mountains with cattle and train. Jacob, behind him, lingered a little, then at the first turning took another way and disappeared."

Coexistence: In his chapter titled "Jacob and Esav: Strategies for Coexistence", Michael Rosenak outlines different paradigms for the relationship between the people of Israel and the nations of the world. Rosenak characterizes Jacob's response to Esav as "an ideology of self segregation" and compares it to other paradigms for coexistence such as the Abrahamic model, which is expressed "not only in his social intercourse and concern for others, but in his passions to teach others his 'universal' monotheistic truth and yet to maintain warm relationships with those who do not accept it." Rosenak suggests there is a need to balance Jacob's self segregation, an appreciation and desire to safeguard Jewish particularity, with an Abrahamic openness and interchange with the non-Jewish world.

Weeping: "When Nebuchadnezzar will send them into exile, and they pass her grave, "there, on the road," Rachel will come out of her grave and cry and ask mercy for them – as it is said, "A cry is heard in Ramah – wailing, bitter weeping – Rachel weeping for her children. She refuses to be comforted for her children, who are gone. Thus said the Lord: Restrain your voice from weeping, your eyes from shedding tears... your children shall return to their own country." *Rashi and the Prophet Jeremiah*

The power of tears : "At that border place, her eternal yearning for her children will generate redemptive force. Her tears will win a response from God: her children will not disappear into the night. Through the sheer power of her yearning for her children, 'who are not' (lit., who are gone), and practiced by much longing for children, who were not, Rachel will bring them back into real, coherent being." *Avivah Zornberg*

Rachel speaks: "Two contractions and the baby has not yet emerged. For two days now my cries fill the emptiness of the tent. They can be heard from one end of the world to the other... I already know that my death is coming. I just have to give birth and bring forth another little boy and afterward, I can sleep, sleep." *Penina Adelman*

Ch.35: 16 – 20   On the way home Rachel went into labour and it was a very difficult birth. Rachel died giving birth to her son and the boy was called Benjamin. Rachel was buried on the road to Efrat and Jacob built a memorial on her grave, still standing today.

Remember when Jacob first met Rachel at the well, he kissed her and then he cried. Jacob cried because at that moment when he first fell in love with Rachel he saw into the future that she would die a young woman, and he would be left without her.

Why did Jacob bury Rachel on the roadside rather than carrying her to the Cave of Machpela, where Abraham and Sarah were buried? We shall see later, when Jacob himself is about to die, that he feels bad about not burying Rachel in the cave. But the Talmud says that if a woman dies in childbirth, out of respect for her she should be buried immediately and not carried on the roadway.

Sages of Old tell that when Rachel died, Jacob saw into the future and knew his descendants would be sent into exile. He saw that they would pass through Efrat and he buried Rachel there so she could pray for them. According to Jewish tradition Rachel does cry and pray for the Children of Israel as they pass her grave on the way into exile. And God listens to Rachel's crying and promises, "Your children shall return to their own country." With her strong wish to have children, her early death as she gave birth and her crying for the exiled Children of Israel, Rachel is remembered as a great and loving matriarch.

Ch.35: 27 – 28   And Jacob journeyed on to see his father in Hebron. Isaac was one hundred and eighty years old and he died, content with his life. His sons Esav and Jacob buried him.

Esav and Jacob, who have now made peace, came together to bury their father. Sages of Old tell that Isaac was buried in The Cave of Machpela, together with Abraham and Sarah, and Rebecca. Rebecca had died whilst Jacob was travelling on the way home from Laban's house. Jacob's grandparents, and now both of Jacob's parents, are dead – a generation has passed. Jacob, the third patriarch, with his twelve sons and one daughter, are now the next generation of Israel.

Coming Home

Vayishlach is the story of Jacob coming home, returning back to where he started from, closing the circle. It is a homecoming woven with mystery, with peace-making and with sadness.

Jacob left his parents' home long ago. He has not seen his father, his mother or brother for over twenty years. He fled, a young man, with nothing. He returns now, a husband, a father of many children, a wealthy man. But still Jacob is nervous about his return, frightened about meeting his family again, especially his brother. Did Esav still hate him, still want to kill him? Jacob didn't know.

Then the mysterious night struggling with the angel-man, wrestling, knotted together in the dust. As Elie Wiesel writes, "A strange adventure, mysterious from beginning to end, breathtakingly beautiful, intense to the point of making one doubt one's senses. Who has not been fascinated by it? Philosophers and poets, rabbis and storytellers, all have yearned to shed light on the enigmatic event that took place that night, a few steps from the river Jabbok." That wrestling match has become a symbol – for our struggle with others, and our struggle with ourselves.

Jacob demanded a blessing, and received a name change. He would no longer be called Jacob but Israel – the one who wrestles with God. Jacob left the struggle, his body injured, limping, but his mind and heart strengthened. He had wrestled with the angel of death, with Esav's guardian angel, with his fears, his guilt, his conscience, we know not which, but Jacob emerged, the winner, a changed man. He was now ready to face his past, and his future; to meet his brother, and continue the journey to his parents' home. And the Jewish people will be called after Jacob's new name, Children of Israel, Those who wrestle with God.

After twenty years of fear the meeting with Esav went well. The brothers grown up and matured, could now be at peace with each other. "Let what you have remain yours," they said, "I have plenty."

But the final leg of Jacob's journey home is shadowed with sadness. Jacob's beloved wife Rachel dies, giving birth to her second son. And when Jacob arrives home he finds that his mother had died some time earlier; she never got to see her son Jacob again or meet her grandchildren. On his return Jacob's father Isaac was already one hundred and eighty years old. Soon after, Isaac died. Jacob and Esav, the two brothers now at peace, buried him together. A generation had passed.

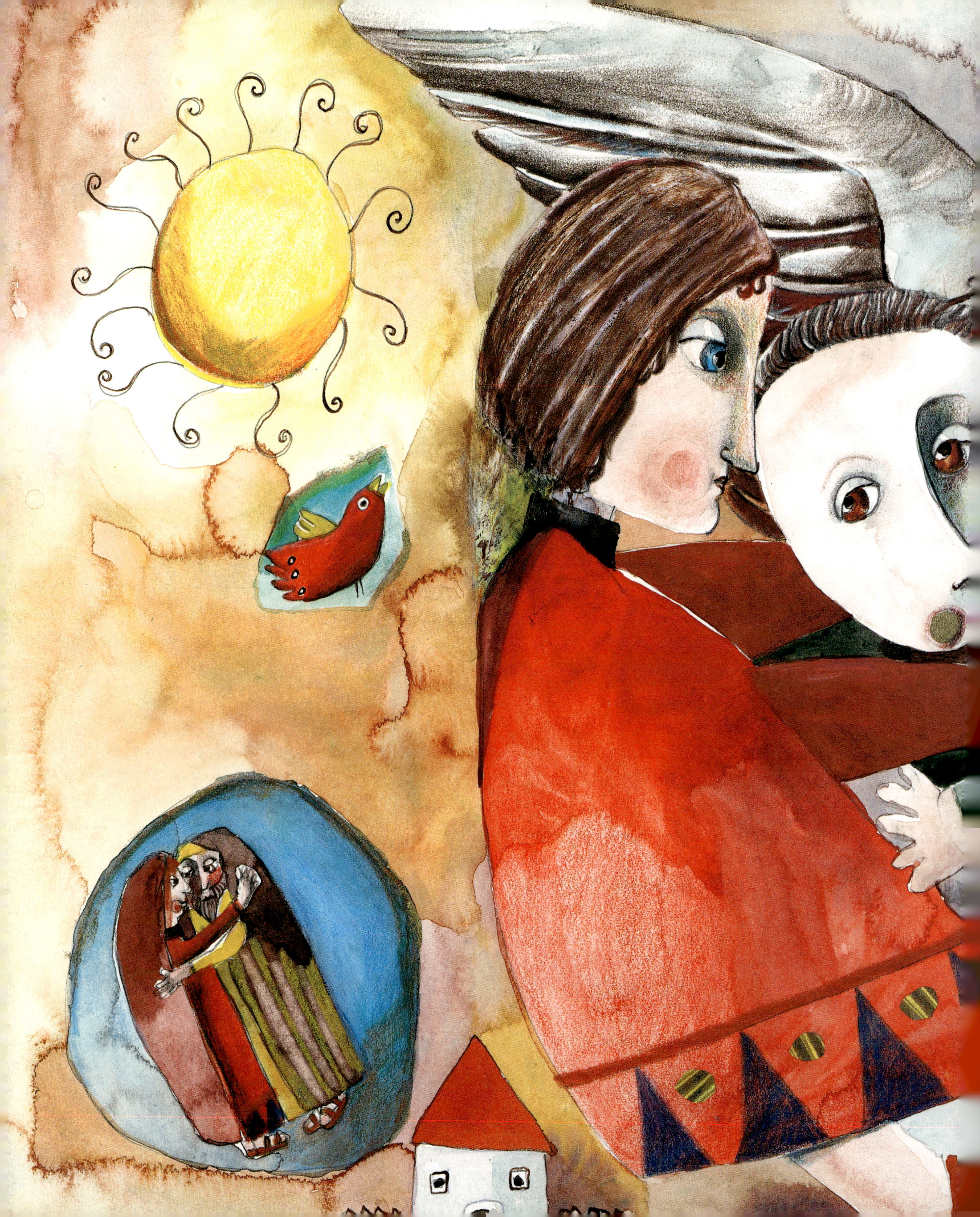

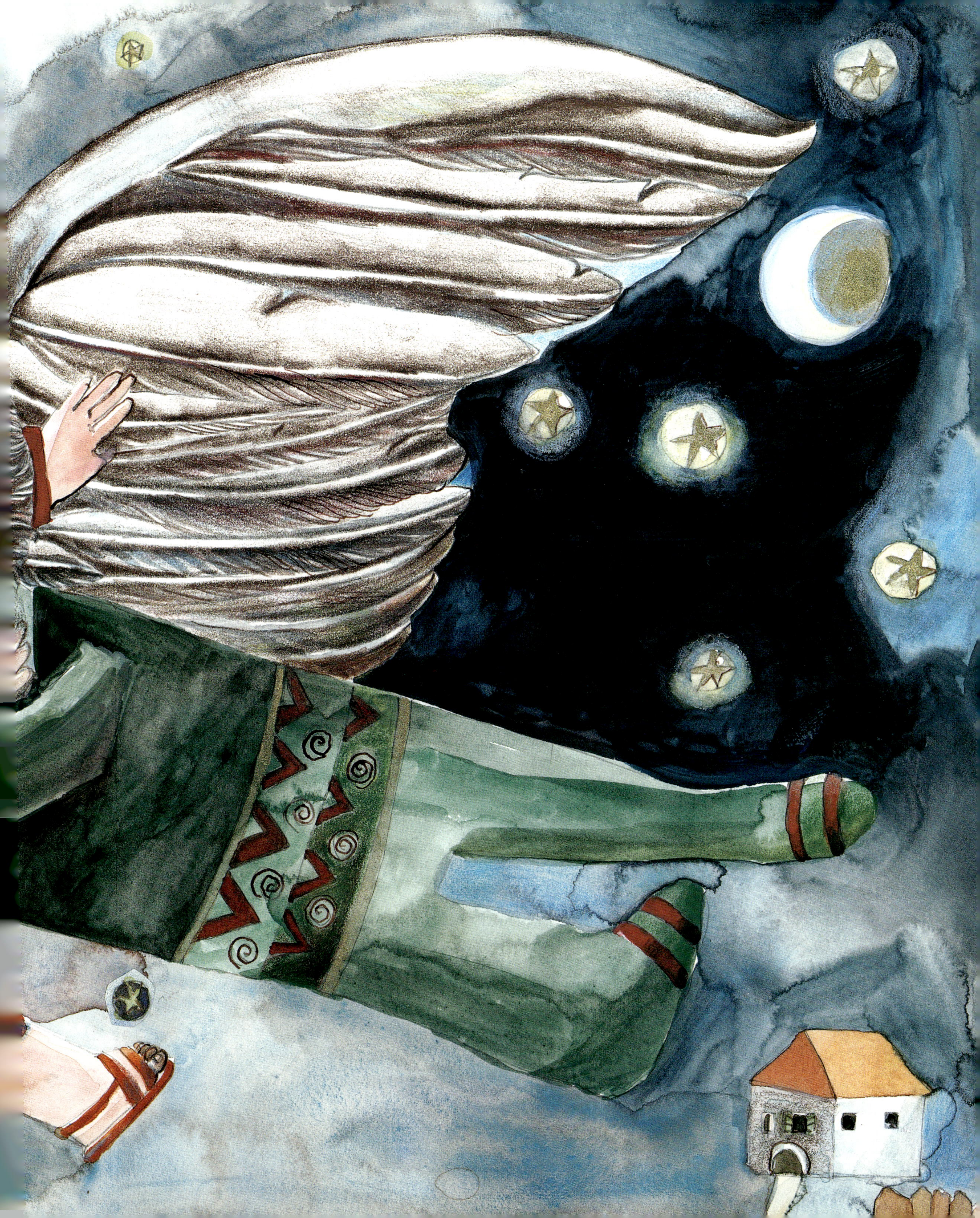

וישב

VAYESHEV

Joseph the dreamer

A yearning to settle: "He would like to settle down in the Holy Land after his years in exile and danger. He would like to read the narrative of his own life as entering a period of fulfilment, of closure, after the difficult conflicts and confrontations of his youth"... but... "the verse, the verb, has been classically read as resonant with forebodings, with a sense that Jacob has fatally misread the structure, the plot, the moral motifs of his own life... Jacob sought to settle in peace – there leapt upon him the agitation of Joseph." Avivah Zornberg

Vayeshev: R. Samson Raphael Hirsch analyzes the Hebrew word used here for "settled" Vayeshev, also the name of this Parasha. "Yashav in accordance with the "sh" sound, a natural, quiet, unobstructed staying: to sit. This is what Jacob hoped to achieve, but it was not to be."

The illusion of peace: "The apparent calm of a wealthy shepherd's pastoral existence forms the setting of the opening chapter of the Joseph cycle, but parental preference, youthful conceit and sibling envy will create a bitter drama." Gunther Plaut

Life's narrative: "To seek to 'settle in peace' is on one level, to seek an ordering of experience, a personal construction of one's own reality, that should be both coherent and realistic... to articulate the narrative of one's own life." Avivah Zornberg

Ch.37: 1 Now Jacob settled in the land where his father had lived, in the land of Canaan.

After returning home from working twenty years at Laban's house, after marrying four wives and having thirteen children, after the fear of meeting his brother and then making peace with him, Jacob now settled in the land. Sages of Old explain that Jacob hoped he could settle down peacefully with his large family, and watch his children grow and become the beginning of the people of Israel. But Jacob's hopes for settling and for peace are not to be. The story that unfolds now is a dramatic one, full of jealousy, anger, dreams and power.

Sages of Old tell that Jacob chose to live in the land where his father had lived, in Canaan. This is the land promised by God to Abraham, Isaac and Jacob, to be their land for their children and children's children. But at that time the land did not belong to them and it would be many generations before they actually owned the land. Even though Jacob did not own the land he chose to live there because he was waiting for God's promise to come true.

Ch.37: 2 – 3 When Jacob's son Joseph was seventeen years old he helped look after the flocks of sheep with his brothers. Now Jacob loved Joseph best of all his sons, for he was the child of his old age, and so he made him a coat of many colours

Why does the Torah bother to tell us exactly how old Joseph was? A Midrash writes, "Joseph was a youth, he acted like a teenager, dressing his hair and adorning his eyes to look handsome." So Joseph was not very different from today's seventeen year olds gelling his hair in front of the mirror! The Midrash tells that the fact that Joseph was a teenager helps us understand some of the ways he behaved. We shall see that Joseph was like many teenagers who think mostly about themselves and have big dreams about what they want to do.

Why did Jacob love Joseph best of all his sons? Scholars of our Time suggest Jacob's special love for Joseph may go back many years, to when he was born. Remember Jacob married the two sisters Leah and Rachel, but he always loved Rachel more. Leah became pregnant easily and had many sons, she already had four sons whilst Rachel was still struggling to have a child. Finally Rachel gave birth to a son, Joseph. Imagine Jacob's happiness that at long last Rachel had a son – that child would have been special to Jacob from the very beginning. (Imagine how Leah's four sons would have felt, to see their father so excited at Joseph's birth.)

Something else may have added to Jacob's special love for Joseph. At the end of the last parasha Rachel died tragically. When she died Jacob poured all the love he felt for her onto Joseph. So Joseph became Jacob's favourite son, a reminder of his favourite wife Rachel.

But how could Jacob favour Joseph so obviously – making him the coat of many colours? How would you feel if your parents loved one of your brothers or sisters the most of all their children, and gave them special things? Jacob knew what it was like when a father loves one son more than the other (as his father Isaac had loved Esav more.) He should have known that when parents have favourites they cause trouble between the children.

Link: "Like many bereaved spouses, Jacob will transfer his emotional attachment to the most tangible link to this dead wife – her child." Naomi Rosenblatt

Foolish youth: Baal Ha-Turim notes that the Hebrew word for youth, na'ar, and the Hebrew word for fool, shoteh, have the same numerical value.

A bad father? Elie Wiesel expresses his frustration at Jacob's poor parenting "Surely Jacob was the real culprit: he must have been a bad father, a poor teacher. What an idea to favour one child, give him more gifts, more attention, more love... Did he not know that such behaviour would eventually harm the boy he wanted to protect?"

? Have you ever seen a parent love or favour one of their children more than the others? What effect did it have?

He should have known better: "As a victim of his own father's favoritism, Jacob would be expected to be more sensitive to his son's feelings. He, better than anyone, should understand the destructiveness of loving his sons unequally... We can only assume that, like many recent widowers, Jacob is too absorbed in his own grief to notice."
Naomi Rosenblatt

Never: The Talmud states, "A man should never single out one child among his other sons."

? Are there people in your family or extended family who don't speak to one another? Do you know why? What are the results?

Ch.37: 2 – 4 Joseph brought bad reports about his brothers to his father. When the brothers saw that their father loved Joseph the most, they hated him so much they could not speak a friendly word to him.

It would be bad enough if your parents loved your brother or sister more than you and gave them special presents. But how annoying would it be if that favourite child "brought bad reports" about you, such as "He hit me!" and "She didn't clean up her room"?

The brothers were so hurt and angry at Joseph that "they could not speak a friendly word to him." You can understand their anger but to be unable to speak to your brother is a dangerous sign. If you don't talk to someone in your family and you don't listen to what they have to say, all the lines of communication are down, and real problems can develop.

Ch.37: 5 – 11 Once Joseph had a dream that he told his brothers. "There we were binding up sheaves of wheat in the field. Suddenly my sheaf stood upright and your sheaves gathered round in a circle and bowed down to my sheaf." "What – do you plan to rule over us and we will bow down to you?" the brothers exclaimed, and they hated him even more because of his dream. Then Joseph dreamed another dream and again he told his brothers and also his father. "In the dream the sun and the moon and eleven stars were bowing down to me." "What sort of dream is this – that I and your mother and your brothers will all bow down to you!" cried Jacob. And the brothers were even more angry at Joseph. But Jacob took note of the dream.

The two dreams that Joseph dreamt have the same meaning – in both of them Joseph is in a position of power above his brothers and parents.

What sort of person would tell others his dreams about ruling over them? Scholars of our Time explain that Joseph was so involved with himself and his dreams that he did not notice, and did not understand his brothers' feelings. Joseph paraded about in his coat of many colours, telling everyone how great he would be, without the slightest awareness of his effect on others.

Today dreams are understood as meaning something about the dreamer's personality, their hopes and fears. But in biblical times dreams were thought to predict the future. Jacob knew about dreams – he too had an important dream of the angels climbing up and down the ladder, and so he took note of Joseph's dream. In fact Midrash tells that Jacob wrote the dream down, wondering whether the events in the dream would really happen, and if so, when.

Narcissism: "Joseph behaves with the narcissism of youth, with a dangerous unawareness of the inner world of others." Avivah Zornberg
"How is it that Joseph is so self absorbed as to seemingly invite his own destruction? His personality and behaviour – from his heedlessly expressed dreams of supremacy to his flaunting of his ornamental tunic – are a precise match for the classic textbook description of narcissistic traits. "A grandiose sense of self-importance or uniqueness, exaggerated tendency to self-dramatization, preoccupations with fantasies of unlimited success and power." Naomi Rosenblatt

Self preoccupied: Elie Wiesel contrasts Joseph's self important dreams with other dreams in the Torah. "Jacob's dreams pertained to the universe, the Pharaoh's dreams to the Egyptian people collectively; Joseph's revolved around his own person, his own career."

Dream analysis: "What is the difference between the two dreams?... the first dream begins in the real life setting inhabited by Joseph and his brothers... an actual agricultural activity they would have been accustomed to perform... 'look we were binding sheaves in the field.'... the second dream does not begin with a realistic setting but with a full blown fantasy... The sheaves of grain of the first dream point forward as a concrete term to the means Joseph will use to exercise power over Egypt: storing up grain in huge silos to dispense to all the inhabitants... whereas the setting of the second dream is – metaphorically – the imperial court of Egypt where the last act of the story will unfold. Joseph surrounded by the celestial bodies is Joseph in the grandeur of Pharaoh's court." Robert Alter

? Have you ever had a dream where you were very powerful? Or a dream where you had no power at all?

War at home: "Bad relationships in a person's home are harder to bear than the war of Gog and Magog."

The pits: "For the essential fact of his (Joseph's) life is that he is a man who was thrown into a pit, into one of many pits, into more than one pit. The experience of the pit is the informing image of his life." Avivah Zornberg

Master of dreams: "Dreams have a critical impact on the course of Joseph's life, and he becomes increasingly involved with dreams as the narrative unfolds. At first he himself is a dreamer, then he interprets the dreams of others, and finally, he provides counsel on the basis of the dreams he interprets, thereby determining the fate of both his family and Egypt as a whole." Dr. Masha Turner

Ch.37: 12 – 20   Once when the brothers had taken the sheep to look for good grazing grass Jacob sent Joseph to them saying, "Go see how your brothers and the sheep are doing, and come back and tell me." When the brothers saw Joseph coming from afar they said to one another, "Here comes the 'Master of dreams'. Let's kill him and throw him into one of the pits – we can say 'A wild animal ate him.' Then we shall see what becomes of his dreams."

How come Jacob sent Joseph out to check on his brothers? Why wasn't Joseph looking after the sheep with them? Sages of Old tell that this was part of Jacob's favouritism – Jacob didn't send his favourite son out to work, he let Joseph stay at home with him.

How did the brothers recognize Joseph from afar? A Scholar of our Time explains it was because he was wearing his coat of many colours. Joseph was so unaware of other people he didn't notice the coat made his brothers angry. When the brothers saw the coat it reminded them again of how their father loved Joseph more than any of them.

But how could the brothers plan to kill Joseph? No matter how angry and jealous they were we are shocked they would consider killing their own brother. And what did they hate most about Joseph? His dreams – if Joseph died his dreams would die with him, and the brothers wanted to be sure of that.

Ch.37: 21 – 24   But Reuben said to his brothers, "Let's not kill him. Let's throw him into this pit in the wilderness instead." Reuben planned to come back later and save Joseph, taking him out of the pit and back to their father. When Joseph reached his brothers they stripped the coat of many colours off and threw him into the pit. The pit was empty – there was no water in it. Then the brothers sat down to eat.

Why was it Reuben who tried to save Joseph? One might think that as Reuben was the oldest of Leah's sons and Joseph was the oldest of Rachel's sons the competition between them would be fierce. But it seems Reuben did not feel this way. As the oldest of all the brothers Reuben may have felt responsible for what happened to his younger brother.

Why do you think the first thing the brothers did was strip the coat of many colours off Joseph? Scholars of our Time explain that the brothers wanted to take away the gift their father had given him, take away the very thing that made Joseph special and different from them.

Why does the Torah seem to repeat itself saying "The pit was empty – there was no water in it." Obviously if the pit (which was a well for storing rainwater) was empty, there was no water in it. But what looks like a repetition gives us a clue that the pit was not empty of other things. Sages of Old tell that it was full of snakes and scorpions. The best way to avoid a snake or scorpion biting you is to stay absolutely still. So Joseph had to remain absolutely still in that deep dark pit with snakes and scorpions all around him.

"Then the brothers sat down to eat." Some say this is the saddest line in the whole of the Torah, the absolute low point. Usually when people are upset they do not think of food. But here the brothers have just thrown Joseph into a pit, probably to die of hunger or thirst. And what do they do next? Sit down and have a meal! Many Sages of Old and Scholars of our Time see the brothers' cruelty to Joseph as one of the worst examples of human behaviour.

Stripped: "The concept of "stripping" occurs here for the first time in the biblical text. It is at root a violent idea, with connotations of flaying skins of animals... Essentially, the desire of the brothers is the absolute destruction of Joseph – of that "excessive" quality in Joseph that is both grace and irritant... (in stripping him of the coat of many colours) they remove that which is additional, unique about Joseph... they tear from him that superlative, individual quality that they most envy." Avivah Zornberg

Howling horror: In his book "Joseph and his brothers" Thomas Mann imagines the scene of the brothers stripping Joseph of his coat. "They fell upon him as the pack of hungry wolves falls upon the prey: it was as though they would tear him into fourteen pieces at least. Rending, tearing apart, tearing off – upon that they were bent, to their very marrow. 'Down, down, down!' they panted with one voice: it was the ketonet they meant, the picture - robe, the veil. It must come off..."

Forgotten: "They cast him into the pit" 37:24 "Wherever the word cast (hashlacha) is used, it means to a depth of at least twenty cubits, that is, to a depth that, in halachic terms, is beyond eyeview. Joseph, therefore, becomes invisible when he is thrown into the bor (pit)... In the fullest sense, he is forgotten by the world." Avivah Zornberg

"Then the brothers sat down to eat" – "There are few more damning lines in the Bible. These men have just thrown their brother into a pit, where they intend to leave him until he dies of hunger or thirst. And what do they do then? Sit down to enjoy a meal." R. Joseph Telushkin

? In what way is the brothers' cruelty to Joseph one of the worst examples of human behaviour?

Hidden plot: "Interwoven into the account of mortal beings is the unseen hand of Divine Providence... underlying the mission that Jacob sent Joseph on to visit the brothers and the flocks... there lay the hidden workings of Providence – God was sending the descendants of Abraham to Egypt." Nehama Leibowitz

Midrashic view: "God wanted to fulfil the decree of 'Know well that your offspring shall be strangers in a land not theirs' (15:13) so He brought about the plot of all this narrative, so that Jacob should love Joseph, and his brothers should hate him, and sell him to the Ishmaelites, who would bring him down to Egypt." Midrash Tanhuma

God's plot: Avivah Zornberg comments on the above Midrash suggesting it poses "...the most provocative challenge to the concept of human freedom... the midrash presents human beings as participants in a drama of God's devising... human beings are for the most part unconscious actors in His plot. How is the Author to get His characters down to Egypt? He achieves His plot through a realistic technique of apparent freedoms – freedom to love, to hate, to kill, to sell into slavery. This apparent lifelikeness granted to the characters is, however, only a tribute to the skill of the Author. In reality, all is decided ahead of time."

Ch.37: 25 – 28 After their meal the brothers looked up and saw a caravan of Ishmaelites with their camels carrying spices down to Egypt. "What do we get out of killing our brother? He is our flesh and blood," said Judah. "Let's sell him to these Ishamaelites instead." So they sold Joseph to the Ishmaelites for twenty pieces of silver, and he was taken to Egypt.

Instead of killing Joseph the brothers decide to sell him as a slave. This is the very beginning of the story of the Children of Israel's slavery in Egypt – where they will stay for two hundred and ten years. Sages of Old explain that the jealousy and hatred between the brothers caused Joseph's sale into slavery and later the slavery of the Children of Israel in Egypt. They would not leave Egypt until the time of Moses, when God takes them out with the Ten Plagues, the splitting of the Red Sea and all the story we read about in the Hagaddah at Pesach.

Midrash tells that the twenty pieces of silver the brothers got for Joseph was not a lot of money. They used the money to buy shoes for themselves.

Ch.37: 31 – 35 **The brothers took Joseph's coat, killed a goat and dipped the coat in its blood. Then they took the coat to their father saying, "We found this. Do you recognize it? Is it your son's coat?" Jacob knew the coat at once and cried out, "Joseph's coat! A wild animal has attacked him and torn him to pieces." And Jacob tore his clothes and mourned for Joseph. All his sons and his daughter tried to comfort him but he would not be comforted.**

The brothers trick Jacob into believing that Joseph was killed by a wild animal. Jacob who tricked his own father to get the blessing, has been tricked before – first by Laban who tricked him into marrying Leah before Rachel, and now by his own sons. Sages of Old and Scholars of our Time wonder – is Jacob still being punished for what he did to his father?

Jacob tore his clothes and mourned for Joseph. A Sage of Old tells that Jacob mourned for Joseph for twenty-two long years and all that time he would not be comforted. Till today Jewish people tear their clothes in mourning. A person sitting Shiva, the seven days of mourning after a close relative has died, often wears clothes with a tear.

Wild animal: When Jacob cries out "A wild animal has attacked him and torn him to pieces" Naomi Rosenblatt explains "He could well be referring to the savage beast of sibling rivalry he has fostered among his own children."

Responsible: The brothers are seen as directly responsible for causing Jacob's anguish. "Know and understand that one who murders or does evil to another is punished not only for that specific victim but for all who sorrow for him, as it is said "Now comes the reckoning for his blood." Sefer Hasidim

Original sin: "The brothers" crime remains throughout Jewish history as a kind of ineradicable original sin...we sacrifice a goat for all communal sin-offerings; the goat that was substituted for Joseph remains a symbol of hatred and violence in the consciousness of the whole people.' Avivah Zornberg

He would not be comforted: "No one can truly console another. One can offer him reasons for taking comfort, the mourner himself must take these reasons to heart if they are to effect a change in his frame of mind. Jacob, however, refused even to attempt to make such a change." R. Samson Raphael Hirsch

? What do you think wearing clothing with a tear symbolizes for a person in mourning?

Faces: "Joseph's growing wisdom is indicated by an apparently minor detail: he becomes sensitive to people's faces, to their changing expressions... Joseph's progress in sensitivity to the human face, which hides and reveals invisible worlds, is a token of the deepening of his wisdom." Avivah Zornberg

Profound change: "Thirteen years as a slave, even though at times a privileged one, left their mark on the young man. He had been his father's favourite, a pampered youth, who told tales on his brothers and who overwhelmed his family with his ambitious dreams. But the trauma of near-death and his subsequent sale into slavery apparently brought on a profound change. Gone were the ornamental tunic and with it the easy arrogance... The gifted son of Jacob developed a sense of humility, and with it his basic qualities of religious sentiment began to change." Gunter Plaut

? In what way is the crime of the butler different to the crime of the baker? How do you think this difference will affect what will happen to each of them?

Ch.39: 1 – 23, Ch. 40: 1 – 6 After the Ishmaelites reached Egypt they sold Joseph to Potiphar, a wealthy man. Later Potiphar sent Joseph to Pharaoh's prison. God was with Joseph in the prison and made him successful. So the prison warden liked Joseph and put him in charge of all the prisoners and all that happened in the prison. One day Pharaoh's cupbearer and baker offended him and he put them in prison. After they had been in prison for some time they each dreamed a dream on the same night. The next morning Joseph saw they were upset and asked, "Why are you so troubled today?"

Joseph would spend the next twelve years locked up in that prison. A Scholar of our Time explains that in many ways the prison was like the pit Joseph's brothers had thrown him into. Both are called *bor* – "pit" in Hebrew. Like a pit the prison was a dungeon dug below the surface of the earth. The biggest danger in falling down a pit is of disappearing and being forgotten by the world. And like in the pit, for a second time Joseph was stuck and forgotten, and did not know if he would get out alive.

Midrash fills in the gaps in the story and tells us why Pharaoh put the cupbearer and baker in prison. Pharaoh found a fly in the goblet of wine given to him by the cupbearer and a pebble in the bread made by the baker. Outraged, Pharaoh threw them both in prison.

What differences can you spot between the "crimes" of the two servants? Sages of Old point out that the fly was not in the goblet when the cupbearer poured the wine, it could have fallen in at any time. But the pebble must have been in the dough of the bread all along. It seems the baker had not been careful enough in sifting the flour. Whilst drinking a dead fly might be disgusting it is not really dangerous. But Pharaoh could break a tooth or choke on the pebble whilst eating the bread.

Joseph understood that the cupbearer and baker were upset when he saw their faces after they awoke from their dreams. What a change from the young Joseph who was so unaware of other people's feelings that he didn't notice his brothers' jealousy and anger. A Scholar of our Time explains that this growth of Joseph's sensitivity to others is the beginning of his growth in wisdom.

Ch.40: 8 – 15 "We each dreamed a dream," they said, "but there is no-one to interpret it for us." "God can interpret dreams" said Joseph, "tell them to me." So the cupbearer told Joseph, "In my dream there was a grapevine with three branches. Its flowers blossomed and the grapes ripened. Pharaoh's cup was in my hand and I took the grapes, pressed them into the cup and gave it to Pharaoh."

"Here is the meaning of your dream," said Joseph. "The three branches are three days. Three days from now Pharaoh will forgive you and you will return to your position as his cupbearer. But when all is well with you again please remember to tell Pharaoh about me, so I can be freed from this prison."

Dream science: "In the two great centres of Near Eastern civilization, Egypt and Mesopotamia, at either extremity of the fertile crescent the science of dreams interpretation was highly developed as a specialized skill, and a vast literature devoted to the subject came into being. One extant Egyptian papyrus, inscribed about 1300 B.C.E and claiming to be a copy of an archetype at least five hundred years older, is actually a reference book of dream interpretations arranged systematically according to symbol and meaning. We are told, for example, that seeing a large cat in a dream is good, for it portends a large harvest. Looking into a deep well, on the other hand, is bad, for it is premonitory of incarceration." Nahum Sarna

Four cups: The word cup is mentioned four times in these verses. The Talmud suggests that because of this four cups of wine are drunk at the Seder on Pesach.

"God can interpret dreams," said Joseph. This is the other big change in Joseph – he has become more sensitive to others and he has become more humble. Scholars of our Time explain that before Joseph dreamt of his own greatness and how he would rule over others. Now he gives credit to God as the one who interprets dreams. Perhaps Joseph also realized that it was in God's hands if his own dreams would come true or if he would be stuck in the prison forever.

Joseph's own dreams had been simple. Joseph, his brothers and his father understood their meaning immediately. But the cupbearer and baker's dreams were not so clear – they needed interpretation. As the Talmud says "An un-interpreted dream is like an unread letter." So Joseph interpreted the dream's meaning for the cupbearer.

Can you think of a different interpretation for the cupbearer's dream? The Sages of Old suggest a meaning of the dream for the Children of Israel. The three branches are Abraham, Isaac and Jacob, the flowers are the foremothers and the grapes are the tribes of Israel. As the vine blossomed and the grapes ripened, so the Children of Israel would flourish in the future.

? The Egyptians had textbooks on how to interpret dreams. How would you interpret these signs in a dream – looking down a well? the shining moon? According to the Egyptian books, looking down a well meant the dreamer would be put in jail. The shining moon is a good sign meaning the gods will forgive you.

Presumed dead: "To be thrown into a pit is, effectively, to be declared dead in the mind of others. The Talmud stated that the presumption of death is so strong that the victim's wife may remarry. An overpowering conviction consigns the 'bor–victim' to death." Avivah Zornberg.

Baker's delight: "The office of chief baker is interesting in light of what is known of Egyptian gastronomy. No less than fifty seven varieties of bread and thirty-eight different types of cake are attested in the texts The baker is reflecting native epicurean propensity when he dreams of baskets containing 'all kinds of food that a baker prepares." Nahum Sarna

? Have you ever planned to remember something, but then forgotten it? What can help keep your memory strong?

Ch.40: 16 – 23 When the baker saw how well the dream interpretation had turned out he said to Joseph, "Explain my dream too. In the dream there were three baskets on my head and in the top basket were all kinds of baked foods ready for Pharaoh, and the birds were eating them." "Here is the meaning of your dream," said Joseph. "The three baskets are three days. In three days time Pharaoh will hang you from a tree and the birds will eat you." On the third day it was Pharaoh's birthday and he made a feast for all his servants. He gave the cupbearer back his position, and he hanged the baker, just as Joseph had said. But the cupbearer did not remember Joseph. He forgot about him, and Joseph stayed in prison.

Joseph's dream interpretations turned out to be correct, with a nasty end for the baker. But even though Joseph asked the cupbearer to remember him he is forgotten, invisible. He lives only in the world of the prison and is not remembered in the real world. Why did the cupbearer forget to tell Pharaoh about Joseph? When things are good often people don't like to be reminded of the bad times in their lives. The cupbearer may have hoped Pharaoh would completely forget that he had been punished and put in prison.

Based on this story, a Scholar of our Time argues that memory must be active and worked at. Unless you actively make a point of remembering a person or an event, it is likely to be forgotten. The story of Joseph is the very beginning of the story of the slavery of the Children of Israel in Egypt. Later in the Torah and in the Haggadah, as Jews we are told many times to remember our time as slaves in Egypt. This is so we will always have understanding and empathy for other people in difficult situations. Without reminders in books like the Haggadah and rituals like the Seder, people might become successful and wealthy, and forget their memory of what it was like to be powerless and poor. This is what happened to the cupbearer. Once he was freed from prison and returned to his respected position serving Pharaoh, he did not want to remember his days in prison or the man who had helped him there.

How to realize your dreams

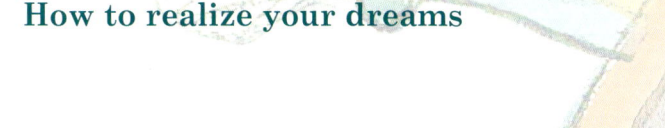

The story of Joseph is a story of dreams and dreamers. Dreams are important in our lives, they give us a vision of how things could be, a direction to follow, a goal to work towards. "Nothing happens unless first we dream."

Joseph is a dreamer, but as a young man he is so involved in his dreams that he thinks only of himself and forgets about others. If you are always wrapped up in your own dreams, you lose touch with other people. Others, even family – especially family, may turn away from you, in frustration and anger.

So there has to be a balance between our dreams and our involvement with others and the world. A famous Jewish woman, Bella Abzug, who had big dreams and who fought passionately for equal rights of women and blacks in the United States once said, "Remember that to realize our dreams, we must keep our heads in the clouds and our feet on the ground."

At first Joseph only had his head in the clouds as he paraded about in his coat of many colours. He had to go through the hurt, the loneliness, and the fear of being thrown in a pit and then imprisoned in jail to find his feet on the ground. Only then did he become more modest and more aware of others' faces and their feelings. So Joseph grew from someone who could think only of his own dreams to a man who could listen to and understand the dreams of others. Our own dreams are important but we must never lose sight of the faces of others.

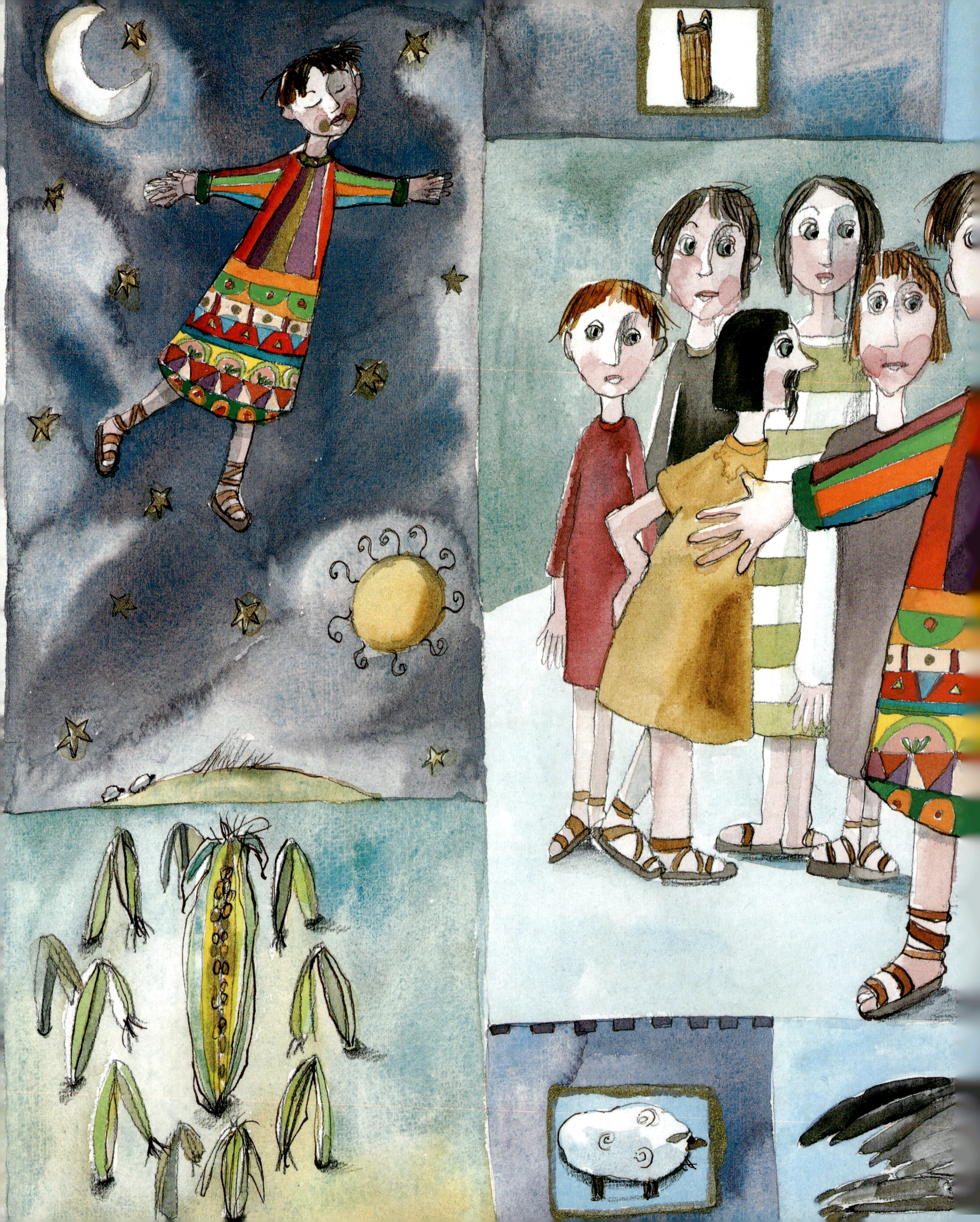

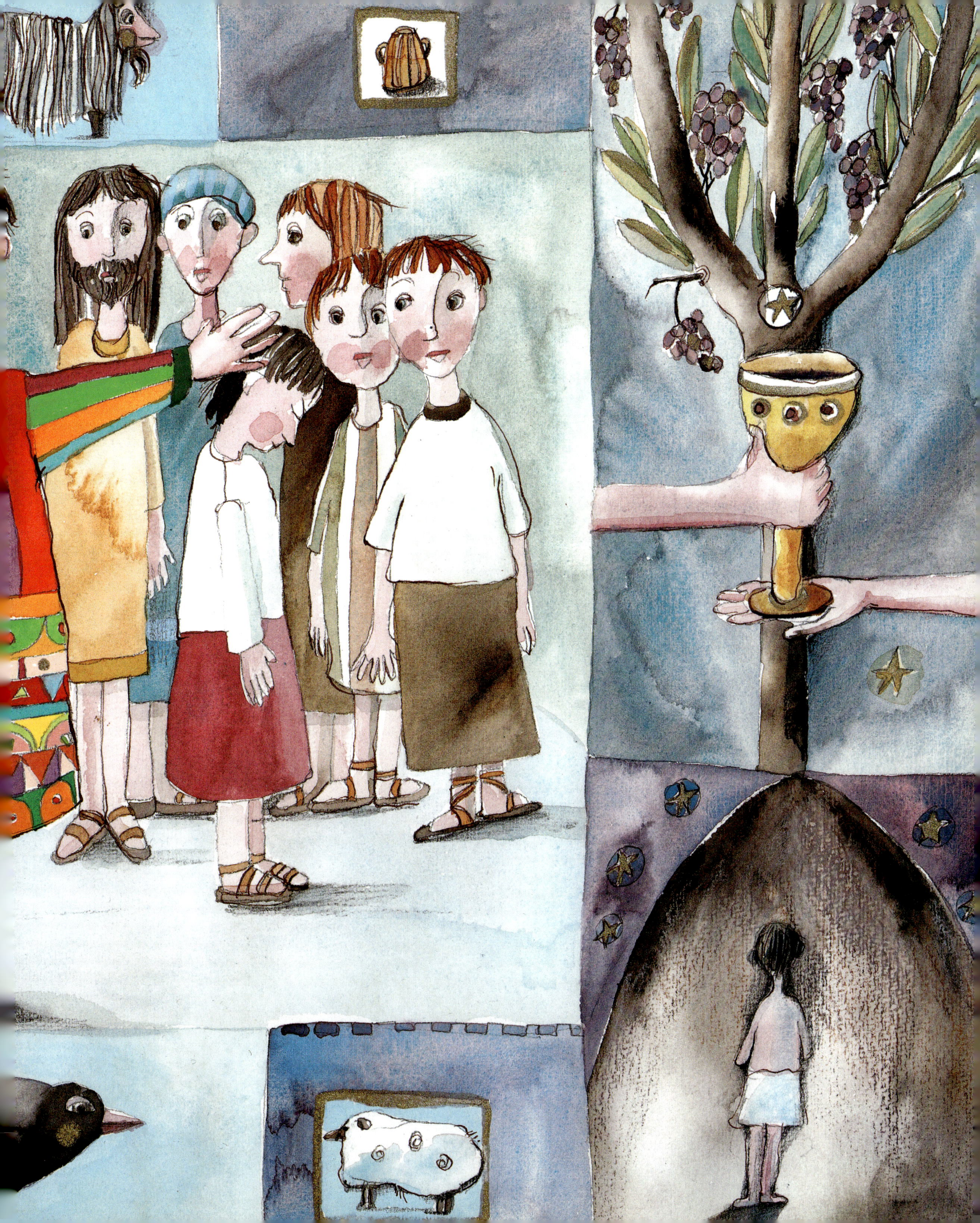

185

מקץ

MIKETZ

Joseph in Egypt

Corn ears: Traditional commentators interpreted the symbolism of the corn. That seven ears of corn grew on a single stalk indicated that the abundant harvests would be centralized in one area, Egypt. In contrast the thin withered ears of corn on separate stalks symbolized that the famine would be widespread throughout the lands.

Wealth of detail: Nahum Sarna explains that the style of the Joseph story is quite unlike previous stories in Genesis. It "is distinguished by a wealth of background material, detailing the customs, practices and conditions of a non-Israelite people – matters outside the scope of interest of Scripture in the preceding patriarchal stories...The river Nile... is called in the Hebrew ye'or, a word corresponding to the Egyptian word for river... The cows, themselves, provide yet another local touch, for they were abundant and important in the Egyptian economy in contrast to sheep which played a very minor role. This is the exact opposite of the situation in Palestine."

? Only when Pharaoh woke up did he realize it was just a dream. Have you ever had a dream that you thought was real?

Ch.41: 1 – 7 Two more years passed and then Pharaoh dreamed a dream. He was standing by the river Nile and out of the river came seven fat and healthy cows to graze among the reeds. After them seven thin and sickly cows came out of the river and stood near the fat and healthy ones. Suddenly the seven thin cows swallowed up the seven fat ones. And Pharaoh woke up. Pharaoh fell asleep again and dreamed a second dream. This time seven healthy ears of corn grew on one stalk, and after them grew seven withered ears of corn. The seven withered ears of corn ate the seven healthy ears. Pharaoh woke up and saw it was a dream.

Two years passed from when Joseph asked the cupbearer to remember him. Sages of Old calculate that Joseph had been locked up in prison now for twelve long years, from when he was eighteen until he was thirty, some of the best years of life. Maybe he was losing hope that he would ever get out.

This is the first time we are introduced to Pharaoh in the Torah. Pharaoh is not the name of a person, but rather the title of the Egyptian king. In the Torah there are a number of different Pharaohs including the well-known Pharaoh during the time of Moses who refused to let the Children of Israel leave Egypt. The story of Joseph is the very beginning of the story of how the Children of Israel went down into Egypt and became slaves there.

We are introduced to Pharaoh through his dreams. In Egypt in those days people believed dreams held important messages and the dream of a Pharaoh was seen to have a message for all the people of Egypt. In the dream Pharaoh was standing by the river Nile. The river Nile was central to all of the economy and agriculture of Egypt; all the watering of crops depended on it. Scholars of our Time tell that the Nile overflowed once every year covering the fields with fertile soil and water for growing crops. As health and famine depended on the Nile so Pharaoh dreamed of the healthy and sickly cows coming out of the Nile. Whilst cows are a symbol of ploughing the land, corn is a symbol of harvesting. So both dreams relate to agriculture.

The dreams were very real and lifelike. The sight of the thin cows swallowing up the fat ones gave Pharaoh such a shock that he woke up. Sages of Old tell that the dream of the corn was so real Pharaoh thought it was actually happening. Only when he woke up did he realize it was only a dream.

Enduring: "After he's forgotten by the cupbearer, Joseph continues to languish in Pharaoh's dungeon for years. Yet his spirit doesn't die... What is it that allows some people to endure long imprisonment?... In Bruno Bettleheim's landmark book about concentration camp inmates, "The Informed Heart," he concluded that 'prisoners with strong identities – whether political convictions or confirmed religious beliefs – had higher survival rates.' Bettleheim found that to the degree we can maintain a larger, more comprehensive vision of who we are and why we need to survive, we remain more resilient in the face of persecution." Naomi Rosenblatt

? Joseph is stuck in Pharaoh's prison for twelve long years and yet he doesn't lose hope. People like Nelson Mandela and Natan Sharansky also survived many long years in prison and then when they came out they still had the strength and courage to become leaders. What qualities do you think such people may have?

Wake-up call : "Why did God give us the ability to dream? A true dream is a wake-up call, warning us to correct our life's direction. Our eyes are opened to a vivid vision of our future, should we not take heed to mend our ways." R. Chanan Morrison

Disclaimer : "Despite the fact that Israel shared with its pagan neighbours a belief in the reality of dreams as a medium of divine communication, it never developed, as in Egypt and Mesopotamia, a class of professional interpreters or a dream literature. In the entire Bible, only two Israelites engage in the interpretation of dreams – Joseph and Daniel – and significantly enough, each serves a pagan monarch, the one in Egypt, the other in Mesopotamia, precisely the lands in which oneiromancy flourished. Moreover, in each case, the Israelite is careful to disclaim any innate ability, attributing all to God." Nahum Sarna

? The dreams of a Pharaoh were believed to contain a message for all the people of Egypt. How would you interpret Pharaoh's dreams: the seven thin cows swallowing the seven fat ones, and the seven withered ears of corn eating the seven healthy ones, so they had meaning for all the people of Egypt?

Ch.41: 8 – 16 **Pharaoh was very troubled by his strange dreams and sent for all the wise men and magicians of Egypt. But none could interpret his dreams. Finally the cupbearer spoke up. "When I was in prison I had a dream and a young Hebrew prisoner interpreted it for me. And all he said came true." So Pharaoh sent for Joseph and Joseph was taken out of prison and washed and dressed and brought before Pharaoh. "I dreamed a dream and no-one can interpret it for me," said Pharaoh. "I have heard that you understand dreams." "Not I," answered Joseph, "but God knows all dreams."**

Sages of Old tell that the wise men and magicians tried to interpret the dreams but Pharaoh knew in his heart that none of their interpretations was true. One wise man suggested that Pharaoh would have seven beautiful daughters but they would all die. Another told Pharaoh that he would conquer seven countries but later they would all rebel against him. Their interpretations had meaning for Pharaoh as a person, but not for Pharaoh as the king of the Egyptian people.

Joseph told Pharaoh that his ability to understand the meaning of dreams all comes from God. This is what he told the cupbearer and baker, and shows how Joseph is changing and becoming more humble.

Dreams seem to follow Joseph throughout his life. Midrash writes: "Joseph fell because of a dream and achieved greatness because of a dream." Joseph's own dreams made his brothers so angry and jealous they sold him as a slave. But soon we shall see that Joseph becomes great when he reveals the meaning of Pharaoh's dreams.

Ch.41: 17 – 36 So Pharaoh told Joseph his two dreams. "It is really one dream," said Joseph. "God has shown Pharaoh what is going to happen. The seven healthy cows and the seven healthy ears of corn are seven good years when the land will blossom and the harvests will be huge. The seven sickly cows and seven sickly ears of corn are seven years of famine. First seven years of wealth and plenty will come to the land of Egypt. But after that seven years of famine will come, famine so harsh that all the plenty will be forgotten. Pharaoh should find a wise man and put him in charge to gather up and store food during the seven good years so it can be used to feed the people during the famine."

Pharaonic record: The concept of seven years of plenty and seven years of famine existed in Egyptian manuscripts of the time. A text from the twenty-eighth century B.C.E. reads "I was in distress in the Great Throne, and those who are in the palace were in heart's affliction from a very great evil, since the Nile had not come in my time for a space of seven years. Grain was scant, fruits were dried up, and everything which they eat was short."

Economics: Joseph instructed that one fifth of the grain be collected from farmers during the years of plenty. R. Samson Raphael Hirsch suggested this was calculated to supply the basic needs of existence. "Let us assume," he writes, "that in years of plenty one uses twice as much as in ordinary years, and, in contrast, in years of scarcity one makes do with half the ordinary quantity. Hence, in a year of abundance one would use four times as much as in a year of famine. If this is so, then it is quite simple that in any case, one fifth of what is produced in a year of superfluity must suffice to feed one famine year even if everything else, the remaining four fifths, are completely consumed."

A Scholar of our Time points out that all six dreams in the Joseph story came in pairs – Joseph's own dreams, the dreams of the cupbearer and the baker, and now Pharaoh's two dreams. The fact that the dreams came in pairs emphasizes their importance.

Joseph understood that Pharaoh's dreams were two halves of a whole, and really one dream. According to Kabbalah, Pharaoh dreamed the dreams on the eve of Rosh Hashana, the New Year, when dreams are especially significant. Between Rosh Hashana and Yom Kippur God decides the fate of each person and each nation, so God was telling Pharaoh what would happen to the Egyptian nation in the coming years.

Joseph told Pharaoh that seven years of plenty would come to the land of Egypt, but no location is given for the seven years of famine. Sages of Old explain that the years of plenty were only in Egypt but the famine spread to many other lands. So the people in other lands could not store up food, and would suffer even more in the famine. In the dream even after the thin cows swallowed the fat cows, they did not look any fatter. Sages of Old explain that this means that the food stored during the seven good years would be just enough to feed the people during the famine years – there would not be extra food and people would not get fat on the stored food. Joseph realized that storing the food during the years of plenty and rationing it out so there would be enough to last for seven bad years required enormous organization. So Pharaoh needed to appoint someone specifically to be responsible for this job.

? Today some parts of the world have plenty to eat while other parts of the world have famine and people are starving. Would Joseph's plan of storing the food from the countries with plenty and rationing it out to the other countries help to deal with world food shortages today? What do you think?

Twinkling eye: "In the rabbinic Midrash there is an expression which has provided solace to suffering Jews for thousands of years: 'Salvation can come in the twinkling of an eye.' Joseph wakes up one morning, as he had for the preceding two years, as a falsely accused prisoner in an Egyptian jail. He goes to sleep that night, second in power only to Pharaoh, truly, Joseph's salvation comes 'in the twinkling of an eye.'" R. Joseph Telushkin

Assimilation: Joseph took on the role of prime minister of Egypt with apparent enthusiasm and conviction. "His outer garb, his changed name, his marriage to a daughter of the High Priest of Re, and his mastery of the Egyptian language were all calculated to make him outwardly indistinguishable from his fellow Egyptians..." Nahum Sarna.

Past and present: "Joseph was the first Hebrew who lived, so to speak, in the Diaspora. He became thoroughly assimilated, adopted the customs of his environment, changed his name, wore Egyptian clothes, swore by Pharaoh's name and married an Egyptian wife... He entered a new life of affluence and power, and the past seemed far away." Gunter Plaut

Foreign power: Could a foreigner rise to such a high office in the Egyptian government? "This problem can be answered with an emphatic affirmative... It was not at all extraordinary for foreigners, and Semites in particular, to be welcomed by the court and to rise to positions of responsibility and power in the government." Nahum Sarna

? If the measure of a wise man in Pharaoh's time was that he knew many languages, what do you think is the measure of a wise man today?

Ch.41: 37 – 46 Pharaoh liked Joseph's plan and he said to his ministers, "Where will we find another man like this, filled with the spirit of God?" And he turned to Joseph, "Because God has made all this known to you, there is none as wise as you. So you shall be in charge of all the land of Egypt, only I will be superior to you." Pharaoh gave Joseph his ring, dressed him in fine clothes and gave him Asenat, daughter of the priest, as a wife. And he gave Joseph a new name, Zaphenat-paneah, meaning "The one who reveals secrets." Joseph was thirty years old when he became Pharaoh's prime minister.

Did Joseph guess that Pharaoh would choose him to be in charge? A Scholar of our Time writes, "Within the space of an hour Joseph had persuaded Pharaoh to choose him – a wretched Hebrew slave and prisoner in his dungeon – as his prime minister." Joseph had not forgotten his own dreams. Perhaps he sensed the turning point in his own life had come and his fate was about to change.

Legend tells that Pharaoh had to convince all his ministers that Joseph was indeed the most wise man to be in charge. In those days the measure of a wise man was that he knew many languages. So God sent the angel Gabriel to teach Joseph all seventy known languages in an instant.

Joseph became Pharaoh's prime minister, the second most powerful man in all of Egypt. He wore Egyptian clothes, married an Egyptian wife and even had an Egyptian name. The story of Joseph raises the question of the balance between keeping one's own culture and blending into the main culture of a society in which one is living. Do you think Joseph became too Egyptian and forgot his own past and traditions? Let's see what happens and you decide.

Ch.41: 47 – 57 During the seven good years Joseph gathered the plentiful grain and stored it. Before the famine began Joseph had two sons with his wife Asenat. Joseph named the older boy Manasseh meaning "God has made me forget my suffering and my father's house." And he named his second son Ephraim meaning "God has made me fruitful in the land of my suffering." The seven years of plenty came to an end and the seven years of famine began. There was famine in all the lands, but only in Egypt was there grain. When the people cried out to Pharaoh for food he told them "Go to Joseph." Joseph opened the storehouses and rationed the grain. So people from all the lands came to Joseph for food.

> *Secretary of agriculture:* "Joseph's chief task was to lay up an adequate store of food during the years of plenty and to be responsible for its distribution during the years of famine. It is one of those strange quirks of history that the shepherd boy, a member of a semi-nomadic clan, should become Secretary of Agriculture, and perhaps Joseph's first dream, dealing with binding sheaves in the field, contained a hint of his future vocation."
> Nahum Sarna
>
> *What's in a name?* "It is in this context of spectacular success as provider of food, of life, to a whole nation, that we read of the birth of Joseph's two sons... nowhere does Joseph reveal as nakedly as in these names his own feeling about the strange vicissitudes of his life... Manasseh is named for forgetfulness. Joseph seems to celebrate the oblivion, not only of his suffering, but of 'all my father's house'...he is grateful not to be haunted by memory... A certain mercy of oblivion has allowed Joseph to turn his back on the world of loves and values and possibilities, to turn his face unequivocally toward the single necessity of the moment."
> Avivah Zornberg

After he came out of prison Joseph became a man of action – he showed good leadership and organization. He gathered the grain and stored it, and then rationed it out as needed during the years of famine.

What do you make of the names Joseph gave to his children? With the name Manasseh Joseph seems to want to forget his past – the cruelty of his brothers and the suffering they caused him. A Scholar of our Time suggests that Joseph had to concentrate on his job of managing food supplies and could not afford to be worried by bad memories from the past. We shall see that although Joseph seemed to want to forget his past, his past will not be left behind.

Emotional vortex: "The brothers' arrival in Egypt plunges Joseph into an emotional vortex. The sight of them bowing before him, like the sheaves in his dream, triggers a flood of emotional memories. Anger, revenge, and heartache mix with tender longings to reunite with his father and younger brother Benjamin. In a reversal of his childhood trauma, Joseph now wields complete power over his brothers' movements, and throughout this episode and those that follow he will manipulate them mercilessly." Naomi Rosenblatt

In another story: "The sense of not being able to understand their own story also constitutes the radical anxiety that Joseph inflicts on his brothers. His technique is a series of enigmatic questions whose drift is opaque to his victims... The brothers experience this undercutting of their own narrative, when Joseph, as Egyptian viceroy, accuses them of spying, and demands that they bring their youngest brother in proof of their story. The illogic of such a demand engenders in them the vertigo of an alternative narrative." Avivah Zornberg

? Have you ever had a dream that came true? Like Joseph's dream seemed to come true?

Ch.42: 1 – 20 When Jacob saw that there was food in Egypt he said to his sons, "Go down to Egypt and buy food for us so we shall live and not die." So the brothers went down to Egypt but Jacob did not send his youngest son Benjamin for he was scared some disaster might befall him. The brothers came to Joseph and bowed low to him. Joseph recognized his brothers but they did not recognize him. He acted like a stranger towards them, speaking roughly. "Where do you come from?" he asked. "From the land of Canaan to buy food," they answered. "You are spies," accused Joseph. "No, we are all twelve sons of one man in Canaan. The youngest is still with our father, the other is no more." "No, you are spies," repeated Joseph. "This is how I will test you. Let one of your brothers remain here in prison while the rest of you take food back to your households. Then bring your youngest brother back to me."

Ten brothers went down to Egypt – the same ten brothers who sold Joseph into slavery. Benjamin was not there when they sold Joseph, he was too young and had stayed at home with his father. Now again he stays home with Jacob.

The brothers do not recognize Joseph. It was twenty-two years ago when they last saw him. He was a teenager of seventeen, now at thirty-nine he is Egypt's prime minister. He has an Egyptian name, dresses like an Egyptian and speaks Egyptian. When the ten brothers appeared before Joseph he must have been shocked to see them. As they stand before him, Joseph's memories come flooding back – of his father, of what his brothers did to him, of his dreams. Remember Joseph's first dream, when the sheaves of wheat gather in a circle and bow down to Joseph's sheaf. Now as the brothers bowed low to Joseph as prime minister of Egypt, it seems Joseph's first dream has come true.

Joseph pretends not to believe the brothers' story. He interrogates them to find out the information he wants to know – that his father and his brother Benjamin are still alive. Why does Joseph trick his brothers – not revealing his true identity to them and then accusing them of being spies? Many Sages of Old and Scholars of our Time have discussed this question What reasons can you think of for Joseph's behaviour?

Ch.42: 21 – 24 **Joseph took Simeon and had him bound before their eyes. The brothers said to one another, "We are being punished for what we did to our brother Joseph. For we saw his suffering and did not listen to his pleading." Reuben reminded them, "Did I not tell you 'Do no wrong to the boy', but you would not listen. Now we must pay for his blood." The brothers did not know that Joseph could understand them, for there was an interpreter between them and him. When Joseph heard their words he turned away from them and wept.**

What made the brothers suddenly remember what they had done to Joseph? Perhaps the shock of seeing Simeon bound before them, the fact that they were about to lose another brother who had to stay in prison in Egypt. Again they would have to face their father with one brother missing.

The brothers remembered clearly that day when they threw Joseph into the pit. Did they think about it often, did they speak to each other about it? Did they regret what they had done? We do not know. "We saw his suffering and did not listen to his pleading." As readers we now find out new details about what happened when the brothers threw Joseph into the pit; like detectives discovering fresh evidence about a crime. In the original story there was no description of Joseph pleading. Now we know that the brothers deliberately ignored Joseph's desperate cries for help – this new detail emphasizes how cruel they were. The Torah itself does not write of Joseph's cries. A Scholar of our Time explains that because the brothers did not listen, it is as though Joseph's cries never existed, and so there is no record of them.

Balancing the scales: "Joseph took his brother Simeon as a hostage, possibly because he was the one who had suggested that Joseph be killed. Thus punishment is exacted and the scales of justice begin to balance." Sefer Ha – Yashar

Flashback: "The recalling of this long buried episode here, at this juncture, represents the awakening of the brothers' conscience. Joseph's heart-rending pleas for mercy, more than they emanate from the pit, now well up from the depths of their own hearts. This constitutes the underlying intention of the narrative in citing this detail here. It is meant to reveal what was going on in the consciousness of the brothers at the moment indicating their remorse." Meir Wiess

Witnessing trauma: Joseph's trauma, his cries in the pit are not recorded in the Torah. Avivah Zornberg suggests that in the pit Joseph is an object, there is no description of his experience, no reference to how he feels. The brothers treat Joseph as a commodity and Torah does too. Recent studies of trauma suggest that where there is no witness to a trauma, it is difficult to speak about it, one's voice is lost. And if one cannot tell the story part of the self is lost.

What has God done to us? "Immediately they sensed that this was no mere coincidence but the intervention of Divine justice repaying them measure for measure." Heketav Vehakaballa

Precedent: "Rashi reads Rachel's death 'on the way' as setting up a dangerous precedent, creating in her family a kind of genetic sensitivity to the derech, to the road between places, that is no place. In the light of this Rashi understands Jacob's reluctance to let Benjamin travel to Egypt with his brothers and comments: 'If he leaves his father, we are anxious he will die on the derech (journey), since his mother died on the derech.'" Avivah Zornberg

? For Jacob the road was a dangerous place. Is there a place for you or your family that is connected with danger, perhaps because something bad happened there in the past?

Ch.42: 24 – 38 Joseph gave orders to his servants to fill the brothers' sacks with grain and to return each one's money to his sack. The brothers loaded up their donkeys and went on their way. That night one of the brothers opened up his sack to feed his donkey and found his money inside. "Look, my money has been returned." The other brothers found that their money too had been returned. Terrified and trembling, they cried to one another, "What has God done to us?" They returned home to their father Jacob and told him all that had happened. "Why are you always causing me to lose my children?" said Jacob. "Joseph is gone, Simeon is gone, and now you would take Benjamin away." Jacob was quiet a moment and then continued, "No, Benjamin will not go with you. His brother is dead and he alone is left. If he meets disaster on the road you will send me to my grave in grief."

The brothers do not understand why their money was returned to them and they are frightened. A Scholar of our Time explains that they are terrified as they realize things are being done to them and they are not in control. They sense they are helpless characters in a story, a story they do not understand.

It seems that Benjamin has taken Joseph's place as Jacob's favourite son. Benjamin is Jacob's last remaining link to his wife Rachel and his lost son Joseph. So Jacob is afraid to let Benjamin travel the road to Egypt with his brothers. Remember Jacob's wife, Rachel, Benjamin's mother, had died on the road as they were travelling. And Rachel's other son Joseph disappeared when he was on the road to meet his brothers. As a Scholar of our Time writes, "There is almost an expectation that the children of Rachel will disappear into nothingness." In Jacob's eyes the road has become a dangerous place, a place where people disappear and die.

Ch.43: 1 – 14 The famine continued for weeks, months and into years. When they had eaten all the food they brought from Egypt, Jacob said, "Go back and buy more food." But Judah reminded Jacob, "The man warned us not to return without our youngest brother – he will not see us if we do not bring Benjamin. Father – send the boy in my care, so we may live and not die. I myself will be responsible for him. If I do not bring him back to you I will stand guilty before you forever." Jacob sighed, "If it must be, then take Benjamin with you. Take also double the money so you can return the money put back in your sacks. May God make the man show mercy towards you so he releases Simeon and Benjamin. As for me, if I am to be bereaved, so be it."

Judah offered to take complete responsibility for Benjamin. Sages of Old explain that Judah promises he will do everything humanly possible to guard Benjamin from danger. He will guard him with his life, and would die himself before allowing harm to come to Benjamin. Judah said "I myself will be responsible for him." He knew that if all the brothers together took responsibility for Benjamin, each one may leave it to the other. So it was better if only one was responsible for him.

According to a Scholar of our Time, Jacob had hoped against hope that he would not have to send Benjamin down to Egypt. But in the end Jacob saw that they would all starve so he gave in. Jacob's last words to Judah are important, "May God make the man show mercy towards you." Jacob had done all he could – the rest was up to God.

Jacob's dilemma: "You may learn from the story of Jacob that it is a man's worst trial to have his children ask him for food when he has nothing to give."
Midrash Hagadol

I will stand guilty before you forever: "This figure of speech contains a valuable lesson, teaching us something not otherwise explicitly alluded to in the Torah: that there is no punishment outside of the sin, sin itself is its own punishment in the Divine scheme of judgement and serves the purpose of reward and punishment. This is the meaning of: 'then shall I bear the blame to my father forever.'"
Benamozegh

I myself will be responsible for him: "On a profound level, Judah must make a place for Benjamin, with himself, so that if he is lost, his 'not – being,' his lostness, is to be thoroughly owned by Judah and his brothers... The legal imagery of 'standing surety' (arev – responsible for him) traces the precise parameters of Judah's commitment to Jacob. In economic situations, the guarantor commits his own resources to cover the debt of others... Surety thus involves an obscuring of boundaries, particularly of the most basic boundary that separates individuals." Avivah Zornberg

Slow motion: Avivah Zornberg notes that this is the second time Joseph weeps "...in the course of his masquerade with his brothers. In fact, Joseph sheds most of the tears in Genesis... each time he weeps, something opens up in him." Zornberg explains how the narrative – Joseph overcome with feeling, on the verge of crying, rushing out, crying in another room, washing his face and regaining composure, is detailed and extended. "The effect is a kind of slow motion lingering on the experience of weeping – before, during, and after."

Joseph's tears: "For he (Joseph) knew the ordeal which he intended to inflict on him (Benjamin), and in what a painful position, even if temporarily he could not avoid placing him."
R. Samson Raphael Hirsch

Joseph's and Benjamin's conversation: "In this Midrashic narrative, Joseph's compassion is stirred, not simply by nostalgia and love for his true brother Benjamin, but because his own existence is suddenly fleshed out in absence... Joseph has lived on in Benjamin's mind, as a continuous presence, manifested in the names of his sons... he has continued to be an object of imagination and regret for his brother."
Avivah Zornberg

? How do you think the brothers will respond to seeing Benjamin being favoured?

Ch. 43: 15 – 34 **So the brothers returned to Egypt. When Joseph saw Benjamin was with them he prepared a feast and brought Simeon to join them for the meal. As Joseph gazed at Benjamin, his little brother, he was so overcome with feelings that tears welled up in his eyes and he rushed out and went into another room to cry. Then he washed his face and returned. Joseph sat the brothers at the table in their correct birth order, from youngest to oldest. The brothers looked at each other in astonishment. Food was served to all but Benjamin's portion was five times bigger than anyone else's.**

Midrash tells of the conversation between Joseph and Benjamin that brought tears to Joseph's eyes. Joseph asked Benjamin, "Have you a full brother, one who has the same mother as you?" "I had a brother," answered Benjamin, "but I do not know where he is." "Do you have sons?" asked Joseph. "I have ten." "What are their names?" "I named them all after my brother and the troubles that befell him. One is called Bela because my brother was *nivla* - swallowed up - and disappeared. Another is called Bechor because he was the *bechor*, the first-born of our mother. A third is called Achi because he was *achi*, my brother and a fourth is called Chuppim because he did not see my *chuppah*, my wedding day. So Benjamin explained the names of his ten sons and Joseph was full of love for his brother and sadness for the time they had not shared together.

Midrash tells a story about how Joseph seated his brothers correctly from youngest to oldest. Joseph wanted to have Benjamin sit next to him but did not know how to go about it. So he picked up his goblet, pretending it had magic powers. He tapped it and called out the brothers' names Reuben, Simeon, Levi, Judah and so on from oldest to youngest. When he came to Benjamin he said, "He has no mother and neither do I. He had a brother who was separated from him at birth and so did I – let him sit next to me."

Why did Joseph give Benjamin five times more food than anyone else? Sages of Old tell that Joseph was testing his brothers. In the past when their father favored him the brothers became so jealous and angry they wanted to get rid of him. How would they react when they saw another brother being favored? Benjamin had become Jacob's favourite son and now the prime minister of Egypt was also favoring him. Joseph wanted to see if his brothers had changed – were they the same jealous, angry men as before or not.

Ch.44: 1 – 13 Then Joseph instructed his servant, "Fill the brothers' sacks with food. And put my silver goblet in the sack of the youngest one." Early the next morning the brothers set off but they had not gone far when Joseph told his servant, "Go after them. And when you catch up say to them, 'Why did you repay good with evil? You have stolen my master's goblet, the one he drinks from and uses for magic. What a wicked thing you have done." So the servant accused the brothers and they answered, "We would not do such a thing. Look, we brought back the money we found in our sacks, why would we steal silver or gold from your master's house? If you find it in one of our sacks let that person die and the rest of us will be slaves to your master." But the servant said, "Only the one who has the goblet will be my master's slave. The rest of you shall go free." So he searched in their sacks, beginning with the oldest and ending with the youngest, and the goblet was found in Benjamin's sack. The brothers tore their clothes in grief and returned to the city.

Reformed?: "Joseph carefully contrives a desperate situation in which the brothers are compelled to show, once and for all, whether they have reformed since the day they so brutally sold him into slavery." Nahum Sarna

A test: "Or perhaps it was that Joseph himself was bent on testing his brothers, manipulating events so as to see if they would once again be guilty of standing idly by as their younger brother (Benjamin, this time) was unjustly taken from them." James Kugel

Reinterpreting: Avivah Zornberg understands Joseph's behaviour as a reassembling of "fragments of his repressed past, imprisoning Simeon as he was imprisoned, insisting on Benjamin being 'brought down' to Egypt, as he was brought down...Joseph and his brothers must reinterpret the fragments."

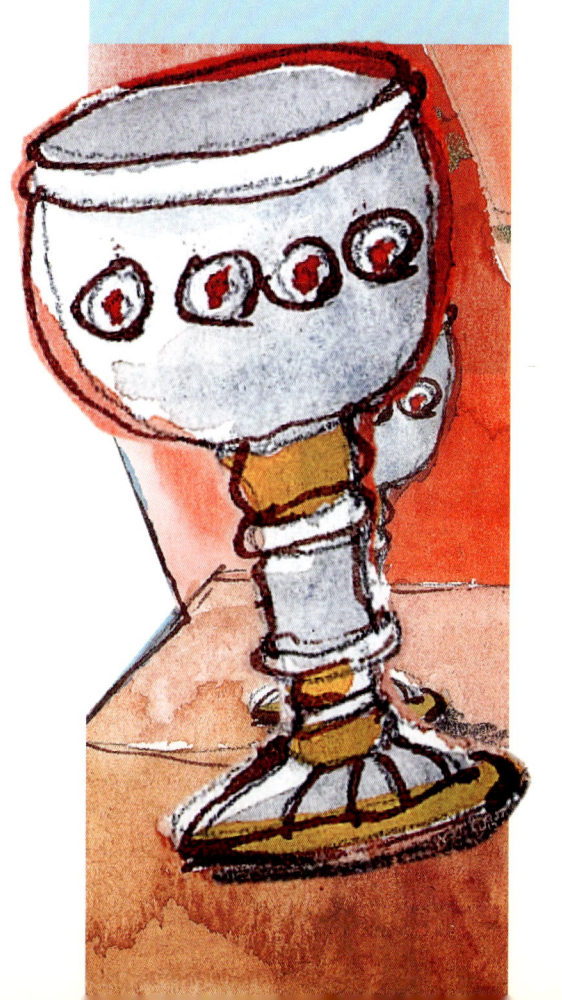

What is Joseph doing to his brothers? First he accused them of being spies and kept Simeon as a prisoner, then he returned their money to their sacks, and now he accuses Benjamin of stealing his silver goblet and demands that he remain in Egypt as his slave.

Was Joseph taking revenge on his brothers, making them suffer as he had suffered? He imprisons Simeon as he was imprisoned. He insists on Benjamin being "brought down" to Egypt as he was brought down.

Sages of Old and Scholars of our Time suggest a different way of understanding Joseph's behaviour. They explain that Joseph needed to see if his brothers had changed since the day they threw him in the pit and then sold him as a slave. He set up conditions where Benjamin was the favoured son as he had been. Would the brothers get rid of Benjamin as they had got rid of him many years before? Or would they show more brotherly caring for one another? Joseph hoped to see a change in his brothers. And if they changed all the brothers would see it too. Only then was there any chance for peace in this family.

Literary structure: Parashat Miketz tells of Joseph's ascent in Egypt, from prison to prime minister of the palace. In juxtaposition to this rise the parasha describes the brothers' decline, they must come down to Egypt to buy food, must bow low to the prime minister and become enslaved. The structure of the narrative itself reflects this ascent and descent. "…the first three aliyot (divisions in the parasha) describe Joseph's rise to greatness and the last three aliyot describe his brothers' fall. The point where they cross comes in the central fourth aliya… in which Joseph and his brothers encounter one another for the first time in Egypt."
R. Dr. Pinchas Hyman

What can we say: "Judah's speechlessness is poignant but enigmatic: his primary response is a gesture of confession, of guilt, that allows of no defence… He cannot justify himself, God has indeed 'found' the sin of all of them…"
Avivah Zornberg.

Ch.44: 14 – 17 When the brothers came to Joseph's house they bowed low before him. "What have you done," said Joseph, "stealing my goblet which has magic powers?" "What can we say, my lord," Judah replied. "God has found out our sin. Here we are ready to be your slaves, both we and the one in whose sack the goblet was found." "No," declared Joseph. "Only the one in whose sack the goblet was found shall be my slave. The rest of you, go home in peace to your father."

What do you think Joseph was thinking while he waited for his servant to bring the brothers back to him? Would the brothers abandon Benjamin in Egypt as a slave (as they had once sold him as a slave) and return home with their sacks full of food? And if they did, what would Joseph, do? Would he keep Benjamin, his one true brother, in Egypt with him? Or would he send him back to his father?

And what do you make of Judah's response? Judah knew that none of them had stolen the cup, not Benjamin nor any of the others. But he did not plead for an easier punishment. Instead he accepted punishment for all of them: "Here we are ready to be your slaves." A Scholar of our Time explains that Judah knew they were being wrongly accused of stealing the cup but he was not confessing to that crime. He was confessing to another crime – the brothers' crime of throwing Joseph in the pit and selling him as a slave. And in relation to this crime he knew that "God has found out our sin."

From prisoner to prime minister

Many people love the story of Joseph. He is larger than life; everything happens to him on a grand scale. At his lowest he is stuck in a pit with snakes and scorpions, and then imprisoned in a dungeon for years with no way out. And then in his glory, he rises to be Pharaoh's prime minister, dressed in fine clothes and gold, the second most powerful man in all of Egypt. Joseph is loved because in his story nothing is impossible. As the Midrash says "A change of fortune can come in the blink of an eye." So Joseph's fortune changes in the blink of an eye and gives hope to others stuck in all sorts of difficult situations, in prisons of others or of their own making.

Joseph's change of fortune is due partly to his own growing abilities. In the last parasha Joseph was busy dreaming his own dreams – he was not aware of the dreams or feelings of others, and that got him into trouble. But in this parasha Joseph goes from dreaming his own dreams to listening to the dreams of others and interpreting those dreams. He goes on to act with vision and skill to save the entire people of Egypt from starvation during the years of famine. It seems that only when Joseph could listen to others, could his own dreams come true.

The story of Joseph is a new sort of hero in the Torah. He is the first from the family of Abraham to become a man of power and success in another nation, amongst the Egyptians. As the famous author Elie Wiesel writes, "He stirs our imagination. After all, he was the first Jew to bridge two nations, two histories; the first to link Israel to the world."

But success and power in another nation bring with it the temptation to fit in and leave one's past behind. And Joseph did fit in, he changed his name and his clothes, he spoke Egyptian fluently. He may have been very tempted to forget his past, especially given what his brothers did to him. But when his family show up, Joseph does not turn them away. Although he does not reveal himself, he is very connected to them and is driven to see if they have changed.

Indeed we start to see changes in the brothers – their guilty conscience about what they did to Joseph, Judah's promise to his father to look after Benjamin in all circumstances. How the brothers deal with the question of responsibility for each other is the key to the future of this family and how the story will unfold.

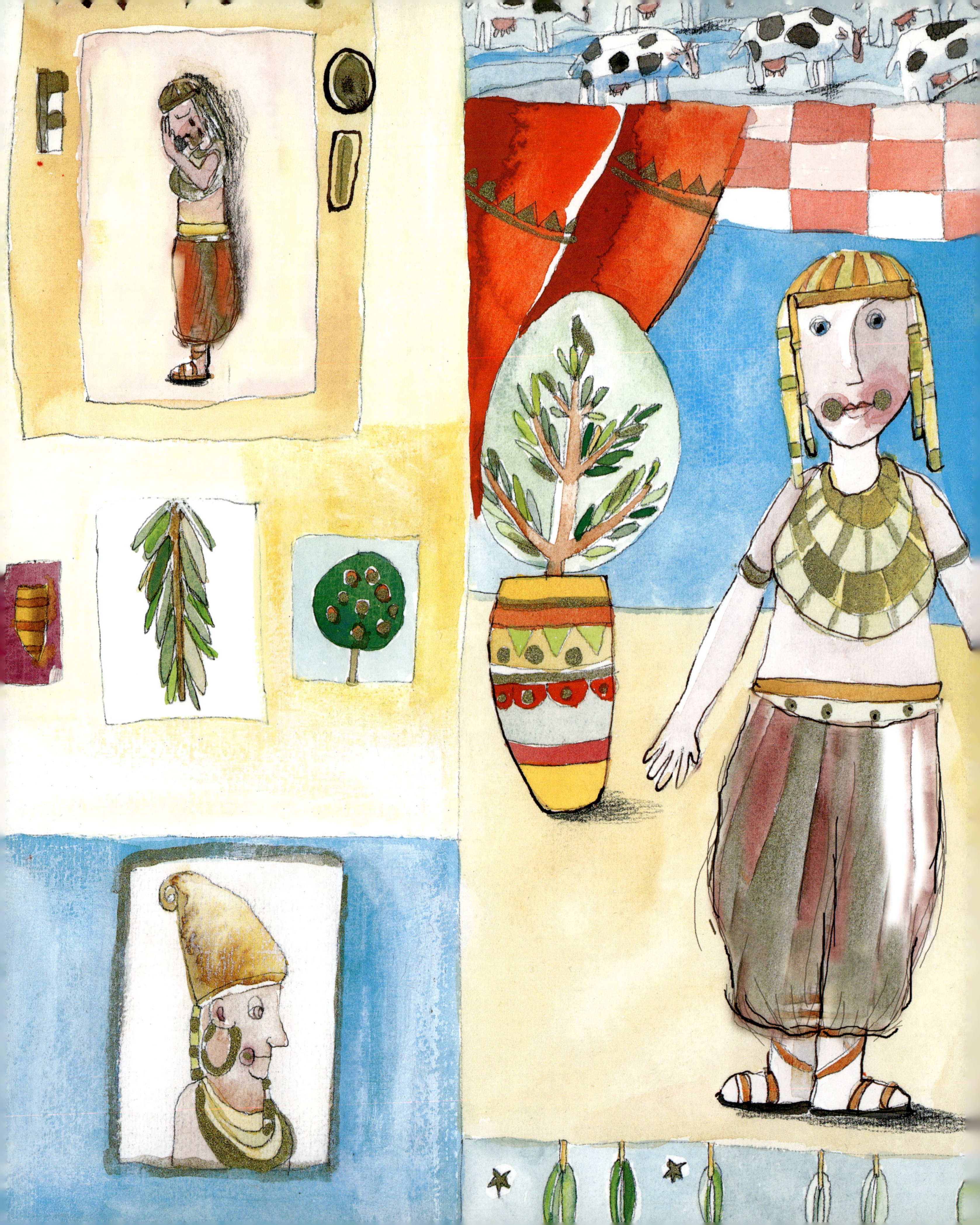

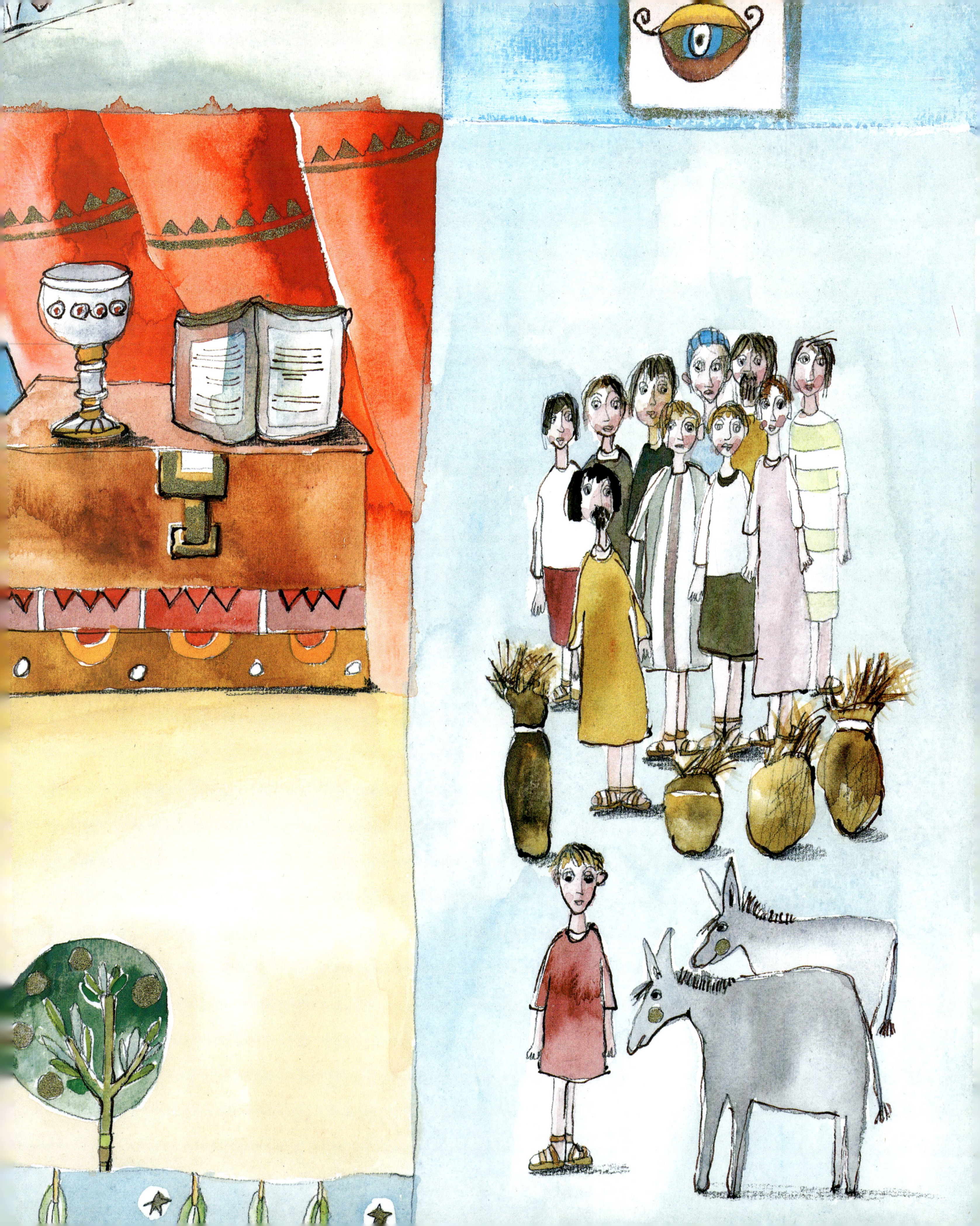

ויגש

VAYIGASH

Joseph and his brothers – the story unfolds

Three ways of drawing close: Various traditional commentators suggest that Judah's drawing close to Joseph is not just a plea for mercy but a challenge, criticizing the prime minister for his past dealings with the brothers. "The word Vayigash which opens the section occurs as an introduction to three different kinds of action: to do battle (II Sam 10:13), to conciliate (Josh 14:6) to pray (I King's 18:36). The three are strangely related: Men are usually ready for any one of the three. So was Judah when he went up." Genesis Rabbah

Close to himself: "Then Judah drew close." To whom? To himself, for only when Judah became himself at his best was he able to speak as he did." Itture Torah

Drawing close: The word Vayigash "And he drew close" recurs a number of times in different forms throughout the parasha. Here Judah draws close to Joseph. Later, as he reveals himself to them, Joseph draws close to his brothers. And the land of Goshen, (comes from the same root as vayigash) where Jacob's children settle together in Egypt, is a land named for reconciliation.

Between the Lines: "What was the point of repeating to Joseph what was already well-known to him. Between the lines however can be detected a note of pathos and grievance – note also the constant repetition of the word "father" with all its emotional undertones. This word which occurs fourteen times in Judah's oration is calculated to arouse compassion…" Nehama Leibowitz

Ch.44: 18 – 29 Then Judah came close - *vayigash* - to Pharaoh's prime minister (we know that he was Joseph, but Judah didn't) and said, "Please, my lord, let me speak to you, who are as powerful as Pharaoh, and do not become angry with me. My lord, you asked my brothers and me, 'Have you a father or another brother?' And we answered, 'We have an old father and a younger brother, the son of his old age, whose older brother died. He is the only son left of his mother and so his father adores him.' And you said, 'Bring him down to me so I may see him.' And we said, 'The boy cannot leave his father, for if he does, our father will die.' But you insisted. So we went home and told our father, and he said, 'If you take my youngest son and some disaster happens to him, I shall die and you shall send me to my grave with grief.'"

Why do you think Judah is the one who goes up to Joseph and speaks on behalf of all the brothers? Although he is not the oldest, it was Judah who promised his father that he would take responsibility for Benjamin. And so he has no choice; he must speak.

What gives Judah the courage, or the chutzpah, to go up to the prime minister of Egypt like that and negotiate with him? Joseph could become angry and make the punishment worse for all the brothers. A Scholar of our Time explains that Joseph's final words in the last parasha – when he told Judah that only Benjamin must stay as a slave and "the rest of you go home in peace to your father" – really upset Judah. For how could the other brothers "go home in peace" without Benjamin? If they did return home without Benjamin there would be no peace for them, and no peace for their father. The peace of the whole family would be destroyed.

Judah's speech to Joseph is the longest speech in all of Genesis. In this part of it he repeats the story of how the brothers came to Joseph as prime minister. But Judah's retelling is more than just a repetition. In it he emphasized the sadness of his old father who has already lost one son and may now lose another.

Ch.44: 30 – 34 "Now if I go home without Benjamin, my father, whose own life is so bound up with the boy's, when he sees that Benjamin is not with us – he will die. And I took responsibility for Benjamin saying, 'If I do not bring him back I stand guilty before my father forever.' So please let me stay as a slave instead of the boy and let him go home with his brothers. For how can I return to my father unless Benjamin is with me? I could not bear to see his suffering."

A Scholar of our Time divides Judah's long speech into three parts. The first part describes what happened in the past, when the brothers went down to Egypt to ask for food from the prime minister. In the second part Judah focuses on what will happen in the present – if Benjamin does not return with them, their father Jacob will die. And then in the third part Judah speaks of his plan for the future. He makes a powerful proposal to Joseph, a plea full of feeling, "Take me instead of Benjamin. Let me remain as your slave and let Benjamin return to our father."

So Judah's speech is moving and dramatic. He is willing to take Benjamin's place and remain a slave himself in Egypt. The speech shows how much Judah has changed. Many years earlier, Judah had agreed to sell a brother into slavery and see his father mourn and grieve year after year. But that time is past. Now Judah is prepared to become a slave himself to save his younger brother. And he can no longer bear to see his father's suffering and will do whatever he can to stop it.

A Scholar of our Time explains that part of what makes this speech so dramatic is that while Judah pleads with the Egyptian prime minister he has no idea he is really talking to his long-lost brother. And then everything he says takes on a double meaning.

Learning empathy the hard way: A Midrash suggests that Judah learnt to become more sensitive to Jacob's mourning for Joseph after Judah himself suffered the death of two of his own children. "His experience of bereavement, the wrenching in the bowels at his own losses, teaches him empathy – belatedly – with Jacob, in his loss." Avivah Zornberg

Double entendre: "What makes the scene so dramatic is that while Judah is consciously trying to evoke the Egyptian viceroy's pity, he has no idea that he is addressing his long-lost brother for whom his words have unbearable associations." Naomi Rosenblatt

Seeing what he sees: Avivah Zornberg describes the climax of Judah's speech as the power and pain of true empathy. "For how can I go back to my father unless the boy is with me? Let me not see the woe that would overtake my father." He has re-described himself in a new vocabulary of intimate relationship: a vocabulary that suggests what it is like to see the other seeing, and not be able to bear seeing what he sees."

? What do you think of Judah's proposal to Joseph – that he will stay as a slave instead of Benjamin? How do you think Joseph will respond?

So it was not you who sent me here but God: "What had originally appeared as a criminal deed of kidnapping now stands revealed in its true perspective, as part of a providential scheme for saving life... But this time it is God and not the brothers who is the initiator and the contrast is now between these two parties 'not you... but God.'" Nehama Leibowitz

God's hand: "At first in the background and now emerging ever more clearly is the guiding hand of God. The human story has a link with divine purpose. Four times in succession Joseph avers that it was not he but God who brought these events to pass.... The tale here foreshadows slavery and exodus: What happens between Joseph and his brothers is therefore an introduction to the story of deliverance that will occupy the second book of the Torah." Gunther Plaut

Do not worry or feel ashamed: "Do not let thoughts of the way and means through which I was brought here disturb the joy over the fact that I am here, which, after all, is great good fortune... I cannot prevent your feelings of regret and sorrow for wrong is wrong, and your feelings are justified. But your minds should temper even this consciousness by teaching you 'to look at the deed with other eyes', as I have long ago come to look at it." R. Samson Raphael Hirsch

Ch.45: 1 – 8 Joseph could no longer control himself. He asked all his servants to leave the room. And then he revealed himself to his brothers. Sobbing and crying, he exclaimed, "I am Joseph! Is my father still alive?" But his brothers could not answer. They could not speak at all, they were so stunned. So Joseph continued, "Come close to me. It is I, your brother Joseph – whom you sold into slavery. But do not worry or feel ashamed that you sold me, for God sent me here to save life. There has been famine in the land for two years, and five more years of famine are still to come. God sent me ahead to save your lives and made me prime minister to Pharaoh and ruler over the whole of Egypt. So it was not you who sent me here but God."

Gashu elai - "come close to me," said Joseph to his brothers. This word, gashu, reminds us of the beginning of this parasha when Judah came close to Joseph. There, we read the word *vayigash* ("and he came close"), which is also the name of this parasha. A Scholar of our Time explains that this parasha really is about people coming close to each other, fixing arguments and hurts from the past.

Joseph had to prove to his brothers that he really was their long-lost brother. "It is me, your brother Joseph – whom you sold into slavery." Outwardly Joseph had changed so much: he was powerful, wealthy, dressed in fine clothes, the prime minister of Egypt! How do you think Joseph could prove his identity to his brothers? A Sage of Old tells that he used two proofs to convince them – he spoke Hebrew and he showed them his circumcision!

Joseph cried so loudly that everyone in Pharaoh's palace heard him. What made him break down and cry, and finally reveal himself to his brothers? After Judah's speech, Joseph saw that his brothers really had changed: they would no longer abandon a brother as a slave, nor could they bear to cause their father more suffering. A Scholar of our Time explains that before, when the brothers threw Joseph into the pit, they treated him like an object and did not listen to his cries. But now the brothers treat their brother Benjamin and their father with feeling and love.

Why did Joseph tell his brothers not to feel ashamed and guilty that they sold him? Joseph presented his brothers with a totally different way of understanding what has happened. By changing the words "you sold me" to "God sent me" he explained that the whole reason he was sold to Egypt was because God was sending him on a mission. In this way Joseph himself, and his brothers, can have a new understanding of their lives. What had happened to them was all due to the guiding hand of God – God's plan for saving life. The story suggests there can be two different ways of understanding reality – a surface level and a deeper level. Although we think we are the masters of our own lives, at times there is another plan, God's plan, at work.

But does the idea of Joseph coming down to Egypt as part of God's plan reduce the brother's crime of throwing him in the pit and selling him? As a Sage of Old says: "A person is not judged by the actual result of his deeds, but by his intent."

> **?** Do you think a person should be judged by the result of his actions or by his intentions? How do the courts judge people?

From betrayal to forgiveness: "As usual, Genesis emphasizes the long slow journey from hurt to healing, from betrayal to forgiveness... (Joseph) stands as a model for any of us struggling to put family hurts behind us and to get beyond the emotional scorekeeping that's so destructive to family harmony... When Joseph reveals himself to his brothers, he also reveals himself to himself."
Naomi Rosenblatt

Overcoming vengeance: "Did he not have valid reasons to repudiate his enemy brothers who had plotted his death?.. It was only normal that he withdrew from this family he could no longer love and thought of vengeance. Yet this was only a first impulse; he quickly pulled himself together: he would not be an avenger. There is rare virtue in foregoing justified reprisals, overcoming well-founded bitterness. It is not easy to resist dealing out deserved punishment. Only a Tzaddik forgives without forgetting."
Elie Wiesel

? What qualities do you need to make peace with someone who has hurt you? William Blake, a famous poet of the nineteenth century wrote, "It is easier to forgive an enemy than to forgive a friend." What do you think?

Ch.45: 9 – 15 "Now hurry home to my father and tell him: 'So says your son Joseph: God has made me prime minister of Egypt. Come down to me, and you with all your family will live near me, in the land of Goshen. And I will provide food for you, for there will be five more years of famine." Then Joseph hugged his brother Benjamin and wept. And he kissed all his other brothers and wept. And at last the brothers were able to talk to him.

Joseph hugged and kissed and wept with his brothers. This is the moment when they finally make peace with each other. Just as Judah and the brothers had to change so there could be peace in the family, so too Joseph had to change. We have already seen that Joseph became more modest and more sensitive to other people. Now Joseph was in a position of great power and he could have taken revenge on his brothers for the terrible thing they did to him. But in order to make peace Joseph had to let go of the feelings of hurt and anger he must have felt towards them.

Only after Joseph finished speaking and the brothers kissed and wept were they "able to talk to him." Twenty-two years earlier the Torah told us that Joseph's brothers "hated him so much they could not speak a friendly word to him." Not talking to each other – that breakdown in communication – had terrible consequences. Perhaps the story of Joseph and his brothers teaches us that no matter how angry or upset we may feel with people in our family, it is important we keep talking to each other.

Ch.45: 16 – 28 Pharaoh heard that Joseph's brothers had come and he was pleased. And Pharaoh said to Joseph, "Say to your brothers – go and bring your father and all the rest of your family to Egypt. I will give you the best of the land in Egypt and any possessions you need. You will settle in the land of Goshen."

Joseph has hinted to Pharaoh that Goshen would be a good place to settle his family, and indeed here Pharaoh tells Joseph to settle the family there. A Scholar of our Time explains that the name Goshen comes from the same word as *Vayigash* – "he came close." Goshen is a place named for the brothers to come close to each other.

Another Scholar of our Time explains why Goshen was a good place for the Children of Israel to settle. The Children of Israel worked as shepherds and Goshen had good grazing land. But Egyptians themselves did not work as shepherds and so did not live in that area. By settling together in one place, where few Egyptians lived, the Children of Israel were less likely to lose their own identity and more able to keep their own traditions and language during the many years they were in Egypt. Indeed the next book of the Torah, the Book of Exodus, tells that two hundred years later the Children of Israel still kept their own language and traditions.

Pharaoh was pleased Joseph's brothers and father had come to Egypt. Some Sages of Old suggest Pharaoh wanted the family to settle in Egypt, not just stay there until the famine was over. Pharaoh saw how talented Joseph was and so he thought that keeping his talented family in Egypt would be good for the country. Joseph himself had succeeded in Egypt by fitting into the Egyptian way of life – as prime minister he had taken an Egyptian name and Egyptian dress. But at the same time he remained connected to his family. Perhaps Pharaoh worried that if Joseph's family was in Canaan Joseph would not be completely focused on his job as prime minister of Egypt and would think about returning there one day. But with his family in Egypt Joseph would stay. This is the beginning of the story we know from Pesach and the Haggadah where the Pharaoh wants to keep the Children of Israel in Egypt. In future time they will become slaves to a new Pharaoh who insists, "I will not let them go."

Land of Goshen: "The area of Israelite settlement in Egypt is known by the name of Goshen in the Bible texts. Joseph suggested the district because of its proximity to his own residence and its excellent grazing facilities. It must have been located in the north-eastern part of the Delta... The data given in the book of Exodus confirm that the land of Goshen was quite near the frontier, and that a 'mixed multitude' of non-Egyptians also resided there. At the same time, since sheep-rearing was an unpopular occupation few Egyptians apparently occupied the region." Nahum Sarna

Joseph the Assimilationist: "Yosef was indeed an assimilationist... but 'assimilate' has two quite contrary meanings. In its primary sense, as a transitive verb, assimilate means 'to take in and appropriate; to absorb into the system.' Only in its tertiary definition, as an intransitive verb, does it mean 'to become assimilated'. Yosef achieved the breathtaking breadth of such assimilating identity in his own life, and this became the pattern for all the hues and tones of the varied exiles of Yisroel." R. Matis Weinberg

Joseph the family provider: "Because of what he has accomplished and the position he has acquired, Joseph has the power and assumes the obligation to preserve his family through the five years of famine still ahead... His brothers and their families – Joseph's entire clan – are totally dependant on him for survival. In this time of famine, he is the one sheaf of wheat still standing." Naomi Rosenblatt

? A Scholar of our Time calls Goshen – "The ghetto of choice." In what ways was Goshen like the ghettos centuries later in Europe? In what ways was it different?

How shall we tell him? "It is passing strange that we shall have to talk to him out of something we once talked him into by means of the bloodstained garment..." Thomas Mann

The truth of a poem: "A poignant Midrashic tradition has it that Jacob is told of Joseph's survival and identity, not by the brothers themselves, but by a young girl, Serah, the daughter of Asher... The effect of music, of rhyme is to induce a dreamlike state, where ideas penetrate, though conscious reason repudiates them. This gives Jacob breathing space, as it were, to adjust gradually to the truth of the poem." Avivah Zornberg

? Remember when the brothers took Joseph's coat of many colors dipped in blood and showed it to Jacob? Now they have to convince Jacob that Joseph is actually alive. How would you break that news gently to Jacob?

Ch.45: 25 – 28 So the brothers went from Egypt to the land of Canaan to Jacob their father. When they came to Jacob and told him, "Joseph is still alive and he rules over the whole land of Egypt," Jacob nearly fainted. He was so shocked he could hardly believe them. But when they told him all that Joseph had said, and when he saw the wagons that Joseph had sent, Jacob's spirit was revived. "My son Joseph is alive!" he exclaimed. "I must go and see him before I die."

Imagine what it would be like for Jacob to be told that Joseph is still alive. For twenty-two years Jacob has believed Joseph to be dead – he cried and mourned for him a long time. Now suddenly he is told that Joseph is alive and well and not only that, he is prime minister of Egypt! It is no wonder Jacob nearly fainted.

Midrash tells that the brothers tried to break the news gently to Jacob, and so reduce his sense of shock. They asked Serah, Jacob's young grand-daughter, to play on her harp and sing Jacob a rhyme about Joseph alive in Egypt. As Jacob listened to the song the idea that Joseph was alive drifted into his mind. And so when he saw the brothers and their wagons and they told him the news Jacob was still shocked but his "spirit was revived."

Ch.46: 1 – 4 **So Jacob set out to Egypt with all his family and he came to Beer-Sheva. There God appeared to Jacob in a vision in the night calling out, "Jacob, Jacob." "Here I am," answered Jacob. And God said, "I am God, the God of your father. Do not be afraid to go down to Egypt, for I will make you a great nation there. I Myself will go down with you to Egypt. And I Myself will bring you up."**

God appeared to Jacob in a night vision calling him, "Jacob, Jacob" and Jacob answered, "Here I am." This reminds us of when God called, "Abraham, Abraham" and Abraham too answered, "Here I am." We feel that something important is about to happen.

Why did God tell Jacob, "Do not be afraid to go down to Egypt"? The story does not describe Jacob as being afraid – what did he have to be afraid of? He was going to see his long-lost son, to a land of plenty, to live under the protection of the prime minister of Egypt. Sages of Old explain that Jacob was not afraid for himself as an individual. Rather he was afraid for the future of the Children of Israel as a nation. Perhaps in Egypt they would enjoy the life of comfort and ease, and not want to return to the Promised Land. Perhaps they would forget their covenant with God and become Egyptians.

Do not be afraid: "Jacob fears that his family's identity may be too fragile to stand up to the temptations of the cosmopolitan Egyptian culture. He's no doubt haunted by the prophecy God spoke to his grandfather Abraham: 'Know well that your offspring shall be strangers in a land not theirs, and they shall be enslaved and oppressed four hundred years.'" Naomi Rosenblatt

In darkness: "This final revelation to Jacob is shrouded in the darkness of impending exile, weighted down by the fears of physical and spiritual bondage, 'in the visions of the night.' The sole ray of light is the Divine promise: 'I will also surely bring thee up again.'" Nehama Leibowitz

The night of exile: God "appeared unto him in the visions of the night, to make him understand that the time had come to shoulder the yoke of exile, that is termed 'night.' The world is then darkened and deprived of the holy spirit, which manifests only for brief periods, according to need, just as lightning flashes punctuate the dark." Ha'amek Davar

? Sages of Old explain that Jacob was afraid for the future of the Children of Israel – that they would enjoy the life of comfort and ease in Egypt and become Egyptians. What parallels can you see for this fear today?

Not just a family visit: "This divine communication serves the purpose of transforming the descent to Egypt from a family visit into an event of national significance, which has its preordained place in God's scheme of things." Nahum Sarna

Prototype of exile: "Ya'akov and his children leave the land of Canaan to join Yosef in Egypt, beginning the first of the exiles prophesied to Abraham: 'Your children shall be strangers in a foreign land' (ch 15 vs 13), prototype of exiles to come." R. Matis Weinberg

Born in exile: "The Torah appears to explain the foundations of Israel's existence through this interplay of divine play and human decision. It shows God knowingly sending His children into Egypt and into subsequent oppression... In Canaan the people of Israel could not or would not become what they were destined to be..." Gunther Plaut

? Remember God has appeared to Jacob in a vison before, in Jacob's dream of the ladder with the angels. How is this vision of God similar to, and also different from, the earlier vision?

What does God mean by saying, "I Myself will go down with you to Egypt. And I Myself will bring you back"? We shall soon see that Jacob dies in Egypt. God does not bring him back to Canaan. A Scholar of our Time explains that God is not speaking to Jacob only, God is speaking to the Children of Israel as a nation. God promises to go with them into exile, and then in the future – after they become slaves in Egypt – God promises to bring them out and take them back to the Promised Land.

The Torah tells us that God came to Jacob in a vision in the night. Why do you think God chose to appear to Jacob in the night? Perhaps the darkness of this vision hints at the darkness of the years of slavery awaiting the Children of Israel.

God's last ever words to Jacob, and indeed to all the Patriarchs and Matriarchs in Genesis are: "I Myself will go down with you to Egypt. And I Myself will bring you back." This is God's promise.

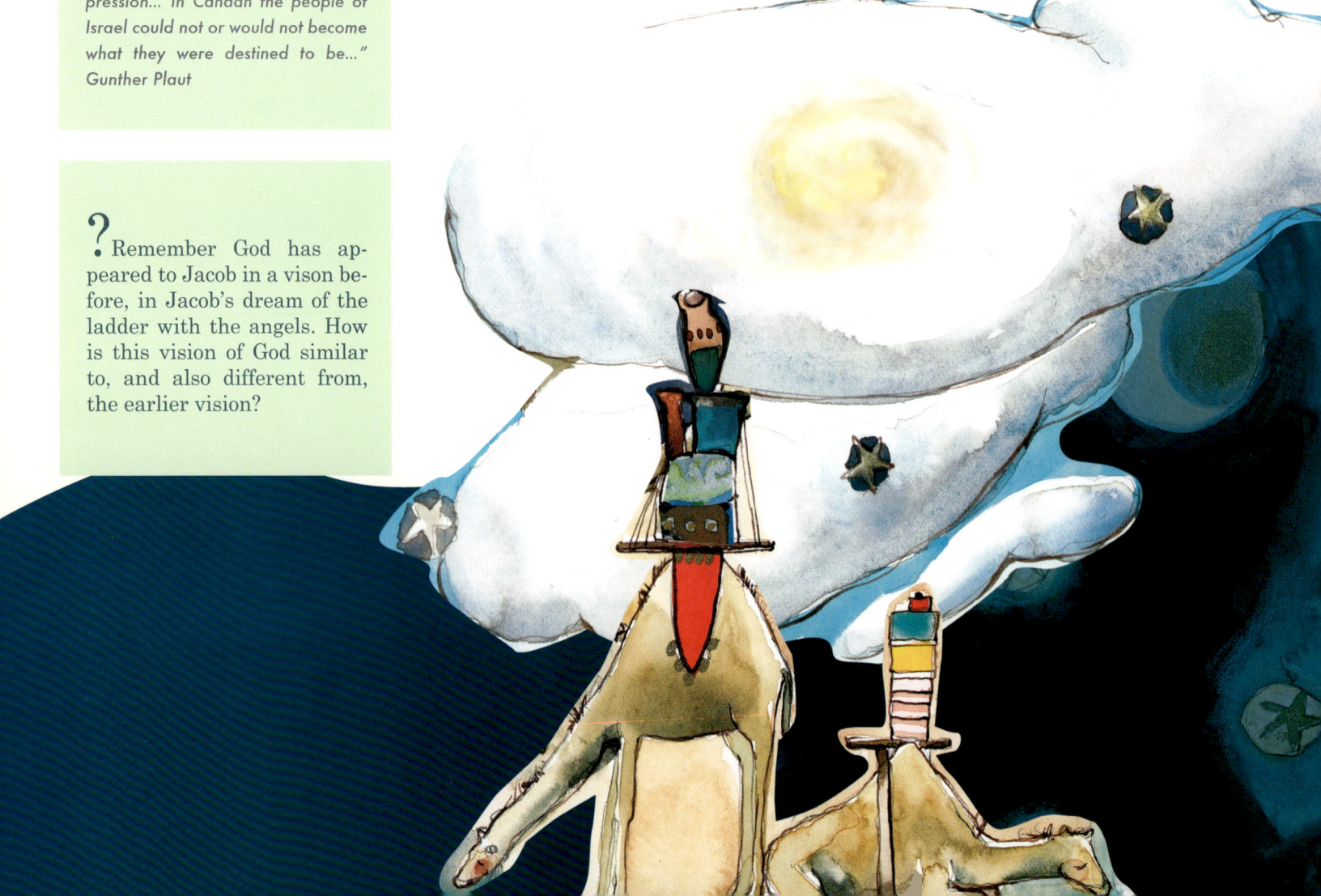

Ch.46: 5 – 31 Ch.47: 29 – 30 **So Jacob and all his family, seventy people in all, went down to Egypt. They went with all their possessions and their animals and many wagons. And Joseph went to meet his father and hugged him and wept for a long time. Then Jacob said to Joseph, "Now I can die, having seen for myself that you are still alive." So the Children of Israel settled in the land of Eygpt, in Goshen, and they made it their own, and they grew and multiplied greatly.**

The Torah lists the names of all the people who went down to Egypt – all of Jacob's family. There were Leah's sons and grandchildren, Rachel's sons and grandchildren and the sons and grandchildren of their two handmaids. But if you add up all the names they come to sixty-nine people – not the seventy people the Torah says went down to Egypt. Who is the missing seventieth person?

A Midrash tells that the seventieth person is Yocheved, Moses' mother. She was not born yet when the family left Canaan but was born just as they were entering the gates of Egypt. What timing! Just as the Children of Israel were entering the land of Egypt – the mother of Moses, who will be the one to lead them out is born!

Alternatively a Sage of Old suggests that the seventieth person is not Yocheved but is actually God! Remember God said to Jacob, "I myself will go down with you to Egypt."

Seventy is a special number in the Torah: Seventy people went down to Egypt. The Sages of Old also tell that there are seventy nations in the world. Just as each of the seventy nations has its own unique role to play in history so each of the seventy members of Jacob's family had their own role to play in the growth of the Children of Israel as a nation.

Only seventy Children of Israel went down to Egypt but the next book of the Torah, the Book of Exodus, tells us that when they left Egypt the Children of Israel numbered six hundred thousand! This shows us just how much they grew and multiplied in the two hundred years they were in Egypt. As we read in the Haggadah at Pesach, "With seventy souls your fathers went down to Egypt, but now God has made you as numerous as the stars of the heavens."

Seventy nations: The Talmudic tradition that there are seventy primary nations in the world is based on the listing of Noah's seventy descendants – those who became the ancestors of the new world after the flood. According to the Mishnah just as there were seventy nations, so the words of the Torah engraved on the Tablets were written in seventy languages so that all the nations might read them.

? Seventy is a special number in the Torah and Jewish tradition. Do you know what numbers seventy?

- Seventy people went down to Egypt

- Noah had seventy descendants

- There are seventy nations in the world (based on Noah's seventy descendants)

- There are seventy languages, and the Torah was written in seventy languages so all the nations could read it.

- The Torah has seventy faces – seventy different ways of interpreting and understanding the letters, words and stories of the Torah. Here in "Genesis - the Book with Seventy Faces" you can discover some of those faces!

Coming Close

The story of Joseph and his brothers is the longest story in the whole of the Book of Genesis. This is already the third parasha about Joseph and his brothers.

This parasha is about people coming close to one another. The very name of the parasha, Vayigash, means "And he came close." In the beginning Judah came close to Joseph and then, later Joseph tells his brothers "come close to me." And the name of the place where the Children of Israel settle in Egypt, Goshen, comes from the same word. So the parasha is about family members who have been hurt and angry, who do not talk to each other, and how they come close with each other again.

How do you make peace with people who have hurt you? It took twenty-two long years for this family to come close again. And this could only happen after all of the brothers had changed.

In the story Judah is the clearest example of the change in the brothers. Judah, the brother who once suggested selling Joseph as a slave, is now prepared to become a slave himself to save his younger brother. In the deepest possible way Judah and the brothers have learned that brothers need to be responsible for one another.

But what does true change mean? Judaism calls it *teshuva* – repentance. Rambam, the great Rabbi, philosopher and doctor from the twelfth century explained that true change only comes about when a person is placed in the same situation where he or she once behaved wrongly and then chooses to behave differently. This is how Joseph tested his brothers – to see if they would abandon Benjamin as a slave the same way they had abandoned him as a slave. Judah's changed behaviour convinced Joseph that his test had gone far enough – his brothers had truly changed and now Joseph could reveal himself to them. Repentance is expressed not in words but in actions. In the thousands of years since the Torah was given, Judah's behaviour continues to be an example of *teshuva* – true change.

As we have seen Joseph too had to change before there could be peace between the brothers. A Scholar of our Time, author and Nobel Peace prizewinner Elie Wiesel writes, "It is not easy to resist dealing out deserved punishment. Only a Tzaddik forgives without forgetting. By forgiving his brothers and promising to care for their children, Joseph finally becomes a Tzaddik, a righteous man… one is not born a Tzaddik, one must strive to become one. And having become a Tzaddik, one must strive to remain one."

Can you notice something different about the end of this parasha? The Torah always has a space between one parasha and the next. In this book that space is shown by a double page picture and an empty page. But there is no space between this parasha and the next one. When you read the next parasha you will find out why.

ויחי

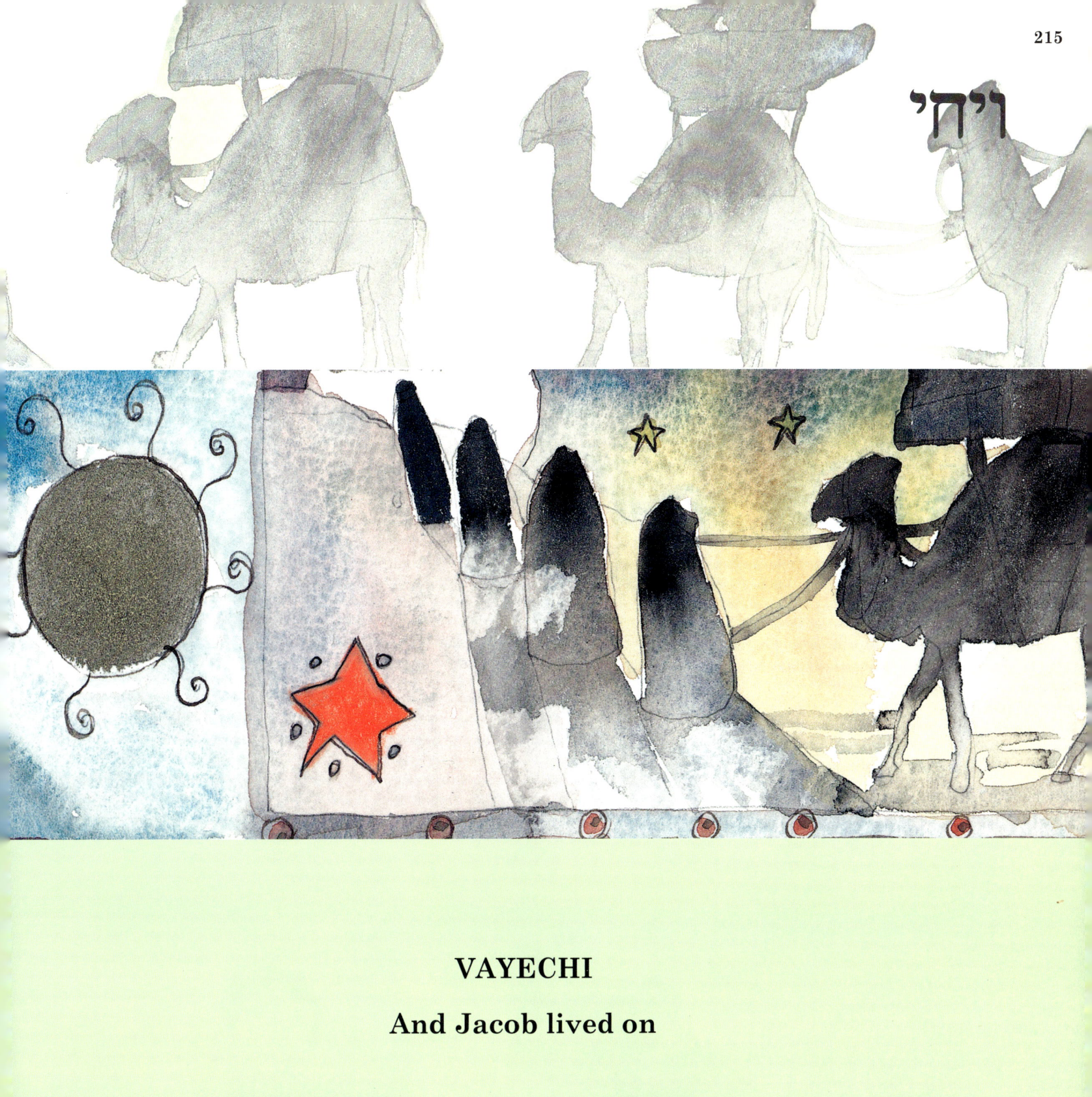

VAYECHI
And Jacob lived on

Deathbed scene: "In speaking to define a reality that he is about to leave, Jacob is unique among the patriarchs. His is, in fact, the only deathbed scene in Genesis, indeed in the whole Torah…. Abraham's death, for instance, is simply narrated after a summary of his years. As the Midrash notices, he conspicuously fails to bless his children… Isaac's death is narrated as following on Jacob's return from Padan Aram. His 'deathbed' blessing to Jacob, masquerading as Esau, occurred twenty-two years earlier." Avivah Zornberg

Jacob's death drew near: Rashi explains that one should fear death during the five year period before and after the age at which one's parents had died. Many people do experience a strange feeling of anxiety and fatefulness as they approach and then pass the age at which their parents died.

Numbers count: "The use of numerical symmetry is Scripture's way of conveying the conviction that the formative age in Israel's history was not a series of haphazard incidents but the fulfillment of God's grand design… the life spans of the three patriarchs constitute a number series when factored; the coefficients decrease by two, while the squared numbers increase by one." Nahum Sarna

? Do you think it is better to die without warning, in your sleep, or in an accident? Or is it better to know ahead of time, so you can prepare for your death?

Ch.47: 28 – 29   Jacob lived seventeen years in the land of Egypt so the span of his life came to one hundred and forty-seven years. And when Jacob's death drew near he called his son Joseph to him.

When the Torah tells us the specific number of things (Jacob lived seventeen years in Egypt, he was one hundred and forty-seven years old when he died) there is a special meaning to the numbers.

Sages of Old tell that Jacob looked after Joseph for seventeen years when Joseph was a child. And now when Jacob is old Joseph looks after him for seventeen years in Egypt. Parents look after their children when they are young and then the cycle of life turns and often children look after their parents when they are old.

Jacob died when he was one hundred and forty-seven years old, Isaac died when he was one hundred and eighty years old and Abraham died when he was one hundred and seventy-five years old. There is a pattern in the ages of the patriarchs – if you are very brilliant at math you might be able to work it out. You can check out the pattern in the endnotes.

Jacob knew he was going to die: "The days of Jacob's death drew near." He is the first person in the Torah who is described as knowing he will die soon. A Midrash tells that before Jacob's death people died suddenly without becoming sick or weak. But Jacob asked God to become sick before he died so he would have time to prepare for his death. This story tells how Jacob prepared.

Ch.47: 29–31, Ch.48: 7 Jacob asked Joseph, "Swear to me that you will not bury me in Egypt. But instead when I die bury me with my parents and grandparents in their burial place. Even though your mother Rachel died when I was traveling back to Canaan, on the road to Efrat, and I had to bury her there on the roadside." And Joseph swore to him.

The story tells us that the place where a person is buried is special, and so it was very important for Jacob not to be buried in Egypt. In the last parasha, the Midrash told us that Jacob was worried about his family getting stuck in Egypt. After seventeen years Jacob saw that his family really was settled very comfortably in Egypt. So Jacob asked to be buried back in the Promised Land to remind them of their homeland. It is as though Jacob is saying to his family, "You may want to live and prosper in Egypt, but I do not wish even to be buried here." For Jacob it is important to be buried with his family in the Cave of Machpela, in the land that God had promised to the Children of Israel.

Why did Jacob suddenly remember and talk about Rachel's death now? Sages of Old explain that Jacob felt bad about Rachel's burial and apologized to Joseph that his own mother was not buried with the rest of the family. Even though Jacob did not manage to bury Rachel in the Cave of Machpela he asked Joseph to make sure he would be buried there.

Perpetual reminder: "He (Jacob) was not afraid of the persecution and the bondage that had been foretold to his forefather Abraham, but rather of the wealth and prosperity that might turn their heads and cause them to repudiate their national destiny to leave Egypt for the Promised Land. That this was Jacob's chief concern is indicated quite clearly from his last words to his favorite son Joseph. He insisted that Joseph should bury his remains in the Holy Land as a perpetual reminder to his descendants of their true homeland which they should always aspire to reach." Nehama Leibowitz

Imagining Jacob's thoughts: Rachel died and I had to bury her on the road to Efrat – "I was so overcome by grief that I could not collect myself to take her to the ancestral tomb at Hebron, but there is no doubt that since then there had been a void in my heart." Sforno

Standing by: "Rachel then is portrayed as the symbol of the Matriarch of Israel standing by to protect her descendants on their way into exile and interceding on their behalf for their eventual return to the homeland." Nehama Leibowitz

? Do you think the place where a person is buried is important?

Ch.48: 3,7,21 And Jacob said to Joseph, "God appeared to me in the land of Canaan and blessed me, saying: 'I will make you many and I give you this land to be yours, for your children and your children's children forever more.' Now I am about to die. But God will be with you and bring you back to the land of your fathers."

This is the special blessing that God gave to Abraham, and then to Isaac and then to Jacob. It is the special blessing God gives to the Jewish people, "I will make you many and I give you this land." Now Jacob passes this blessing on to his son Joseph.

Ch.48: 1 – 2 Some time later Joseph was told, "Your father is sick." So Joseph took his two sons Manasseh and Ephraim to visit him. When they came, Jacob gained some strength and sat up in bed.

Why do you think Joseph took his two sons with him to visit Jacob? Perhaps Joseph wanted to show his sons how important it is to visit a sick person, and especially look after your parents when they are sick. Maybe Joseph wanted his sons to spend some more time with their grandfather, enjoy and learn from him, before he died. Or perhaps Joseph knew that having his grandchildren near him would cheer up Jacob. Indeed the Torah tells that when they came, Jacob gained strength and sat up in bed.

This is the second time in Genesis we read of visiting the sick – remember the first time was when God visited Abraham after his circumcision. These stories emphasize how important it is to visit a sick person, and not leave them lying in bed on their own. In fact Midrash tells that whoever visits a sick person helps them feel one sixtieth better!

Visiting the sick: Recognizing how psychologically important it is that the sick not feel abandoned, the Rabbis declared that whoever visits a sick person removes one sixtieth of his illness (Bava Mezia 30b), while he who ignores a sick person hastens his death. An extensive series of ordinances and suggestions were drawn up to guide people making sick calls. Most of the laws have little to do with ritual, being mainly concerned with interpersonal sensitivity. "Enter the room cheerfully," the medieval Rabbi Eliezer of Worms taught, "Because an invalid carefully monitors the reactions of visitors, and any look of shock on a guest's face will be terribly demoralizing." R. Joseph Telushkin

Helping to change bandages: R Joshua Ben Levi asked the prophet Elijah, "Where shall I find the Mesiah?" "At the gate of the city," Elijah replied. "How shall I recognize him?" "He sits among the lepers." "Among the lepers?" cried Rabbi Joshua. "What is he doing there?" "He changes their bandages," Elijah answered. "He changes them one by one." Babylonian Talmud

? In what way does visiting a sick person help them feel better?

A sort of knowledge: "I know, my son, I know" answers many specific unspoken anxieties; but its resonance seems to transcend such specifics... it evokes Jacob's own most radical experience of firstborns displaced, of deception and error in the context of blessing. An intimate and ultimate sense of order radiates from these words, a patriarchal confidence..." Avivah Zornberg

Binding: "The words of a dying man are as binding as a deed which is written and delivered." Talmud

Right or left: "In most cultures the right hand takes linguistic and emotional preference over the left e.g. in English "right" also means just; while "left" has negative meanings." Gunther Plaut

Needing a blessing: Ephraim's pre-eminence was not the result of Jacob's blessing, rather it was because Ephraim was destined for more greatness that he needed a more intensive blessing. Whoever plays a more prominent role needs more of a blessing so that he can carry out his mission successfully. Haamek Davar

Ch.48: 8 – 14   Jacob said to Joseph, "Bring the boys close to me so I may bless them." Now Jacob's eyes were dim with age so he could not see well. Joseph brought the boys close and Jacob kissed them and hugged them. "I had not thought to see your face again, and here God has let me see your children as well."

And Jacob stretched out his right hand and laid it on Ephraim's head, though he was the younger, and he laid his left hand on Manasseh's head, thus crossing his hands, for Manasseh was the first-born. When Joseph saw this it seemed wrong to him and he tried to move Jacob's right hand from Ephraim to Manasseh, saying, "Not so, my father; Manasseh is the first-born. Lay your right hand on his head." But Jacob refused, saying, "I know, my son, I know. He too will become a tribe and he too shall be great. But his younger brother shall be greater than he."

What is going on here with the crossing of hands? Sages of Old tell that the custom in those days was that a father blessed his older son with his right hand on his head. But Jacob put his right hand on the second-born, Ephraim's, head. Was Jacob old and blind and making a mistake? That's what Joseph thought and so he tried to move Jacob's hand. But Jacob knew what he was doing ,"I know, my son, I know." He wanted to give the first-born blessing to Ephraim – but why?

Sages of Old explain that the Hebrew word used for crossing *sikel* is very similar to the Hebrew word for wisdom *sekhel*. And so when Jacob crossed his hands, "He guided his hands with understanding and wisdom." Jacob's answer "I know, my son, I know" with its repetition and its certainty seems to speak not only of Ephraim and Manasseh but also of other stories in their family history. Many years ago in his father's tent, Jacob had been blessed ahead of his older brother Esav. And now Jacob blesses Joseph's younger son ahead of the older. It is as though the same moment is repeating itself. When Jacob says "I know", what he knows is that sometimes it is right to change the blessings around. He knows now that it was right that he and not Esav received the blessing of the firstborn. It was right that he and not Esav had the responsibility to carry on God's covenant. So it was meant to be.

Although Jacob blessed Ephraim before Manasseh, the younger before the older, the story does not tell of jealousy and anger between them as there was between Esav and Jacob. Perhaps this is a story where the brothers accepted the differences between them and both knew that one was more suited to be a leader than the other.

My father's God: "Jacob speaks of the God of his father; this is his link with the past. God is his Lord because of tradition – but not only because of tradition. He is his God also through personal experience and relationship. This remains the basic nature of Jewish worship: God is approached as the God of history, especially Jewish history, but beyond that each generation has to rediscover for itself the God who was the God of the Father." Gunther Plaut

Renewing connections: "Blessing one's children was ordained in the Torah, when Jacob gave two of his grandchildren and then twelve of his children a personalized blessing... In recent centuries many parents have begun to bless their children every Shabbat and holiday eve. Using the words of the priestly benediction they place both hands on the head of each child... In formulating a personal blessing, you may wish to acknowledge what you most admire in your child or express a particular wish for that child." Noam Zion

Blessing the children: For a boy: May God make you like Ephraim and Mannaseh. For a girl: May God make you like Sarah, Rebbeca, Rachel and Leah. For all: May God bless you and guard you. May God's face shine on you and be gracious to you. May God's face smile at you and grant you peace.

Ch.48: 15 – 16, 20 And so Jacob blessed Joseph's sons: "The God in whose ways my fathers Abraham and Isaac walked, the God who has been my shepherd all my life long to this day, the angel who has protected me from all harm. Bless these boys and make them grow to be many on the earth. And when the Children of Israel bless their sons they shall say 'May God make you like Ephraim and Manasseh.'"

Jacob's blessing to his grandsons is very personal – he speaks of shepherds and angels, things he knows about. What does Jacob mean by calling God "my shepherd?" A shepherd looks after the sheep from the day they are born to the day they die. He protects the sheep from predators, leading them to fields of grass to eat, guiding them away from danger. So Jacob felt God looked after him. Jacob knew very well what being a shepherd involved – he had worked hard as a shepherd for over twenty years.

Jacob had a lot of experience with angels as well. Remember his dream with the angels climbing up and down the ladder – the angels who would look after him on his journey as he ran away from his brother's anger. And then the angels appeared again to protect Jacob as he crossed back into Canaan, returning to his parents' home. So Jacob knew what it was to be protected by angels.

Jacob's blessings have a special place in Jewish tradition. Every night before closing your eyes there is a prayer that asks "the angel who has protected me from all harm" to look after you as you sleep. The idea of parents blessing their children has also remained. After making the blessings over the wine and challah on Shabbat evening, some parents bless their children. They bless their sons by saying, "May God make you like Ephraim and Manashe" and their daughters by saying, "May God make you like Sarah, Rebecca, Rachel and Leah."

Ch.49: 1 – 28 Then Jacob called all his sons and said, "Gather together so I can tell you what will happen at the end of days. Keep together and listen my sons, listen to Israel your father." And Jacob blessed his sons – he blessed each one in turn, speaking to each of his strengths and his weaknesses, his past and his future. And so Jacob blessed Reuben, Simeon, Levi, Judah, Zebulun, Issachar, Dan, Gad, Asher, Naftali, Joseph and Benjamin, each with his own special blessing; all these sons who would later grow to become the tribes of Israel, twelve in number.

Jacob blessed each son personally But even as he spoke to each one as an individual he emphasized how important it was that they stay together as brothers. By telling his sons to "gather together" and "keep together" he reminded them that they will be strong as a people only if they are united, understanding their shared past and future. And so a people can be made up of individuals who are all very different but are still bonded together.

What does Jacob mean when he calls his sons to tell them what will happen "at the end of days?" Sages of Old explain that Jacob had wanted to tell his family what would happen to them in the future, what their destiny as a people would be. He wanted to reveal to them a good future waiting for them at the end of the difficulties of their journey. But he does not tell them about any future. Instead he blesses each son individually. What happened to Jacob's vision of the future? As he lay dying Jacob had a glimpse of the future and a knowledge of what would be, but that vision lasted only a few moments and then disappeared. His glimpse into the future was closed.

This closing up of Jacob's vision into the future has been built into the very way this parasha is written in the Torah. In the Torah there is always a division between one parasha and the next – some empty lines and white space are left to separate between them. In this book that division is shown by a double page picture and an empty page separating one parasha from the next. But there is no such division between the last parasha, Vayigash, and this one. Such a parasha, where there is no division, is called a "closed parasha" – *parasha stuma*. The parasha is "closed", like Jacob's vision into the future.

Blessing : "The most enduring legacy we can bequeath to our children is a clear articulation of who we are and what we stand for... if we can make clear to our children who we are, where we have come from, and what we value, then they can begin to build their own personal identity based on a solid foundation." Naomi Rosenblatt

God departed : "He wished to reveal the end to them but the Presence of God departed from him, and he began to say other things." Rashi

Closed vision : "Why should Jacob have wanted to reveal the date of the end of days to his sons? Because exile is easier to bear if one knows in advance when it will end. But God wanted Israel's exile to be difficult and therefore He closed Jacob's vision from him so that the Children of Israel should not learn the date of their final redemption." R. Simchah Bunam

? Jacob told his sons to "Keep together." Do you think it is important for brothers and sisters to stay together?

Life's completion: "Jacob sees his life spread before him. He is aware of the continued presence of God and acknowledges it with deep feeling. Past and future are now fused… His life is completed; the blessing of Abraham, which Isaac bestowed on him, has now passed down." Gunther Plaut

Gathered to my people: The verb asaf "gather" often connotes the ingathering of an object to its proper place. Whenever it is stated in reference to death it connotes this ingathering of souls. Rashi

Gathering souls: The Yizkor prayer is said in synagogue to recall the souls of the departed. In this prayer we ask that the soul of the departed be "bound up in the Bond of Life, together with the souls of Abraham, Isaac, and Jacob; Sarah, Rebecca, Rachel, and Leah; and together with the other righteous men and women in the Garden of Eden."

? What do you think about the idea that when a person dies their soul goes to join the other souls in heaven?

Ch.49: 29 – 33   And Jacob instructed his sons saying, "I am about to be gathered to my people. Bury me with my fathers in the Cave of Machpela. There Abraham and Sarah, Isaac and Rebecca were buried and there I buried Leah." When Jacob finished his instructions to his sons he breathed his last breath and was gathered to his people.

As Jacob blessed his children he gives us an example of passing on what you have learnt in life to those coming after you. Jacob again tells his sons to bury him with the family, in the cave that Abraham bought. He wants to make sure the next generation will not forget where they had come from. And so Jacob's instructions for his burial and his blessings for his sons tie together the past and the future of the family.

What does Jacob mean when he says, "I am about to be gathered to my people?" Sages of Old explain that he means he will join his ancestors who have died before him and his soul will be gathered together with all the other souls. You may remember (from the first parasha Bereshit) that before a baby is born a soul is chosen especially for that person from all the souls gathered in heaven. And so when a person dies, his or her soul returns again to join the souls in heaven.

Ch.50: 1 – 14 Joseph wept over his father and kissed him. Then he ordered the doctors to embalm him. And the Egyptians mourned Jacob for seventy days. Then Joseph and his brothers and all their families went to bury Jacob, and with them went all Pharaoh's officials and the elders of Egypt. And when they reached the land of Canaan they mourned for Jacob another seven days. And they buried him in the Cave of Machpela. Then Joseph and all his brothers, and all who had gone to bury Jacob, returned to Egypt.

Eyes closed: "When Jacob died the eyes of Israel became, as it were, closed, because then they really entered into exile and the Egyptians enslaved them." Zohar

The closed life of slavery: "For when Jacob our father died, the eyes and hearts of Israel were closed because of the affliction of the bondage with which the Egyptians began to afflict them." Rashi "...slavery brings with it, even in its incipient stage, a condition in which the victims are diminished in their basic ability to read and understand their own reality." Avivah Zornberg

---

Still today when someone dies, we sit Shiva for seven days to mourn them, as the brothers mourned for Jacob seven days in the land of Canaan. So the Jewish custom of seven days of mourning dates back to this story.

A Midrash tells that when Joseph was coming back from his father's funeral he made a detour and visited the pit where long ago his brothers had thrown him – where the story began. For a long time Joseph looked into the pit and gazed into the darkness. Joseph's brothers saw him and worried that he would become angry with them as he remembered what they had done to him. But then they saw that Joseph made a blessing – "Blessed be God who made a miracle for me in this place." Joseph thanked God for saving him from the pit. But in another way Joseph also thanked God for his time in the pit – for it was there that Joseph began his journey of change – his growth from being a teenager who thought only about himself to a wise man.

Joseph and all his brothers returned to Egypt and they ended up staying there a long time. Over time the Children of Israel became slaves in Egypt and stayed there for two hundred and ten years. Sages of Old explain that as slaves their eyes were closed because they did not understand what was happening to them.

Kabbalah explains that when a parasha is closed, and there is no white space between one parasha and the next, there is no chance to stand back and get some perspective on what is happening. In the same way the Children of Israel could not stand back and see what was happening to them, that gradually during their stay in Egypt they were becoming enslaved. And so for these reasons too this parasha, Vayehi, is closed.

? Have you gone to visit a relative or friend as they sat Shiva for seven days?

Coffin and ark: "The word for both (coffin and ark) is aron. Why? So that in their wanderings through the desert the Children of Israel would carry with them both the aron (coffin) of Joseph and the aron (ark) containing the Tablets of the Law, to show that in one aron was a man who fulfilled the commandments contained in the other." Talmud

God in Genesis: "God is not finished. His highest divine attribute is His creativeness and that which is creative exists always in the beginning stage. God is eternally in Genesis." Isaac Bashevis Singer

? Moses carried Joseph's bones all the way to the Promised Land. Do you know where Joseph's bones are buried in Israel?

Ch.50: 22 – 26 So Joseph and his family lived in Egypt, and Joseph lived to see his great grandchildren. He lived to be one hundred and ten years old. And Joseph said to his brothers, "I am about to die. God will remember you and bring you up from this land to the land promised to Abraham, Isaac and Jacob. When God remembers you, you must carry my bones from here." So Joseph made the Children of Israel promise. And Joseph died and he was embalmed and placed in a coffin in Egypt.

Like Jacob before him, it was very important for Joseph not to be buried in Egypt but rather to be buried in the Promised Land. Many, many years after Joseph's death, after the end of the Book of Genesis, the next book of the Torah, the Book of Exodus tells that Moses led the Children of Israel to the land that God promised to Abraham, to Isaac and to Jacob. And there it is written: And Moses took the bones of Joseph with him for Joseph had made the Children of Israel swear "God will surely remember you and you will carry my bones away with you." (Exodus Ch.13: 19)

The last word of the Book of Genesis is Egypt. This word is a bridge to the next book, the Book of Exodus, which tells of how the Children of Israel were slaves in Egypt until God took them out. As God had promised: "I Myself will go down with you to Egypt. And I Myself will bring you back."

So ends the Book of Genesis. It started with the creation of the world and moved on to the stories of the Patriarchs and Matriarchs, and the creation of the Children of Israel. But Genesis "Bereshit" means beginning. The Book of Genesis is only the beginning of the long story of the Children of Israel, the Jewish people.

Endings and Beginnings

The Book of Genesis tells of many things – the creation of the world and the creation of the first people. The lives of the Patriarchs and Matriarchs – Abraham and Sarah, Isaac and Rebecca, Jacob, Leah and Rachel unfold – stories of love and anger, laughter and jealousy, dreams and fears. As the Book of Genesis tells of many births so here in this parasha there is a story of death. Perhaps it is fitting that the last parasha of Genesis tells of the death of the last patriarch, Jacob. The parasha tells us, almost in slow motion, of how Jacob prepared for his death, what he wanted to pass on to his children, to those he left behind.

As we read the stories of the Patriarchs and Matriarchs we see the journeys their lives take. They go through many changes: leaving their parents' homes, confronting difficulties and challenges in the world and, with time, growing wiser. A Scholar of our Time reminds us that through their journeys two calls are heard and repeated many times throughout the Book of Genesis – Go Forth and Fear Not.

Go Forth tells us not to wait for life to come to us but to go out into the world and discover the journey of our own life. *Lech lecha* – Go Forth, Go for yourself, – Go learn, laugh, grow, make friends, be part of a family, and a community, create, help fix the world.

And together with this Fear Not. Although life is uncertain, although the future is unknown, although we all make mistakes, fear should not stop us. Each one of us was created unique with our own contribution to make to this world.

A saying tells that there are only two lasting things parents can pass on to their children. One of these is roots, an understanding of where you have come from, your history. The other is wings. So you can fly to your future.

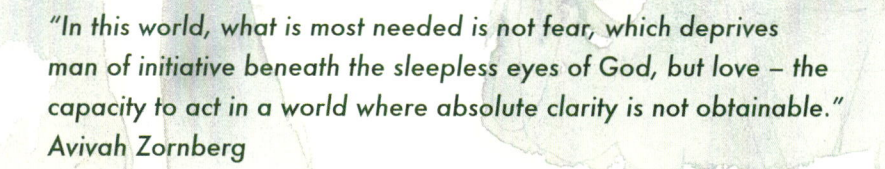

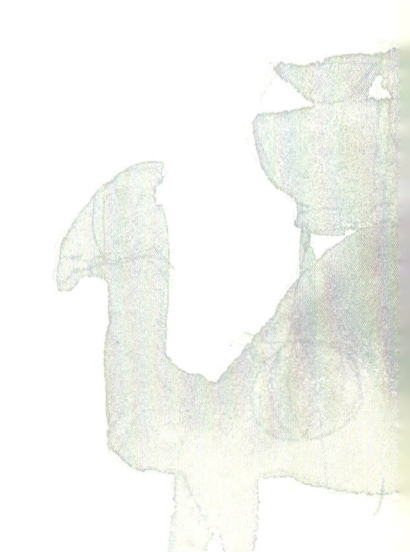

"In this world, what is most needed is not fear, which deprives man of initiative beneath the sleepless eyes of God, but love – the capacity to act in a world where absolute clarity is not obtainable."
Avivah Zornberg

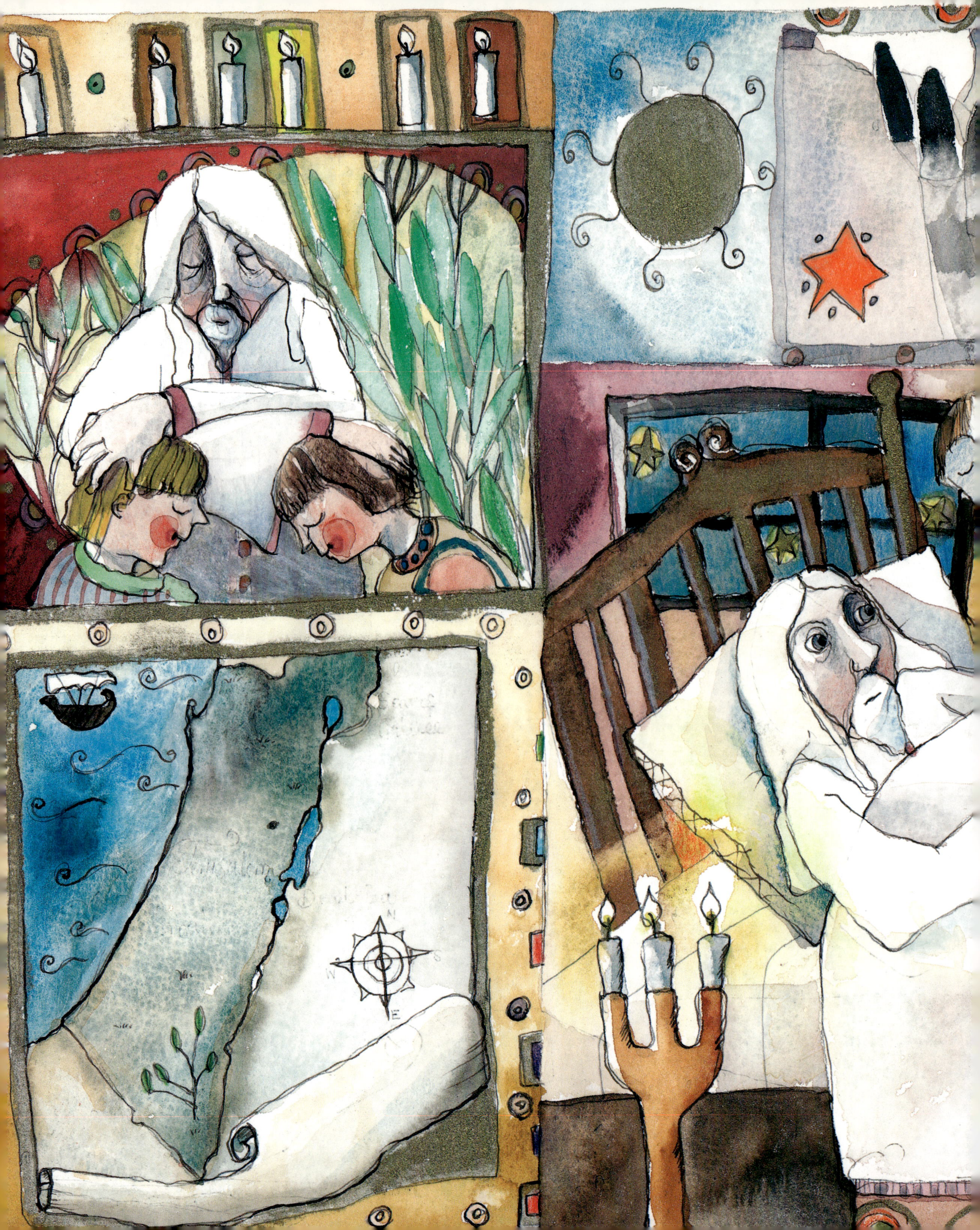
N
S
W
E

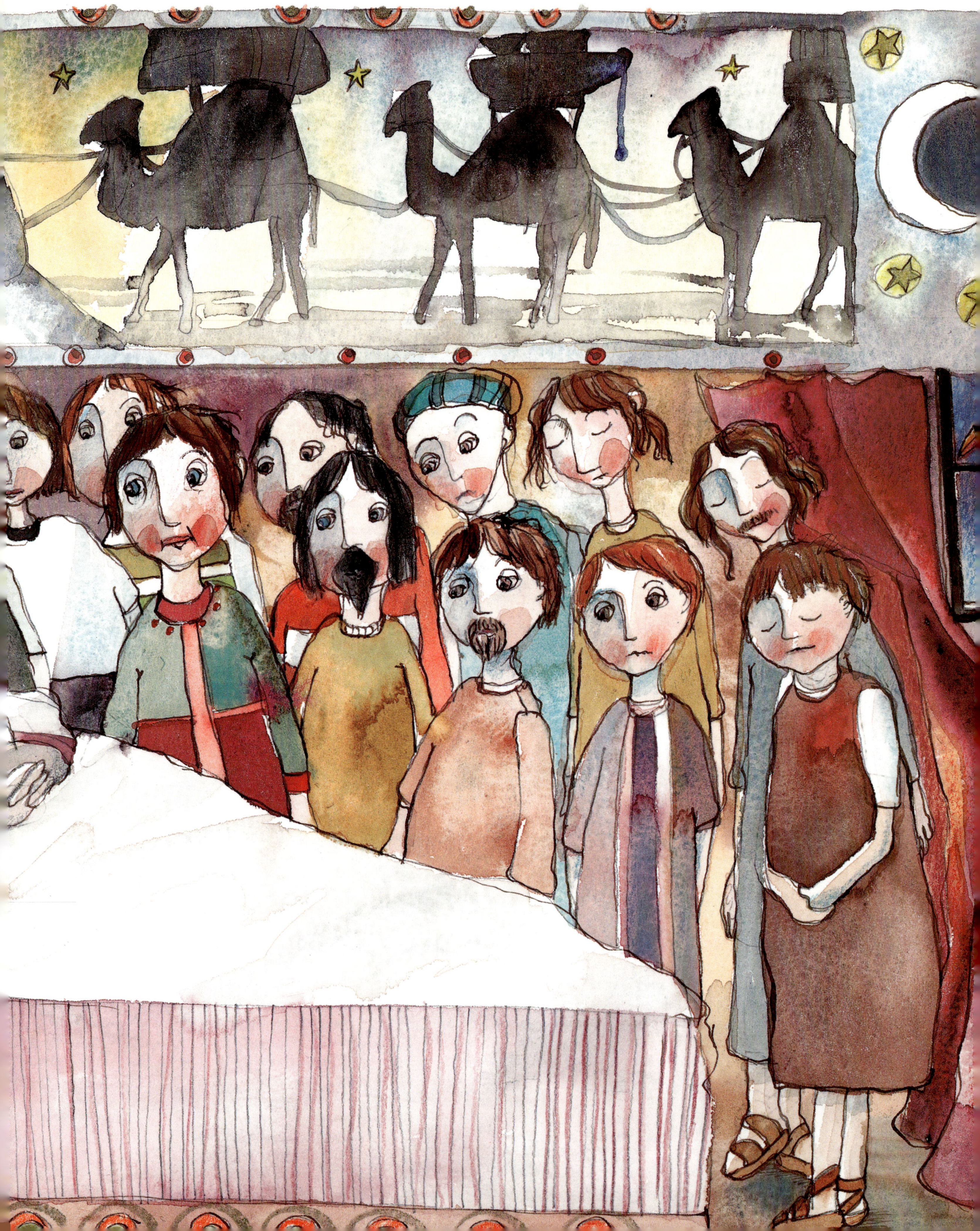

ENDNOTES

References for Sages of Old, Scholars of our Time, Midrash, Legend and Kabbalah, and references for the margin boxes (in italic and bold font as in the text) are given in the order they appear in the text of each page. Where I have been unable to confirm page numbers for quotations, I have referenced n.p. In the Endnotes R. is used in place of Rabbi.

HOW TO READ THIS BOOK Endnotes

Barry Holtz, "On Reading Jewish Texts" in *Back to the Sources: Reading the Classic Jewish Texts*
Prof Edward Greenstein, "Medieval Bible Commentaries" *ibid*, p213
Michael Rosenak, *Commandments and Concerns*, p160

BERESHIT Endnotes

P.16
Sages of Old: Avot 1:4, as cited in R. Michael L. Munk, *The Wisdom in the Hebrew Alphabet*
Intolerable chaos: R. Samson Raphael Hirsch, *Hirsch Commentary on the Torah*, p7

P.17
Scholar of our Time: R. Samson Raphael Hirsch, *Hirsch Commentary on the Torah*
Sages of Old: Sefer Habahir, Meam Loez
Kabbalah: These ideas are based on Lurrianic Kabbalah, developed by Rabbi Isaac Luria in the 6th century. For a detailed description of Lurrianic Kabbalah, see *Nine and a Half Mystics: The Kabbalah Today* by Herbert Weiner.

P.18
Sages of Old: Mishnah Avot 5:1
Midrash: Midrash Rabbah
Beyond the singular: Talmud
The dark ages: For a description of the parallel between the world before creation and the world at the time of the flood, see Nahum Sarna, *Understanding Genesis*.

P.19
Sages of Old: Rashi, Rambam
Scholar of our Time: R. Samson Raphael Hirsch, *Hirsch Commentary on the Torah*, p15
Water wheel: *ibid*, p12

P.20
Scholar of our Time: R Samson Hirsch
Sages of Old: Mishnah Chulin 5:5
Trees and us: R. Samson Raphael Hirsch, *Hirsch Commentary on the Torah*, p20

P.21
Midrash: R. Simeon Ben Pazzi
Kabbalah: Sefer Habahir

P.22
Legend: References to various strange and wondrous creatures are scattered through different sources such as Bava Basra 73b, 74b, 75a, Agudat, Psalms, and collected in Louis Ginzburg, *Legends of the Jews* and *Legends of the Bible*
Legendary Ziz: Louis Ginzburg, *Legends of the Bible*, p15

P.23
Sages of Old: R. Simeon Ben Halafta
Uncompleted: R. Simcha Burnam, quoted by Louis Newman, *The Hasidic Anthology*, p6
Ongoing pattern of creation: W. Gunther Plaut, *The Torah: A Modern Commentary*, p22

P.24
Sages of Old: Ahavat Yonatan
Midrash: Gen Rabbah 8:5
Translators' problem: Talmud (Megillah 9a)

P.25
Sages of Old: Rashi
Midrashim about the creation of the soul are found in Tanhuma Pekudai.
Body and soul; **Three souls each**: For further explanation of the concept of the soul in Jewish thought, see Gershom Scholem's *Kabbalah* (1974).

P.26
Sages of Old: Rashi, Chizkuni, Sforno
In God's image: Naomi Rosenblatt, *Wrestling with Angels*, p14
Human dignity: Leo Baeck, cited in *The Torah: a Modern Commentary*, p22

P.27
Scholars of our Time: W. Gunther Plaut, *The Torah: A Modern Commentary*
Earth and earthling: Arthur Waskow in *Torah of the Earth*, p10
Rule over the earth: Robert Gordis, cited in *The Torah: A Modern Commentary*, p25
Environmental Judaism: For more thoughts on Judaism as an ecologically responsible religion, see Arthur Waskow in *Torah of the Earth*, Chapter 13.

P.28
Sages of Old: Mishnah Sanhedrin 4:5
Sages of Old: Rashi, Abarbanel
Other Sages of Old: Targum Yonatan
Sages of Old: Rashi
Side by side: Judith Antonell, *In the Image of God*
Alone not lonely: Rabbi Soloveitchik, *The Lonely Man of Faith*

P.29
Eve and Isha: Avivah Zornberg, *The Beginning of Desire*, p303
Women's beginning: Naomi Rosenblatt, *Wrestling with Angels*, p32
A woman reveals: R. Abraham Kook, Olat Refiah 1:62

P.30
Scholar of our Time: Abraham Joshua Heschel
Sacred time: Michael Lerner, *Jewish Renewal*, p346
Hope for progress: Abraham Joshua Heschel, *The Sabbath* p28
True rest: Arthur Green, *These are the Words: A Vocabulary of Jewish Spiritual Life*, p257

NOAH Endnotes

P.36
Sages of Old: Rashi
Sages of Old: Rashi

P.38
Sages of Old and Scholars of our Time: Rashi, Avivah Zornberg, Alan Dershowitz
Scholar of our Time: R. Matis Weinberg, *Frameworks*
Spoiled world: Naomi Rosenblatt, *Wrestling with Angels*, p67
The ruin of human wickedness: Nahum Sarna, *Understanding Genesis*, p55

P.39
Sages of Old: Rashi
Safe ark: Naomi Rosenblatt, *Wrestling with Angels*, p66
Mass destruction: Avivah Zornberg, *The Beginning of Desire*, p45–46
A learning God: Alan Dershowitz, *The Genesis of Justice*, p64

P.40
Sages of Old: Rashi
Compare and contrast: Morris Adler, as cited in *The Torah: A Modern Commentary*, p65

P.41
Midrash: Targum Yonatan, Kli Yakar
Midrash: Genesis Rabbah (30:7)
Sage of Old: Rashi
The flood in other cultures: For a comparison of flood stories in other cultures, see Nahum Sarna, *Understanding Genesis*

P.42
Legends: *Legends of the Bible* by Louis Ginzberg
Scholar of our Time: Avivah Zornberg
Floating prison: Avivah Zornberg, *The Beginning of Desire*, p63
Legendary: Louis Ginzberg, *Legends of the Bible*, p75

P.43
Scholars of our Time: Nahum Sarna, *Understanding Genesis*
Scholars of our Time: Avivah Zornberg, *The Beginning of Desire*
Creation unravelling: Nahum Sarna, *Understanding Genesis*

P.44
Legends: Louis Ginzberg, *Legends of the Bible*
Scholars of our Time: R. David Cohen; R. Mordechai Gifter, *Bereshis* (Artscroll Tanach Series), vol. 1(a)
Bridge to a new world: ibid, p215
Learning to care: ibid, p216

P.45
The Sages of Old: Rashi
A renewed creation: For a description of the parallel between events after the flood and the first days of creation, see Nahum Sarna, *Understanding Genesis*

P.46
Scholar of our Time: Nahum Sarna

P.47
Midrash: As cited in R. Yehuda Nachshoni, *Studies in the Weekly Parasha*
Scholar of our Time: Naomi Rosenblatt, *Wrestling with angels*
Let out: R. Samson Raphael Hirsch, *Hirsch Commentary on the Torah*, p159

P.48
Sages of Old and Scholars of our Time: Abarbanel, Or Hachaim, Michael Lerner,
R. Matis Weinberg
Sage of Old: Abarbanel, as cited in R. Yehuda Nachshoni, *Studies in the Weekly Parasha*
Scholar of our Time: R. Matis Weinberg, *Frameworks*
Part of the food chain: ibid, p25
Lerner's vegetarianism: Michael Lerner, *Jewish Renewal*, p339–340

P.49
Sage of Old: R. Or Hachaim, as cited in Nachshoni, *Studies in the Weekly Parasha*
Scholar of our Time: Michael Lerner, *Jewish Renewal*
Temporary concession: R. Abraham Kook

P.50
Scholar of our Time: R. Matis Weinberg, *Frameworks*
A change of view: ibid, p24
Realistic view of humans: Naomi Rosenblatt, *Wrestling with Angels*, p76
Not a mirror image: R. David Hartman, *A Living Covenant*, p28
The seven Noahide laws are: no killing, no robbery, no worshipping idols, no blasphemy, no incest, no eating flesh cut from a living animal and establishing courts of justice

P.51
Scholar of our Time: R. Samson Raphael Hirsch, as cited in Nachshoni, *Studies in the Weekly Parasha*
Rainbow symbols: As discussed in Nachshoni, *Studies in the Weekly Parasha*
God in a rainbow: Midrash Rabbah (Bereshit 35)
Umbrella of trust: Naomi Rosenblatt, *Wrestling with Angels*, p73

LECH LECHA Endnotes

P.58
Scholar of our Time: Avivah Zornberg, *The Beginning of Desire*
Infertility and rootlessness: ibid, pp76–77

P.59
Midrash: Rabbah 38:13
Midrash Bhmz: *The Book of Legends* (Hayim Bialik)
Abram the iconoclast: R. Matis Weinberg, *Framework*, p49

P.60
Sages of Old: Rashi
Scholar of our Time: Haketav Vehakabbda
Self transformation: Avivah Zornberg, *The Beginning of Desire*, p78
Left behind: Anatole France, French novelist n.p.
Abraham the patriarch: Micheal Rosenak, *Tree of Life, Tree of Knowledge*, p29

P.62
Scholars of our Time: Dr. Avram Davis, *The Way of the Flame*
Sages of Old: Radak, Rambam
Kabbalah: Sefer Habahir
What does it mean to bless and be blessed?: Dr. Avram Davis, as cited in *Judaic Mysticism*, p81
Feeling blessed: Naomi Rosenblatt, *Wrestling with Angels*, p100

P.63
Midrash: Sifri
Land of blessing: Naomi Rosenblatt, *Wrestling with Angels*, p102
Believing a promise: ibid, p102

P.64
Midrash: Hagadol
Sages of Old: Rashi

P.65
Sages of Old: Sechel Tov
Good intentions but: Naomi Rosenblatt, *Wrestling with Angels*, p138
Claiming a child: Nahum Sarna, *Genesis/Bereshit: the Traditional Hebrew Text with New JPS Translation*, p119
Barrenness: Noam Zion and Steve Israel, *The Troubling Family Triangle: Sarai, Avram and Hagar*, n.p.

P.66
Midrash: Hagadol
Sages of Old: Rambam
Sages of Old: Rambam
Sages of Old: Abarbanel, Sforno
Stuck in a triangle: Dana Fewell and David Gunn Gender, *Power and Promise*, p46
Shifted status: Noam Zion and Steve Israel, *The Troubling Family Triangle: Sarai, Avram and Hagar*, n.p.

P.67
Sages of Old: Sforno
Symbol of oppression: Phyllis Trible, *Texts of Terror*, p28

P.69
Circumcision and birth: Judith Antonelli, *In the Image of God*, p270; Naomi Rosenblatt, *Wrestling with Angels*, p154
Historical context: ibid, p153

Exposed to God: Zohar 98b

P.70
Sages of Old: Rashi
Sages of Old: Ralbag
Midrash: Bereshit Rabbah 53:6
What's in a name: Nahum Sarna, *Understanding Genesis*, p130
Sarah: Miki Raver, *Listen to her Voice*, p35

VAYEIRA Endnotes
P.76
Sages of Old: Rashi, Rav Chama (Bava Metzia 86b)
Kabbalah: Sefer Habahir
Midrash: Talmud Bava Metzia 86b

P.77
Sages of Old: Rashi
Legend: Louis Ginzberg, *Legends of the Bible*
Angelic duties: based on Rashi
What a host!: Naomi Rosenblatt, *Wrestling with Angels*, p162

P.78
Midrash: Tanchuma
Midrash: Bereshit Rabbah 53:6
God's marital therapy: based on Rashi

P.79
Scholar of our Time: R. David Hartman, *A Living Covenant*
Midrash: Pirkei d'R. Eliezer
In relationship: R. David Hartman, *A Living Covenant*, p29
Moral thermometer: W. Gunther Plaut, *The Torah: A Modern Commentary*, p132

P.80
Kabbalah: Zohar
Sages of Old: Abarbanel
Scholar of our Time: R. David Hartman
Sages of Old: Akeidat Yizchak
The symphony of argument: W. Gunther Plaut, *The Torah: A Modern Commentary*, p133
The responsibility to question: Naomi Rosenblatt, *Wrestling with Angels*, pp169–170
An image problem: Rashi
Fully awake: R. David Hartman, *A Living Covenant*, p31

P.81
Sages of Old: Talmud Betsah 32b
The merit of the few: W. Gunther Plaut, *The Torah: A Modern Commentary*, p133
Timeless: Naomi Rosenblatt, *Wrestling with Angels*, p171

P.82
Midrash: Rashi
Midrash: Bava Metzia 87a
Laughter: Naomi Rosenblatt, *Wrestling with Angels*, p171
Laughable: R.Samson Hirsch, *Hirsch Commentary on the Torah*, p352

P.83
Midrash: Bereshit Sanhedrin 89b
Sage of Old: Rambam, *Guide to the Perplexed*
Advance knowledge: Prof. Uriel Simon, as cited in R. Joseph Telushkin, *Biblical Literacy*, pp37–38

P.84
Sages of Old: Rashi
Unmatched power: Elie Wiesel, *Messengers of God*, p70
Mistranslation: R. Joseph Telushkin, *Biblical Literacy*, p37

P.85
Sage of Old: Rashi

Lech lecha x 2: based on Nahum Sarna, *Understanding Genesis*
Moral conflict: R. Joseph Telushkin, *Biblical Literacy*, pp38–39

P.86
Sages of Old: Tanchuma Yashan, Sefer Hayashar
Scholar of our Time: R. Gur, Sefat Emet
Scholar of our Time: Lippman Bodoff
Imagining Abraham's internal dialogue: Lippman Bodoff, *The Binding of Isaac: Religious Murders and Kabbalah*, pp74–75
Not really God's will: R. Gur, Sefat Emet 1:67
The Sages and Sarah: *Bereshis* vol 1 (Artscroll Tanach Series), p786
Sodom and the Akeida: R. David Hartman, *A Living Covenant*, p60

P.87
Sages of Old: Sforno
Midrash: Tanhuma
Scholar of our Time: Nehama Leibowitz
Sages of Old: Sforno, Rashi
Scholar of our Time: Elie Wiesel
The old man and the river: Nehama Leibowitz, *Studies in Bereshit (Genesis)*, p195
A double-edged test: Elie Wiesel, *Messengers of God*, p91
Proceed as commanded: Lippman Bodoff, *The Binding of Isaac: Religious Murders and Kabbalah*, p73

P.88
Scholar of our Time: Elie Wiesel
Moriah and Golgotha: Elie Wiesel, *Messengers of God*, p76

P.89
Legend: *The Book of Legends* (Hayim Bialik), p41
Beating heart: Elie Wiesel, *Messengers of God*, p73
Heart wrenching: R. Joseph Telushkin, *Biblical Literacy*, p40

P.90
Scholar of our Time: R. David Hartman
Midrash: attributed to R. Menachem Mendl of Kotzk, cited in *Gabriel's Palace*
Stayed: Samuel Driver, as cited in *The Torah: a Modern Commentary*, p153
Two different models: R. David Hartman, *A Living Covenant*, p42
Model of submission: R. Joseph Soloveitchik, "Majesty and Humility", in *Tradition* 17:2, pp36–37

P.92
Midrash: Genesis Rabbah 56:15
Prayer: From the Musaf service on Rosh Hashana

CHAYEI SARAH Endnotes
P.98
Midrash: Pirkei d'R. Eliezer, Chapter 32
Midrash: Tanhuma Vayeira 23
Scholars of our Time: Phyllis Trible, "Women in the Hebrew Bible" in *Beginning Anew: Woman's Companion to the High Holy Days*
Inexplicable cost: Avivah Zornberg, *The Beginning of Desire*
All or part of me: R. Kalonymous Shapira, *Sacred Fire*, p14
Transforming: Midrash Aggadah, quoted in Torah Shelemah Bereshit Ch. 23

P.99
Midrash: Genesis Rabbah 60:16
Legend: Louis Ginzberg, *Legends of the Bible*
At home in a tent: R. Soloveitchik, *The Warmth and the Light*

P.100
Scholar of our Time: R. Matis Wienberg, *Frameworks*
Legend: Louis Ginzberg, *Legends of the Bible*
Back to the real world: Ibn Ezra Rambam
Practical details: R. Burton Visotsky, *The Genesis of Ethics*, p116
Love and burial: R. Matis Weinberg, *Frameworks*, p101
A bargain?: Nahum Sarna, *Understanding Genesis*

P.101
Scholar of our Time: R.Matis Weinberg, *Frameworks*
Obedience and marriage: Rama in Yirah Deah 240:25
Ageing: R. Matis Weinberg, *Frameworks*, p113
Choosing a bride: Naomi Rosenblatt, *Wrestling with Angels*, p217

P.102
Sages of Old: Rashbam Ibn Ezra

P.103
Sages of Old: Sforno
Scholar of our Time: Naomi Rosenblatt, *Wrestling with Angels*

P.104
Scholar of our Time: Naomi Rosenblatt, *Wrestling with Angels*
Kabbalah: Sefer Habahir
Healing energy: Avivah Zornberg, *The Beginning of Desire*, p139

P.105
Midrash: Or Hachaim
Well done: Naomi Rosenblatt, *Wrestling with Angels*, p220

P.106
Sages of Old: Abarbanel
Greedy hospitality: Rashi, Sforno

P.107
Scholar of our Time: Naomi Rosenblatt, *Wrestling with Angels*
Sages of Old: Rashi
Rebecca's cloth: Naomi Rosenblatt, *Wrestling with Angels*, p223

P.108
Midrash: Talmud Berachot 26b
Scholar of our Time: Naomi Rosenblatt *Wrestling with Angels*
Sages of Old: Rashi
Sages of Old: Radak Yalkut Shimoni
Midrash: Rabbah
Scholar of our Time: Avivah Zornberg, *The Beginning of Desire*
Future shock: *ibid*, pp142–143

P.109
Midrash: Hagadol 24:67
Loss and comfort: R. Samson Raphael Hirsch, *Hirsch Commentary on the Torah*, pp412–413

TOLDOT Endnotes
P.116
Midrash: Hagadol
Sages of Old: Rashi, Tanchuma
Kabbalah: Zohar
Harmony and balance: R. Laibl Wolf, *Practical Kabbalah*

P.117
Sages of Old: Sforno
Sages of Old: Rashi
Midrash: Resh Lakish
Barrenness: Noam Zion and Steve Israel, *The Troubling Family Triangle: Sarai, Avram and Hagar*, n.p.

P.118
Midrash: Ibn Ezra, based on Midrash
Sages of Old: Rashi
Midrash: Aggadah
The children clashed inside her: Avivah Zornberg, *The Beginning of Desire*, p169

P.119
Sages of Old: Rashi, Radak
Midrash: Hagadol
Scholars of our Time: *Etz Hayim: Torah and Commentary*, p147
In context: For examples of traditional commentators' characterizations of Esav and Jacob, see *Bereshis* (Artscroll Tanach Series), Parashat Toldot, and James Kugel, *The Bible As It Was*, p206
Comforting: *ibid*, p206

P.120
Midrash: Hagadol
Sages of Old: Rashi
The fight to be first: Midrash Hagadol
Antihero: James Kugel, *The Bible As It Was*, p202; Michael Rosenak, *Tree of Life, Tree of Knowledge*, p79

P.121
Sages of Old: Racanati, Radak
Midrash: Hagadol
Scholars of our Time: Avivah Zornberg, *The Beginning of Desire*; R. Bradley Artson, *The Bedside Torah*
Modern insights: R. Joseph Telushkin, *Biblical Literacy*, p54; James Kugel, *The Bible As It Was*, p208; Michael Rosenak, *Tree of Life, Tree of Knowledge*, p81
Psychological differences: Avivah Zornberg, *The Beginning of Desire*, p164

P.122
Sages of Old: Rashi, Nachshoni
Scholars of our Time: R. Samson Raphael Hirsch, *Hirsch Commentary on the Torah*; Michael Rosenak, *Tree of Life, Tree of Knowledge*
Scholar of our Time: R. Samson Raphael Hirsch, *Hirsch Commentary on the Torah*
Courting disaster: Michael Rosenak, *Tree of Life, Tree of Knowledge*, p88
Progressive proverb: Proverbs 22:6
Simple yet diverse: R. Samson Raphael Hirsch, *Hirsch Commentary on the Torah*, p425
Nature or nurture: See chapter "Bringing up a problem child" in Michael Rosenak, *Tree of Life, Tree of Knowledge*

P.123
Scholars of our Time: Avivah Zornberg, *The Beginning of Desire*; Naomi Rosenblatt, *Wrestling with Angels*
Kabbalah: Zohar
Marital tension and male bonding: Naomi Rosenblatt, *Wrestling with Angels*, pp244, 251
Opposites attract: R. Samson Raphael Hirsch, *Hirsch Commentary on the Torah*, p427

P.124
Scholars of our Time: Nahum Sarna, *Understanding Genesis*
Sages of Old: Ohel Yaakov
Scholars of our Time: *Genesis: A New Teacher's Guide*
Justifying Jacob: R. Yehuda Hachassid in Da'at Zekeinim
The power of translation: Robert Alter, *The World of Biblical Literature*, p93

P.125
Scholars of our Time: Nahum Sarna, *Understanding Genesis*
Midrash: Bereshit Rabbah
Sages of Old: In Da'at Zekeinim
Darkness imprinted: Avivah Zornberg, *The Beginning of Desire*, p157

P.126
Sages of Old: Malbim
Scholars of our Time: Nehama Leibowitz, *Studies in Bereshit (Genesis)*
Scholars of our Time: *Etz Hayim: Torah and Commentary*; *Genesis: A New Teacher's Guide*
Vacuum: Naomi Rosenblatt, *Wrestling with Angels*, p252
Needing therapy: R. Joseph Telushkin, *Biblical Literacy*, p54

P.127
Scholar of our Time: R. Samson Raphael Hirsch, *Hirsch Commentary on the Torah*
Sages of Old: Rashi, Yalkut, Bereshit Rabbah 67
Scholars of our Time: Nehama Leibowitz, Nahum Sarna
Stuck: Naomi Rosenblatt, *Wrestling with Angels*, p251
The moral issue: Nahum Sarna, *Understanding Genesis*, p183
Proactive pragmatist: Naomi Rosenblatt, *Wrestling with Angels*, p252

P.128
Scholars of our Time: Avivah Zornberg, *The Beginning of Desire*
Face to face: Naomi Rosenblatt, *Wrestling with Angels*, p247
Transformation: Avivah Zornberg, *The Beginning of Desire*, p171

P.129
Sages of Old: Beresit Rabbah 67; Rashi
Scholars of our Time: Nehama Leibowitz; R. Joseph Telushkin; Nahum Sarna
Consequences: Nehama Leibowitz, *Studies in Bereshit (Genesis)*

P.130
Scholar of our Time: Avivah Zornberg, *The Beginning of Desire*
Legally blessed: Avivah Zornberg, *The Beginning of Desire*, p145
Terror: This Midrash and its explanation are based on Avivah Zornberg, *The Beginning of Desire*, p152
Unconscious insight: R. Joseph Telushkin, *Biblical Literacy*, p52

P.131
Sages of Old: Yalkut
Scholars of our Time: R. Joseph Telushkin
Esau's pain: R. Joseph Telushkin, *Biblical Literacy*, p50
Tragic: R. Bradley Artson, *The Bedside Torah*, p41
Sympathy: R. Joseph Telushkin, *Biblical Literacy*, p50

P.132
Right or wrong: R. Joseph Telushkin, *Biblical Literacy*, p52

VAYETZE Endnotes
P.138
Scholars of our Time: Avivah Zornberg, *The Beginning of Desire*
Kabbalah: Zohar
Setting out alone: Naomi Rosenblatt, *Wrestling with Angels*, pp260–261

P.139
Sages of Old: Rashi
Sages of Old: Rashi
Crash: Avivah Zornberg, *The Beginning of Desire*, p187
Dark night of the soul: *ibid*, p185

P.140
Scholar of our Time: Naomi Rosenblatt, *Wrestling with Angels*
Sages of Old: Rashi
A ladder upwards: Naomi Rosenblatt, *Wrestling with Angels*, p263
A ladder to God: Nahum Sarna, *Understanding Genesis*, p193
The ladder as history: Pirkei d'R. Eliezer
A ladder in Poland: Elie Wiesel, *Messengers of God*, p138

P.141
Scholars of our Time: Avivah Zornberg
Sages of Old: Rashi
"I am with you": Michael Rosenak, *Tree of Life, Tree of Knowledge*, pp64–65
Vertical and horizontal: Avivah Zornberg, *The Beginning of Desire*, p193

P.142
Sages of Old: Rashi
Midrash: Pirkei d'R. Eliezer
Upward ladders: Naomi Rosenblatt, *Wrestling with Angels*, p264
Dreaming: Avivah Zornberg, *The Beginning of Desire*, p190

P.143
Scholar of our Time: Avivah Zornberg, *The Beginning of Desire*
Sages of Old: Radak
Sages of Old: Rashi
Sages of Old: Sforno
Midrash: Genesis Rabbah
Flying: Avivah Zornberg, *The Beginning of Desire*, pp200–201
The well of meeting: Naomi Rosenblatt, *Wrestling with Angels*, p267
Love at first sight: Miki Raver, *Listen to her voice*, p63

P.144
Midrash: cited by Rashi
Sages of Old: Sforno
Bride price: Nahum Sarna, *Understanding Genesis*

P.145
Sages of Old: Sforno Da'at Zekeinim

P.146
Midrash: Torah Temimah
Two kinds of love: Adin Steinsalz, *Biblical Images*, p60
What's in a name: R. Bradley Artson, *The Bedside Torah*, p51
To be a woman: Naomi Rosenblatt, *Wrestling with Angels*, p279

P.147
Sages of Old: and Scholars of our Time: Radak, Rambam, Naomi Rosenblatt
Give me children or I will die: Noam Zion and Steve Israel, *The Troubling Family Triangle: Sarai, Avram and Hagar*, n.p.
Rachel speaks: Penina Adelman, *Praise her Works*, p37

P.148
Sages of Old: Rashi
Sages of Old: Rambam
Textual life span: Ilana Pardes, *Out of the Garden*, p38
Echoes of rivalry: Adin Steinsalz, *Biblical Images*, p58

VAYISHLACH Endnotes
P.154
Sages of Old: Rambam
Sages of Old: Rashi
Sages of Old: Rashi
A stranger: Avivah Zornberg, *The Beginning of Desire*, p229

P.155
Scholars of our Time: Roberta Hestenes in *Genesis: A Living Conversation*
Frozen in time: *ibid*, p297
Fright and anxiety: Rashi, based on Genesis Rabbah 76:2

P.156
Sages of Old: Rashi
Scholars of our Time: *Genesis: A New Teacher's Guide*
Courage: Rashi
Out to impress: Avivah Zornberg, *The Beginning of Desire*, p230
Tomorrow: Elie Wiesel, *Messengers of God*, p105

P.157
Scholars of our Time: Naomi Rosenblatt, *Wrestling with Angels*
Solitude: Elie Wiesel, *Messengers of God*, p125
Crossing the Jabbok: W. Gunther Plaut, *The Torah: A Modern Commentary*, p221

P.158
Sages of Old and Scholars of our Time: Rashi, Tanchuma, Naomi Rosenblatt,
Avivah Zornberg, Elie Wiesel
Sages of Old: Rashi
Surreal: Elie Wiesel, *Messengers of God*, p106
The struggle in me: Bill Moyers, *Genesis: A Living Conversation*, p299

P.159
Kabbalah: Sefer Habahir
Confusing: Elie Wiesel, *Messengers of God*, p107
He did not know: W. Gunther Plaut, *The Torah: A Modern Commentary*, p222

P.160
Sages of old and Scholars of our Time: Rashi, Bill Moyers
Struggling with God: John Barth in *Genesis: A Living Conversation*, p304
Inner victory: Naomi Rosenblatt, *Wrestling with Angels*, p299
Meaning in suffering: Esther Spitzer in *The Torah: A Modern Commentary*, p223

P.161
Sages of Old: Sefer Hachinuch
Limping: John Barth in *Genesis: A Living Conversation*, p305
Alone: Jesse Sampter Brand in *The Torah: A Modern Commentary*, p223
Different encounter: Irving Fineman, *Jacob*, pp179–180

P.162
Sages of Old: Rashi citing sages in Sifrei B'ha'alosecha; Ibn Ezra Ralbag
Scholar of our Time: Gunther Plaut, *The Torah: A Modern Commentary*
Reconciliation: *ibid*, p222
Jacob and Israel: Avivah Zornberg in *Genesis: A Living Conversation*, p304

P.163
Scholars of our Time: Naomi Rosenblatt, *Wrestling with Angels*
Separate ways: Thomas Mann, *The Tales of Jacob*, p130-131
Coexistence: Michael Rosenak, *Tree of Life, Tree of Knowledge*, Chapter 10

P.164
Sages of Old: Rashi
Weeping: Jeremiah 31:14-16
The power of tears: Avivah Zornberg, *The Beginning of Desire*, p213
Rachel speaks: Penina Adelman, *Praise her Works*, p37

VAYESHEV Endnotes
P.170
Sages of Old: Rashi
Sages of Old: Or Hachaim
A yearning to settle: Avivah Zornberg, *The Beginning of Desire*, pp243–244
Vayeshev: R. Samson Raphael Hirsch, *Hirsch Commentary on the Torah*, p539
The illusion of peace: W. Gunther Plaut, *The Torah: A Modern Commentary*, p243
Life's narrative: Avivah Zornberg, *The Beginning of Desire*, p257

P.171
Midrash: Bereshit Rabbah 84:7
Scholar of our Time: Naomi Rosenblatt, *Wrestling with Angels*
Link: *ibid*, p319
A bad father?: Elie Wiesel, *Messengers of God*, p155

P.172
He should have known better: Naomi Rosenblatt, *Wrestling with Angels*, p323

P.173
Scholars of our Time: Naomi Rosenblatt, *Wrestling with Angels*
Midrash: Hagadol
Narcissism: Avivah Zornberg, *The Beginning of Desire*, p253; Naomi Rosenblatt, *Wrestling with Angels*, p325
Self preoccupied: Elie Wiesel, *Messengers of God*, p157
Dream analysis: Robert Alter, *The World of Biblical Literature*

P.174
Sages of Old: Rambam
Scholar of our Time: R. Joseph Telushkin, *Biblical Literacy*
War at home: Berachot 76
The pits: Avivah Zornberg, *The Beginning of Desire*, p290
Master of dreams: Dr. Masha Turner in *A Divinely Given Torah*, pp107–108

P.175
Scholars of our Time: Avivah Zornberg, *The Beginning of Desire*
Sages of Old: Rashi
Sages of Old and Scholars of our Time: Rashi, R. Joseph Tellushkin
Stripped: Avivah Zornberg, *The Beginning of Desire*, p267
Howling horror: Thomas Mann, *Joseph and his Brothers*, p373
Forgotten: Avivah Zornberg, *The Beginning of Desire*, p291
"Then the brothers sat down to eat": R. Joseph Telushkin, *Biblical Literacy*, p69

P.176
Sages of Old: Rashi
Midrash: Pirkei d'R. Eliezer 38
Hidden plot: Nehama Leibowitz, *Studies in Bereshit (Genesis)*, p394
Midrashic view: Midrash Tanhuma
God's plot: Avivah Zornberg, *The Beginning of Desire*, p255

P.177
Sages of Old: Ramban, Sforno
Scholars of our Time: R.Joseph Telushkin, *Biblical Literacy*; Naomi Rosenblatt, *Wrestling with Angels*
Wild animal: Naomi Rosenblatt, *Wrestling with Angels*, p324
Responsible: Sefer Hasidim 131
Original sin: Avivah Zornberg, *The Beginning of Desire*, p271
He would not be comforted: R.Samson Hirsch, *Hirsch Commentary on the Torah*, p552

P.178
Scholar of our Time: Avivah Zornberg, *The Beginning of Desire*
Midrash: Talmud Berachot 55b
Scholar of our Time: Avivah Zornberg, *The Beginning of Desire*
Faces: *ibid*, p253
Profound change: Gunther Plaut, *The Torah: A Modern Commentary*, p271

P.179
Scholars of our Time: Naomi Rosenblatt, *Wrestling with Angels*
Sages of Old: Chullin 92a
Dream science: Nahum Sarna, *Understanding Genesis*, p213
Four cups: Talmud Yerushalmi Pesachim

P.180
Scholar of our Time: R. Joseph Telushkin, Biblical Literacy
Presumed dead: Avivah Zornberg, *The Beginning of Desire*, p292
Baker's delight: Nahum Sarna, *Understanding Genesis*, p218

MIKETZ Endnotes
P.186
Sages of Old: Seder Olam
Corn ears: Rashbam, Ha'amek Davar
Wealth of detail: Nahum Sarna, *Understanding Genesis*, p218

P.187
Scholars of our Time: Nahum Sarna, *Understanding Genesis*
Sages of Old: Rashbam
Enduring: Naomi Rosenblatt, *Wrestling with Angels*, pp341–342

P.188
Sages of Old: Rashi Sforno
Wake-up call: R. Chanan Morrison, *Gold from the Land of Israel*, p83
Disclaimer: Nahum Sarna, *Understanding Genesis*, p218

P.189
Scholar of our Time: Robert Alter, *The Art of Biblical Narrative*
Kabbalah: Zohar
Sages of Old: Rambam
Pharaonic record: Cited in *The Torah: A Modern Commentary*, p272
Economics: R. Samson Raphael Hirsch, *Hirsch Commentary on the Torah*, pp580–581

P.190
Scholar of our Time: Naomi Rosenblatt, *Wrestling with Angels*
Legend: Louis Ginzberg, *Legends of the Bible*
Twinkling eye: R. Joseph Telushkin, *Biblical Literacy*, p81
Assimilation: Nahum Sarna, *Understanding Genesis*, p222
Past and present: Gunther Plaut, *The Torah: A Modern Commentary*, p271
Foreign power: Nahum Sarna, *Understanding Genesis*, p221

P.191
Scholar of our Time: Avivah Zornberg, *The Beginning of Desire*
Secretary of agriculture: Nahum Sarna, *Understanding Genesis*, p220
What's in a name?: Avivah Zornberg, *The Beginning of Desire*, p285

P.192
Scholar of our Time: Naomi Rosenblatt, *Wrestling with Angels*
Emotional vortex: ibid, p356
In another story: Avivah Zornberg, *The Beginning of Desire*, p263

P.193
Scholar of our Time: Avivah Zornberg, *The Beginning of Desire*
Flashback: Meir Weiss, as cited in Nehama Leibowitz, *Studies in Bereshit (Genesis)*, p464
Witnessing trauma: Notes from Avivah Zornberg lecture

P.194
Scholar of our Time: Avivah Zornberg, *The Beginning of Desire*
Scholar of our Time: ibid, p304
What has God done to us?: Haketav Vehakabbalah
Precedent: Avivah Zornberg *The Beginning of Desire*, p304

P.195
Sages of Old: Bechor Shor
Scholar of our Time: Naomi Rosenblatt, *Wrestling with Angels*
Jacob's dilemma: Midrash Hagadol
I will stand guilty before you forever: Benamozegh Em Lamikra

I myself will be responsible for him: Avivah Zornberg, *The Beginning of Desire*, p299

P.196
Midrash: Cited by Rashi
Midrash: Cited in *The Book of Legends* (Hayim Bialik)
Sages of Old: Ramban, Sforno
Slow motion: Avivah Zornberg, *The Beginning of Desire*, p307
Joseph's tears: R. Samson Raphael Hirsch, *Hirsch Commentary on the Torah*, p609
Joseph's and Benjamin's conversation: Avivah Zornberg, *The Beginning of Desire*, p308

P.197
Sages of Old: Or Ha-Chaim, Ramban
Scholars of our Time: Nahum Sarna, James Kugel, R. Samson Raphael Hirsch
Reformed: Nahum Sarna, *Understanding Genesis*, p223
A test: James Kugel, *The Bible As It Was*, p267
Reinterpreting: Avivah Zornberg, *The Beginning of Desire*, p275

P.198
Scholar of our Time: Avivah Zornberg, *The Beginning of Desire*
Literary structure: R. Dr. Pinchas Hyman in *A Divinely Given Torah*, p116
What can we say: Avivah Zornberg, *The Beginning of Desire*, p31

VAYIGASH Endnotes
P.204
Scholar of our Time: Avivah Zornberg, *The Beginning of Desire*
Three ways of drawing close: Genesis Rabbah 93:6
Close to himself: Itture Torah, cited in *The Torah: A Modern Commentary*, p389
Between the lines: Nehama Leibowitz, *Studies in Bereshit (Genesis)*, p484

P.205
Scholar of our Time: Nehama Leibowtiz, *Studies in Bereshit (Genesis)*
Scholar of our Time: Naomi Rosenblatt, *Wrestling with Angels*
Learning empathy the hard way: Avivah Zornberg, *The Beginning of Desire*, p326
Double entendre: Naomi Rosenblatt, *Wrestling with Angels*, p364
Seeing what he sees: Avivah Zornberg, *The Beginning of Desire*, p330

P.206
Scholar of our Time: R. Matis Weinberg, *Frameworks*
Sage of Old: Rashi
Scholar of our Time: Avivah Zornberg, *The Beginning of Desire*
So it was not you who sent me here but God: Nehama Leibowitz, *Studies In Bereshit (Genesis)*, p497
God's hand: Gunther Plaut, *The Torah: A Modern Commentary*, p280
Do not worry or feel ashamed: R. Samson Raphael Hirsch, *Hirsch Commentary on the Torah*, p619

P.207
Sage of Old: Abarbanel

P.208
From betrayal to forgiveness: Naomi Rosenblatt, *Wrestling with Angels* p358
Overcoming vengeance: Elie Wiesel, *Messengers of God*, pp165–166

P.209
Scholar of our Time: R. Matis Weinberg, *Frameworks*
Scholar of our Time: Nahum Sarna, *Understanding Genesis*
Land of Goshen: ibid, p225
Joseph the assimilationist: R. Matis Weinberg, *Frameworks*,

p299
Joseph the family provider: Naomi Rosenblatt, *Wrestling with Angels*, p368

P.210
Midrash: Hagadol 45:26
How shall we tell him: Thomas Mann, *Joseph and His Brothers*, p1124
The truth of a poem: Avivah Zornberg, *The Beginning of Desire*, pp280–281

P.211
Sages of Old: Hizkuni, Ha'amek Davar
Do not be afraid: Naomi Rosenblatt, *Wrestling with Angel*, p371
In darkness: Nehama Leibowitz, *Studies in Bereshit (Genesis)*, p511
The night of exile: Ha'amek Davar

P.212
Scholar of our Time: Nehama Leibowitz, *Studies in Bereshit (Genesis)*
Not just a family visit: Nahum Sarna, *Understanding Genesis*, p224
Prototype of exile: R. Matis Weinberg, *Frameworks*, p293
Born in exile: Gunther Plaut, *The Torah: A Modern Commentary*, p291

P.213
Midrash: Bava Basra 123a
Sage of Old: as discussed in *Genesis* (Artscroll Tanach Series) vol 1b, p2020
Sages of Old: Talmud, Radak

VAYEHI Endnotes
P.216
Sages of Old: Radak
Maths: 147 = 3 x (7x7); 180 = 5 x (6x6); 175 = 7 x (5x5). The coefficients increase by two and the squared numbers decrease by one (as cited in Nahum Sarna, Understanding Genesis, p84).
Midrash: Hagadol 48:1
Deathbed scene: Avivah Zornberg, The Beginning of Desire, p353
Numbers count: Nahum Sarna, Understanding Genesis, pp84–85

P.217
Sages of Old: Rashi
Perpetual reminder: Nehama Leibowitz, Studies in Bereshit (Genesis), pp536–537
Standing by: ibid, p541

P.219
Midrash: Yalkut Shimoni
Visiting the sick: R. Joseph Telushkin, Jewish Literacy, p585
Helping to change bandages: Babylonian Talmud Sanhedrin 98a

P.220
Sages of Old: R. Bachya
Sages of Old: Rashi
A sort of knowledge: Avivah Zornberg, The Beginning of Desire, pp349–350
Right or left: Gunther Plaut, The Torah: A Modern Commentary, p304

P.222
My father's God: Gunther Plaut, The Torah: A Modern Commentary, p305
Renewing connection: Noam Zion, A Day Apart: Shabbat at Home, pp49–50

P.223
Sages of Old: Rashi
Blessing: Naomi Rosenblatt, Wrestling with Angel, p376

Closed vision: R. Simchah Bunam, Wellsprings of Torah, pp93–94

P.224
Sages of Old: Rashi
Life's completion: Gunther Plaut, The Torah: A Modern Commentary, p305

P.225
Midrash: Bereshit Rabbah 91;13
Sages of Old: Rashi
Kabbalah: Zohar
Eyes closed: Zohar 11 216b
The closed life of slavery: Avivah Zornberg, The Beginning of Desire, p356

P.226
Coffin and ark: Talmud, After Sotah 13a
God in Genesis: Isaac Bashevis Singer, cited in Wrestling with Angels, p385

ENDINGS AND BEGINNINGS Endnotes
P.227
Scholar of our Time: Naomi Rosenblatt, Wrestling with Angels
In this world what is most needed . Avivah Zornberg, The Beginning of Desire, p278

BIBLICAL COMMENTATORS AND COMMENTARIES
(Sages of Old and Scholars of our Time)

Alter, Robert: Professor of Hebrew and comparative literature at the University of California, author of a new translation of Genesis and other books on the Bible

Abarbanel, Don Isaac (1437–1508): Spanish commentator on the Bible, philosopher and statesman

Akeidat Yitzchak: Philosophic commentary on the Torah by Spanish Talmudist Isaac Arma (1420-94)

Bechor Shor: French Talmudist of the 12th century

Benamozegh, Elijah ben Avraham (1822–1900): Italian Rabbi and professor of theology

Buber, Martin (1878–1965): Professor of sociology of religion at the Hebrew University and author, he combined involvement with the Zionist movement with a modern philosophic restatement of Judaism and close study of the Bible.

Da'at Zekeinim: Compendium of Torah commentary originating with the Tosafists (13th century) and first printed in 1783

Gur Aryeh: Super-commentary to Rashi by Judah Loew ben Bezalel, known as Maharal of Prague (1525–1609)

Ha'amek Davar: Commentary to the Torah by Naftali Zvi Yehuda Berlin, known as the Netziv (1817–1893)

Haketav Vehakabbalah: Commentary to the Torah combining Kabbalah and written text, by Jacob Zvi Mecklenburg (1785–1865)

Hirsch, Samson Raphael (1808–1888): German rabbinical leader and commentator on the Torah

Ibn Ezra, Abraham (1080–1164): Spanish commentator on the Bible, poet and grammarian

Kli Yakar: Commentary on the Torah by Ephraim Solomin ben Hayyim of Luntshitz (1550–1619)

Kook, Avraham Yizchak Hakohen (1865–1935): First Chief Rabbi of Israel after the Balfour Declaration, he wrote important works on the Talmud, rabbinic law and Jewish thought.

Leibowitz, Nehama (1905-1997): Biblical scholar, teacher and commentator, awarded the Israel Prize in 1956 for her work in furthering greater understanding and appreciation of the Bible.

Malbim: Initials for Meir Yehuda ben Yehiel Mikhal (1809–1880), Russian rabbi who wrote commentary on the Torah Hatorah Vehamitzvah

Midrash Hagadol: Collection of Midrashim on the Bible compiled from ancient Tannaitic sources by David ben Amram Adnai, a Yemenite scholar of the 13th century

Midrash Rabbah: collection of Midrashim from various periods on the Torah and the Five Scrolls

Pirkei d'Rabbi Eliezer: a Midrashic work that retells much of the Torah, focusing on the workings of God in creation, written in the 8th or 9th century

Plaut, W. Gunther: Rabbi of Reform Judaism, author of The Torah: a Modern Commentary, the standard humash used by the Reform movement

Radak: Initials for Rabbi David Kimchi (1157–1236), author of commentary on the Torah

Rambam: Initials for Rabbi Moshe ben Maimon, or Maimonides, (1135–1204), author of a master code of Jewish law, Mishneh Torah, a philosophical handbook to Judaism (Guide to the Perplexed), and a compendium of the 613 commandments, Sefer Ha-Mitzvot; also a famous physician and leader of Egyptian Jewry

Ramban: Initials for Rabbi Moshe ben Naham, or Nahmanides (1194–1270), Spanish biblical and Talmudic commentator

Rashi: Initials for Rabbi Shlomo Yitzchaki, foremost commentator on the Torah (1040–1105), who lived in France. His commentary, with its remarkable brevity and clarity, has been the key to unlocking the Torah for students and scholars since his time

Rosenblatt, Naomi: Psychotherapist, lecturer, author and adult education teacher of Bible studies in Washington and New York

Sarna, Nahum: Professor of Biblical Studies, Chairman of Near Eastern and Judaic Studies at Brandeis University, noted author

Sefat Emet: Collected writings of Judah Aryeh Leib Alter (1847–1905), Jewish leader in Poland and head of the Hasidim of Gur

Sforno, Ovadiah ben Yaacov (1475-1550): Italian Talmudist, physician and commentator on the Torah

Soloveitchik, Joseph Dov (1903–1993): Spiritual leader of modern orthodoxy in the United States, professor of Jewish philosophy and Talmud at Yeshiva University and author

Talmud: Code of Jewish law, lore, philosophy, and ethics, compiled between 200 and 500 B.C.E.

Telushkin, Joseph: Rabbi, spiritual leader, lecturer and author of many acclaimed books

Weinberg, Matis: Dean at the Hebrew Institute of California and Rosh Yeshiva of Kerem Yeshiva, author

Wiesel, Elie: Holocaust survivor, political activist, author of over 40 books, professor and winner of the Nobel Peace Prize

Yalkut Shimoni: Collection of Midrash compiled from more than fifty works, composed around the 12th or 13th century

Zohar: Mystical commentary on the Torah and the most important text of Jewish mysticism, attributed to R. Shimon barYohai, but first publicised in 13th century Spain

Zornberg, Avivah Gottlieb: Lecturer in Bible and Midrash in Jerusalem, the
United States, Canada and the United Kingdom, and award-winning author

BIBLIOGRAPHY

Adelman, Penina, *Praise her Works*, Philadelphia: Jewish Publication Society, 2005.

Alter, Robert, *The World of Biblical Literature,* New York: Basic Books, 1992.

Antonelli, Judith, *In the Image of God: a Feminist Commentary on the Torah,* New Jersey: Jason Aronson, 1995.

Artson, Bradley, *The Bedside Torah,* New York: Contemporary Books, 2001.

Bereshis vol. 1(a) and 1(b) (Artscroll Tanach Series), New York: Mesorah Publications, Ltd, 1995.

Bodoff, Lippman, The Binding of Isaac: Religious Murders and Kabbalah, Jerusalem: Devorah Publishing Company, 2005.

The Book of Legends (Sefer Ha-Aggadah): Legends from the Talmud and Midrash, Edited by Hayim Nahman Bialik and Yehoshua Hana Ravnitzky, New York: Schocken Books, 1992.

Davis, Avram;Mascetti, Manuela, Judaic Mysticism, New York: Hyperion, 1997.

Davis, Avram, The Way of the Flame, New York: HarperCollins, 1996.

Dershowitz, Alan, The Genesis of Justice: Ten Stories of Biblical Injustice That Led to the Ten Commandments and Modern Law, New York: Warner Books, 2000.

A Divinely Given Torah in our Day and Age: Studies on the Weekly Torah Readings, edited by Aryeh A. Frimer, Ramat Gan: Bar-Ilan University, 2002.

Etz Hayim: Torah and Commentary, David L. Lieber, Ed., New York: The Jewish Publication Society, 2001

Fewell, Dana; Gunn, David, Gender, Power and Promise, Nashville: Abingdou Press, 1993.

Fineman, Irving, Jacob, New York: Random House, 1941.

Gabriel's Palace: Jewish Mystical Tales, Selected and retold by Howard Schwartz, New York: Oxford University Press, 1993.

Genesis/Bereshit: the Traditional Hebrew Text with New JPS Translation, commentary by Nahum M. Sarna, Philadelphia: The Jewish Publication Society, 1989.

Genesis: The Student's Guide Part II, Louis Newman, editor, The Melton Research Centre of The Jewish Theological Seminary of America and The United Synagogue Commission on Jewish Education, 1969.

Ginzberg, Louis, Legends of the Bible, Philadelphia: Jewish Publication Society, 1992.

Green, Arthur, These Are the Words: A Vocabulary of Jewish Spiritual Life, Woodstock: Jewish Lights Publishing, 1999.

Hartman, David, A Living Covenant: The Innovative Spirit in Traditional Judaism, Woodstock: Jewish Lights Publishing, 1997.

Heschel, Abraham Joshua, The Sabbath, New York: Harper & Row, Publishers, 1966.

Hirsch Commentary on the Torah, Volume 1 Bereishith/Genesis, translation and commentary by Rabbi Samson Raphael Hirsch, London: The Judaica Press, 1966.

Holtz, Barry, Back to the Sources: Reading the Classic Jewish Texts, New York: Touchstone, 1984.

Kook, Abraham, Olat Re'iyah, Jerusalem: Mossad HaRav Kook, 1983.

Kugel, James, The Bible As It Was, Cambridge: The Belknap Press of Harvard University Press, 1997.

Leibowitz, Nehama, Studies in Bereshit (Genesis): *In the Context of Ancient and Modern Jewish Commentary,* Jerusalem: World Zionist Organization Department for Torah Education and Culture, 1981.

Lerner, Michael, Jewish Renewal: A Path to Healing and Transformation, New York: G.P. Putnam's Sons, 1994.

Mann, Thomas, Joseph and His Brothers, New York: Knopf, 1948.

Morrison, Chanan, Gold From the Land of Israel: A New Light on the Weekly Torah Portion: From the Writings of Rabbi Abraham Isaac Hakohen Kook, Jerusalem: Urim Publications, 2006.

Moyers, Bill, Genesis: A Living Conversation, New York: Double Day, 1996.

Nachshoni, Yehuda, Studies in the Weekly Parashah, New York: Mesorah Publications, 1999.

Newman, Louis, The Hasidic Anthology: Tales and Teachings of the Hasidim, New York: Block, 1994.

Out of the Garden: Women Writers on the Bible, edited by Christina Buchmann and Celina Spiegel, New York: Fawcett Columbine, 1994.

Raver, Miki, Listen to her Voice: Women of the Hebrew Bible, San Francisco: Chronicle Books, 1998.

Rosenak, Michael, Commandments and Concerns: Jewish Religious Education in Secular Society, Philadelphia: Jewish Publication Society, 1987.

Rosenak, Micheal, Tree of Life, Tree of Knowledge: Conversations with the Torah, Colorado: Westview Press, 2001.

Rosenblatt, Naomi; Horwitz, Joshua, Wrestling with Angels: What the First Family of Genesis Teaches Us About Our Spiritual Identity, Sexuality and Personal Relationships, New York: Delacorte Press, 1995.

Sarna, Nahum M., Understanding Genesis: The World of the Bible in the Light of History, New York: Schocken Books, 1970.

Scholem, Gershom, Kabbalah, Jerusalem: Keter Publishing House, 1974.

Shapira, Kalonymous, Sacred Fire: Torah from the Years of Fury 1939–1942, New Jersey: Jason Aronson, 2002.

Soloveitchik, Joseph, The Lonely Man of Faith, New York: Doubleday, 1992.

Soloveitchik, Joseph, "Majesty and Humility", Tradition 17:2 Spring, 1978.

Steinsalz, Adin, Biblical Images, New Jersey: Jason Aronson, 1994.

Telushkin, Joseph, Biblical Literacy: The Most Important People, Events and Ideas of the Hebrew Bible, New York: Harper Collins, 1997.

Telushkin, Joseph, Jewish Literacy: The Most Important Things to Know about the Jewish Religion, Its People and Its History, New York: William Morrow and Company, 1991.

The Torah: A Modern Commentary, Commentaries by W. Gunther Plaut, et al., New York: Union of American Hebrew Congregations, 1981.

Torah of the Earth: Exploring 4,000 Years of Ecology in Jewish Thought, Edited by Ari, Woodstock: Jewish Lights Publishing, c2000.

Trible, Phyllis, Texts of Terror: Literary-Feminist Readings of Biblical narratives, London: SCM Press, 1992.

Trible Phyllis, "Women in the Hebrew Bible" in Beginning Anew: A Woman's Companion to the High Holy Days, Gail Twersky Reimer & Judith Kates, eds., New York: Simon & Schuster, 1997.

Visotsky, Burton, The Genesis of Ethics, New York: Three Rivers Press, 1996.

Weinberg, Matis, Frameworks: Genesis, Boston: The Foundation for Jewish Publications, 1999.

Weiner, Herbert, Nine and a Half Mystics: The Kabbalah Today, New York: Touchstone, 1997.

Wiesel, Elie, Messengers of God: Biblical Portraits and Legends, New York: Random House, 1976.

Wolf, Laibl, Practical Kabbalah: A Guide to Jewish Wisdom for Everyday Life, New York: Three Rivers Press, 1999.

Zielenziger, Ruth, Genesis: A New Teacher's Guide, The Melton Research Centre of the Jewish Theological Seminary of America and The United Synagogue Commission on Jewish Education, 1980.

Zion-Sachs, Noam;Fields-Meyer, Shawn, A Day Apart: Shabbat at Home, Jerusalem: Zion Holiday Publications, 2004.

Zion-Sachs, Noam;Israel, Steve, The Troubling Family Triangle: Sarai, Avram and Hagar, Jerusalem: Sholom Hartman Institute, n.d.

Zornberg, Avivah Gottlieb, The Beginning of Desire: Reflections on Genesis, New York: Doubleday, 1996.

ACKNOWLEDGMENTS

It has been my pleasure and very real privilege to spend many hours over the last years reading the works of great minds and writers – the traditional commentators and our contemporary scholars. There are many whose thoughts on Genesis, and insights on life in general, I have found to be deeply moving, full of wisdom and depth, powerful and inspiring. So my research has been a real learning, an expanding of the heart and mind.

I am honoured and wish to thank Avivah Zornberg for writing the foreword. I have learnt so much from her book *The Beginning of Desire: Reflections on Genesis* and was enriched by her shiurim during my recent sabbatical in Jerusalem.

I wish to thank all those I have studied with – teachers and friends – and those I have given the manuscript to for feedback: Mark Baker, Naor Bar-Zeev, Lynette Chazan, Paul Forgasz, Deborah Miller, Alex Skovron, Deborah Stone and Debbie Weissman. Your input has been greatly appreciated.

There are many others to thank: Yaacov Peterseil, from Pitspopany Press, who with openness and courage agreed to take on my manuscript when I arrived one day in his office in Jerusalem, and who has contributed his thoughtful editing;

Anna Pignataro, whose beautiful illustrations bring the Genesis stories to life;

Dalit Bar, my talented designer, with whom it has been a pleasure to work;

Allon Baron and the staff at abCreative for their generosity in putting up with me as I sat many hours in their office typing changes into the manuscript;

Andrew Majzner for his design advice;

Staff at Makor Jewish Community Library for their patience and good nature as I borrowed books for months at a time, and particularly Ruth Leonards for her expert assistance in editing the endnotes, bibliography and commentaries;

Judy Bierwirth for her generous and detailed proof-reading;

Ariel BenMoshe and the staff at Tal Torah, who provided me with a peaceful place to work on the book during my recent sabbatical in Jerusalem.

Special thanks go to the family and friends who have encouraged me over the long years of working on this book. I am grateful to my parents, Tesse and Moshe Lang, for their support for this book, their ongoing interest and availability to discuss and workshop ideas, their belief in me.

Finally, I express my thanks and appreciation to my family, who lived through the slow gestation and growth of the manuscript, as it spread over the kitchen table (pushed down to one end for dinner) and encroached into most other rooms and parts of our lives, leaving a trail of books and papers in its wake. Very special thanks to my husband, Robert, who read numerous drafts of the manuscript, sharing his insights, and providing support and encouragement during the long journey. I wrote this book with my children – Gabriel, Yona and Alon – in mind. It is my hope that one day they share it with their own children.